Environmental Strategy

There are as many ways for companies to improve their environmental performance as there are stakeholders who are calling upon them to do so. If companies make the right choices, they can satisfy their stakeholders, enhance their financial position, and help address the climate crisis. The wrong choices invite stakeholder scorn and risk wasting valuable resources. What problems do companies need to solve, and how can they solve them, to achieve the promise of shared value environmental performance? This book presents a framework for companies to design, develop and implement an effective environmental strategy that identifies environmental improvements, enables value exchanges with stakeholders, and improves competitive advantage. The step-by-step guide through this framework, illustrated with many examples, shows the promise of environmental initiatives that align with strategic opportunities and resources and the pitfalls of those that do not.

MATTHEW POTOSKI is a Professor in the Bren School of Environmental Science and Management, University of California, Santa Barbara. He is co-author of *The Voluntary Environmentalists* (with Aseem Prakash, 2009) and *Complex Contracting*, which won a Best Book award from the American Society for Public Administration and an Honorable Mention recognition from the Academy of Management's Public and Nonprofit Division.

Organizations and the Natural Environment

Series Editors

Jorge Rivera, George Washington University
J. Alberto Aragon-Correa, University of Surrey

Editorial Board

Nicole Darnall, Arizona State University
Magali Delmas, University of California, Los Angeles
Ans Kolk, University of Amsterdam
Thomas P. Lyon, University of Michigan
Alfred Marcus, University of Minnesota
Michael Toffel, Harvard Business School
Christopher Weible, University of Colorado

The increasing attention given to environmental protection issues has resulted in a growing demand for high-quality, actionable research on sustainability and business environmental management. This new series, published in conjunction with the Group for Research on Organizations and the Natural Environment (GRONEN), presents students, academics, managers, and policy-makers with the latest thinking on key topics influencing business practice today.

Published Titles

Grabs, *Selling Sustainability Short?*
Sharma and Sharma, *Patient Capital*
Marcus, *Strategies for Managing Uncertainty*
Marcus, *Innovations in Sustainability*
Bowen, *After Greenwashing*
Albright and Crow, *Community Disaster Recovery*
Oetzel, Oh and Rivera, *Business Adaptation to Climate Change*

Forthcoming Titles

Gouldson and Sullivan, *Governance and the Changing Climate for Business*
Matisoff and Noonan, *Ecolabels, Innovation, and Green Market Transformation*
Potoski, *Environmental Strategy for Businesses*

Environmental Strategy for Businesses

MATTHEW POTOSKI

University of California, Santa Barbara

Shaftesbury Road, Cambridge CB2 8EA, United Kingdom

One Liberty Plaza, 20th Floor, New York, NY 10006, USA

477 Williamstown Road, Port Melbourne, VIC 3207, Australia

314–321, 3rd Floor, Plot 3, Splendor Forum, Jasola District Centre,
New Delhi – 110025, India

103 Penang Road, #05–06/07, Visioncrest Commercial, Singapore 238467

Cambridge University Press is part of Cambridge University Press & Assessment,
a department of the University of Cambridge.

We share the University's mission to contribute to society through the pursuit of
education, learning and research at the highest international levels of excellence.

www.cambridge.org
Information on this title: www.cambridge.org/9781009098991

DOI: 10.1017/9781009106733

First published 2023

A catalogue record for this publication is available from the British Library.

Library of Congress Cataloging-in-Publication Data
Names: Potoski, Matthew, 1969– author.
Title: Environmental strategy for businesses / Professor Matthew Potoski,
University of California, Santa Barbara.
Description: 1 Edition. | New York, NY : Cambridge University Press, 2023. |
Includes bibliographical references and index.
Identifiers: LCCN 2022032034 | ISBN 9781009098991 (hardback) |
ISBN 9781009106733 (ebook)
Subjects: LCSH: Business enterprises – Environmental aspects. |
Industrial management – Environmental aspects. | Sustainable development.
Classification: LCC HD30.255 .P68 2023 | DDC 658.4/08–dc23/eng/20220707
LC record available at https://lccn.loc.gov/2022032034

ISBN 978-1-009-09899-1 Hardback
ISBN 978-1-009-10733-4 Paperback

Contents

List of Tables   *page* ix

Preface   xi

1 Introduction   1
   1.1 Environmental Impacts as Opportunities   2
   1.2 A Framework for Environmental Strategy   5

2 Foundations and Background   13
   2.1 Markets and Environmental Problems   15
   2.2 Solving Environmental Problems   17
   2.3 Companies, Environmental Impacts, and
        Stakeholder Exchanges   19
        2.3.1 Environmental Stakeholders   21
        2.3.2 Transaction Costs and Coasian Exchanges   22
   2.4 Conclusion   29

3 Environmental Strategy Choices and Challenges   31
   3.1 Search and Screening: Identifying Environmental
        Improvements, Costs, and Stakeholders   32
        3.1.1 Identifying Supply: Environmental Impacts,
               Improvements, and Costs   32
        3.1.2 Identifying Demand: Environmental
               Stakeholder Analysis   35
   3.2 Bargaining and Transfer: Channels for
        Exchanging Value   39
        3.2.1 Market Channels   40
   3.3 Monitoring and Enforcement: Mechanisms for
        Credibility   43
        3.3.1 Measurement and Reporting   45
        3.3.2 Company Brands and Culture   45
        3.3.3 Certifications   47

3.4   Market Environmental Strategies   48
3.5   Conclusion   51

4 Nonmarket Strategy   52
   4.1   Stakeholders and Institutions   54
          4.1.1   Governments   55
          4.1.2   People and Communities   57
          4.1.3   Environmental NGOs   58
          4.1.4   Companies   60
   4.2   Institutions and Nonmarket Strategy   62
          4.2.1   Engaging Environmental Institutions   65
          4.2.2   Collaborating and Institutions   66
   4.3   Conclusion   73

5 Environmental Strategy and Strategic Resources   75
   5.1   Resources for Environmental Strategy   77
          5.1.1   Assessing Environmental Impacts and Costs   79
          5.1.2   Resources for Stakeholders
                   Analysis Engagement   80
          5.1.3   Channels, Resources, and Capabilities   81
          5.1.4   Credibility and Resources   82
   5.2   Organizational Structure and Human Resources for
          Environmental Improvements   84
          5.2.1   Information and Incentive Problems for
                   Environmental Improvements   87
          5.2.2   Organizational Structure, Capabilities, and
                   Sustainability within Companies   89
   5.3   Conclusion   97

6 Green Products and Services   98
   6.1   Strategy for Green Products and Services   100
   6.2   Identifying Green Products' Environmental Benefits
          and Costs   103
   6.3   Demand for Green Products   105
          6.3.1   Co-benefits and Green Products   106
          6.3.2   Complexities with Green Products and
                   Their Co-benefits   110
          6.3.3   Stonyfield's Yogurt and Its Benefits to
                   Consumers   113
   6.4   Channels for Selling Green Products   115

6.5 Green Lemons and the Credibility Challenge   115
    6.5.1 Certifications   116
    6.5.2 Co-benefits and Credibility   117
    6.5.3 Branding   119
6.6 Conclusion   121

7 Employee Engagement   123
  7.1 Employee Engagement and Companies'
    Environmental Performance   127
    7.1.1 Environmental Improvements for
        Employee Engagement   128
    7.1.2 Stakeholder Demand and Employee
        Engagement   129
    7.1.3 Channels for Capturing Value   130
    7.1.4 Credibility and Employees   133
  7.2 EEE Programs   134
    7.2.1 Environmental Problems for Engagement
        Programs   135
    7.2.2 Employee Demand and Environmental
        Engagement Programs   136
    7.2.3 The Value of EEE Programs   139
    7.2.4 Credibility and EEE Programs   142
  7.3 Conclusion   144

8 Environmental Groups   146
  8.1 Environmental Groups and Sustainability   148
  8.2 Environmental Groups and Their Strategy   149
  8.3 Environmental Groups and Activist Campaigns   152
    8.3.1 Targeting for an Activist Campaign   153
    8.3.2 Nonmarket Stakeholders and Demand
        for Environmental Improvements   155
    8.3.3 Channels: The Value Consequences of
        Activist Campaigns   158
    8.3.4 Holdup Problems, Credibility, and Activist
        Campaigns   161
  8.4 Partnerships between Companies and
    Environmental Groups   163
    8.4.1 Environmental Problems for Partnerships   164
    8.4.2 Demand and Partnerships: Environmental
        Groups and Their Stakeholders   165

	8.4.3 Partnerships and Channels for Capturing Value	166
	8.4.4 Credibility and Partnerships	172
8.5	Conclusion	173
9	Conclusion	175
9.1	Environmental Strategy Overview	178
9.2	Nike, Environmental Apparel, Production, and Design	184
References		191
Index		218

Tables

2.1 Transaction cost categories   *page* 23
3.1 Sources of stakeholder influence   36
3.2 Mechanisms for environmental credibility   44
4.1 Nonmarket stakeholders   55
5.1 Examples of senior environmental position titles   90
5.2 Potential areas of responsibility in a CSO's portfolio   91
5.3 Human resource capabilities for developing and
    implementing environmental strategy   95
6.1 Green products and co-benefits   112
7.1 Co-benefits from EEE programs   140
9.1 Environmental strategy framework   180

Preface

When people asked what I was working on, I would tell them, "I'm writing a book about why some businesses do good things for the environment." What I really thought I was writing was a book about "how can we give people incentives to do what is good for society as a whole?" The environment as a business issue was just the setting for thinking through the question. I have come to realize that I have been thinking about this question since I was a kid, when for some reason, my siblings and I devised our own institutions to channel our individual incentives toward collective goods. Before each meal, we made the last kid to arrive at the table act as the "servant" for the rest of us – fetching milk, salt, or whatever else our whims called for – as a humiliating price for making the rest of us wait to start the meal. Of course, the Potoski kids never used terms like "collective action" and "institutions"; we had just grown tired of waiting to start eating.

In graduate school, I found a broader theoretical framework – the concepts, terms, and relations among them – to help me understand what we Potoski kids had been doing. Our institutions were rules for who got to sit where at the table and roles like being the "servant," and our circumstances were those surrounding the "Potoski dinner table." We had designed our institutions to fit our circumstances and move toward the outcomes we collectively wanted: Each kid had incentives to arrive at the dinner table at a reasonable time.

Many of the scholars I admired – Elinor Ostrom, Gary Libecap, Robert Putnam, and Robert Axelrod – made it look so easy: Pick a defining problem of social interaction, pull together insights from many academic traditions, and offer a framework for how institutions can be tailored to address collective action problems across different circumstances. I was particularly drawn to Elinor Ostrom's book *Governing the Commons* (Ostrom 1990). For academic research, *Governing the Commons* defined the important questions and theoretical perspectives in the field and offered a framework through which research could be analyzed and integrated into academic disciplines. Students could read the book to learn theory and practice on environmental management as well as institutionalist approaches for how to understand social interaction. The book was a lodestar for how I pursued my early research and teaching, and it even helped me understand my siblings' efforts to corral the five of us to the dinner table on time.

After finishing my PhD, my research and teaching drifted toward business sustainability, and I started looking for a framework that would help orient my work in the way I had learned in graduate school. I wanted a framework to define the important questions and problems, their potential solutions, and the theoretical constructs for how the pieces would fit together in different circumstances. Over the years, I read the literature, taught classes, talked to managers working in corporate sustainability. A few years ago, I felt I had learned and aged enough that I needed to write it all down to keep things organized. The result is this book.

I have many people to thank. I'll start with my family, who taught me many lessons about organizing individuals for collective action, starting before the "dinner table servant" was even a thing. In 2008 I spent a sabbatical year at the Bren School of Environmental Science and found myself in a community of smart, creative, and curious faculty, staff, and students, all committed to harnessing the power of collaboration to solve environmental problems. I was happy to join the Bren School's faculty a few years later and have been grateful every day since.

Just about everything I have published has been the product of collaboration. Even though only my name is on the cover, this book is no different, because it contains so much that I have learned from my collaborators. I owe particular thanks to Sarah Anderson, Trevor Brown, Patrick Callery, Nicole Darnall, Seonghoon Kim, Hunter Lenihan, Aseem Prakash, Jeff Talbert, Robert Urbatsch, David Van Slyke, and Neal Woods. I should list my students as collaborators since I have learned so much from them as well. I thank them all. The Bren School has hosted scores of business-sustainability managers and executives, many of whom have spent an afternoon guest teaching, thanks to the generous financial support of former Bren School dean, Dennis Aigner. While I was the course instructor on paper, I was really just the organizer and was learning as a student in all those classes. I owe special thanks to those who taught multiple sessions of the course: Joe Bialowitz, Diana Glassman, Dana Jennings, Ryan McMullan, Gwen Migita, Roberto Piccioni, and Dimitri Shanin. Shelby Smith and Robert Urbatsch read the manuscript and provided detailed feedback. Anna Zauner and Shelby Smith helped with research. I am responsible for any remaining errors. Finally, I grateful for Benjamin and Oliver, from whom I have learned the daily joy of being Papa.

1 | Introduction

On a Monday morning in June 2009, Timberland CEO Jeff Swartz woke up to find his inbox jammed with emails accusing Timberland of destroying Amazon rainforests and exacerbating global warming by using leather allegedly sourced from cattle that were being grazed on cleared rainforest land. Over the next few weeks, the emails totaled 65,000. His company had become a target of a campaign organized by Greenpeace, an environmental activist organization with a strong history of exposing companies' environmental negligence. As Swartz recounted, "I figured if that many people were taking the time to send an email, there must be at least half a million not sending emails ... That's a big number. Our brand's reputation was at stake" (Swartz 2010: 39).

At that moment, the environment was a strategic issue for Timberland. Sustainability had always been important to its brand – its logo was a tree, after all – and for decades, Timberland had company programs for its employees to contribute to its corporate social responsibility (CSR) and sustainability initiatives. How Timberland responded to the Greenpeace challenge would have a material impact on the future of its business.

Timberland needed an environmental strategy.

Timberland is not alone. These days, virtually every company confronts environmental sustainability as a strategic challenge. All companies have some impact on the natural environment. A company's potential for environmental impacts exists across the life cycles of its products, from the production of raw materials, through manufacturing and distribution, use, and disposal. The environmental impact of an automobile starts with the extraction of natural resources, continues through the manufacturing process and the distribution of the finished product, extends as the automobile is used, and often ends with disposal of the automobile in a wrecker's yard. Even companies that don't produce material products have environmental impacts.

Management consultants travel for business on airlines that consume fossil fuels and work from offices that are typically heated, cooled, and electrically powered by more fossil fuels, all of which emit greenhouse gasses.

1.1 Environmental Impacts as Opportunities

Every environmental impact is, of course, an opportunity for improvement. A company might offer products with environmentally beneficial features, improve efficiency in its production processes, reduce the risk of environmental spills or mishaps, or implement programs to engage its workforce in sustainability programs, to name only a few.

Environmental impacts also mean that a company may face demands from stakeholders who want to see improvements in environmental performance. Until the last few decades, people did not expect companies to do more than make profits and comply with government laws and regulations. Some companies might produce more environmental goods than regulations required, perhaps by planting some trees in a park or even keeping their smokestacks cleaner, motivated by the same sense of community commitment that led them to sponsor Little League teams or donate emergency supplies in times of civic crisis. Through the 1980s, a few large companies, usually closely owned businesses like Patagonia or Ben & Jerry's, started practicing sustainability on broader, more systematic scales. In 1985, Patagonia pledged to contribute 1 percent of its sales to environmental causes. In 1988, Ben & Jerry's offered ice cream flavors such as "Rainforest Crunch," which touted the company's environmental initiatives. For most companies, however, managing environmental impacts did not extent beyond complying with government regulations.

These days, a clean record of regulatory compliance is no longer sufficient in the arena of public expectations. Consider some examples:

> Consumers increasingly weigh companies' environmental practices in their purchasing decisions. Nearly every imaginable product or service available to consumers has a "green" or sustainable purchasing option. People can have their teeth cared for by a "green" dentist, duly certified by the Eco-Dentistry Association. They can use environmentally friendly cleaning products or hire a green home-cleaning service. When they buy a home, they can do so with the guidance of a certified sustainable real-estate agent.

Environmental groups today represent just about every cause one can imagine. Some groups focus on motivating activists for campaigns and protests and are searching for their next company targets for a campaign. Other groups are looking for opportunities to cooperate with companies in next-generation sustainability practices.

Companies' environmental and social performance has become a larger focus among investors. The number of funds that incorporate environmental, social, and governance factors in their investments has grown from 55 funds investing $639 billion in 1995 to 1,204 funds investing $17.1 trillion in 2020. (US SIF 2020)

Employees want to work for companies that go beyond the requirements of government regulations to produce environmental and social value. A 2016 survey reported that 75% of the Millennial generation (roughly, those born between 1982 and 1996) would take a pay cut to work for a socially responsible company. (Cone Communications 2016)

Investors are weighing environmental performance into their financial evaluations of companies. According to a survey by the consulting company McKinsey (2020), most senior executives said they would be willing to pay 10 percent more to acquire a company with a positive record of environmental, social, and governance performance compared to a company with a negative one.

Trends like these are not confined to the United States and the financially well-off countries in western Europe. Around the world, consumer demand for green products is on the rise. Activist protests are becoming more common, even in the developing world. In 2021 in Gujarat, India, hundreds of people protested against Suzlon, an Indian wind turbine manufacturer. Suzlon had proposed a wind energy project in Sangnara village, which protestors believed would endanger the local forest, long held sacred by the community (Bavadam 2021). Citizen demand for improved environmental conditions is likewise growing across China, even resulting in citizen protests (Khanna 2020).

Even if a company's local surroundings are quiet, it may still experience strong demands for environmental performance through its positioning in global supply chains, as Timberland's Jeff Swartz experienced through Greenpeace's Amazon campaign. Companies are increasingly expecting their suppliers to have stronger sustainability programs. Only 27 of the 1,832 European Union (EU) companies surveyed by the International Trade Centre in 2019 reported that sustainability was not a consideration when considering input sourcing.

For companies around the world, these stakeholder voices – from diverse sources, on diverse issues, and with varying tone and intensity – present both opportunities and threats. The opportunities are to implement environmental improvements that stakeholders demand. Gratified stakeholders may then bestow value on companies who produce the environmental improvements they want: consumers may pay higher prices for environmental products; employees may stay in their jobs longer; insurers may offer better terms. The threat can be the loss of competitive advantage when a company fails to meet stakeholder expectations. Just as stakeholders can bestow value, they can also act in ways that reduce the value a company receives. Stakeholders' protests can damage a company's brand and hurt its product sales. Stakeholders can deny access to key strategic resources, such as material inputs, the license to produce and operate, and access to markets to sell products and services.

More than twenty-five years after Patagonia and Ben & Jerry's made sustainability core to their business, sustainability as a core business practice has become mainstream. Over half the Fortune 500 companies have published annual corporate sustainability reports. Most large companies have a C-suite-level corporate sustainability executive and a department staffed with personnel whose job is to improve the company's environmental performance. By 2022, 622 out of the 2,000 largest publicly traded companies in the world had committed to a strategy to reach net-zero climate emissions (CRE Finance Council 2021). Yet popularity does not always mean success. All too often, companies' sustainability efforts fall short of their goals, leaving managers questioning whether their investments were worthwhile and the public skeptical of companies' sustainability claims.

An environmental strategy serves to guide a company to make choices about how it interacts with the environment, its stakeholders, and various forms of institutions, such as governments, industry associations, and multisector collaborations. An environmental strategy is an integrated set of choices about how a company should interact with the natural environment. It includes deciding which resources and material it uses, where it should source them, how it should handle those that do not end up in products (e.g., waste, by-products, or pollution), and how the company communicates its environmental efforts to its stakeholders. It also includes deciding when and how to engage with others to influence government regulations and nongovernmental institutions so that the company can better achieve its environmental goals. An environmental strategy addresses how a company can enhance its long-term financial returns by improving its environmental performance, mitigating risk, and/or identifying and capturing new sources of value.

The promise of an effective environmental strategy is realized when companies develop, implement, and execute environmental programs that deliver value for itself, its stakeholders, and the environment (what some commentators call the "triple bottom line"): companies earn higher profits, the environment becomes cleaner, and companies have more positive relations with happier stakeholders. As we will see in Chapter 8, Timberland's Jeff Swartz developed an environmental strategy that transformed the threats of Greenpeace's campaign into an opportunity to achieve a leadership position in the eyes of consumers and stakeholders who cared about the Amazon's plight. Nearly two months after Greenpeace's email deluge, Swartz announced that the company and its supplier were moving toward a moratorium against deforestation in the Amazon biome, while at the same time praising Greenpeace's activism for bringing the issue to light. A few days later, Greenpeace issued a statement praising Timberland's leadership on the matter. The Amazon ecosystem benefited from better management practices, Greenpeace benefited by displaying its leadership to its members, and Timberland benefited from a better public image.

1.2 A Framework for Environmental Strategy

No company can make every environmental improvement available to it – environmental improvements are costly and a company will always make an environmental impact of one kind or another, no matter how well it is managing its operations. Environmental strategy is about making choices. Which impacts should a company improve? Stakeholder voices can help guide these choices, but they are not a panacea: a company cannot respond to every stakeholder demand for environmental improvements. Which stakeholders should matter?

The goal in this book is to present an environmental strategy framework that helps companies make choices about which environmental performance improvements to target and how to implement improvements. The framework identifies the important choices facing a company and how it can identify and analyze opportunities for improvement:

Identifying which dimensions of environmental performance improvements can create business value. What environmental improvements can a company implement at a relatively low cost that deliver value to its environmental stakeholders? This means assessing the company's environmental impacts, opportunities for improvements, and the different types of stakeholders and how they value its environmental improvements.

Ensuring channel for value transfer. Just because companies can satisfy stakeholder demand for environmental improvements does not necessarily mean they will receive value for making these improvements. A channel helps stakeholders transfer value to the company that produces the environmental improvement. Sometimes, the channels transfer financial value, such as through consumer purchasing. Often, the value is nonfinancial, such as when an environmental group endorses a company's environmental practices.

Ensuring credibility. Companies need to communicate the value of environmental improvements to stakeholders and ensure confidence that the terms of the exchange will be met. Very rarely are stakeholders able to assess the quality of a company's environmental improvements. Effective communication strategies, such as certifications, company brands, and endorsements, can help a company communicate the integrity of their environmental improvements to their stakeholders. Formal and informal contract terms can ensure that the company and its stakeholders will uphold their side of the exchange.

Capturing sustainable value from environmental improvements. Companies need to ensure that this environmental improvement contributes to a strategic competitive advantage. An environmental strategy can extend existing competitive advantages, or, in rarer cases, an environmental strategy can create new sources of competitive advantage.

Engaging environmental institutions. A company can have opportunities to engage its institutional environment and change how institutions facilitate or impede its ability to achieve its environmental goals. Such engagement requires understanding how institutions influence the distribution of costs and benefits from environmental improvements and other stakeholders' incentives for pursuing institutional change.

An important insight from this book is that a successful environmental strategy needs to be tailored to the unique circumstances of the company implementing it (Starik & Marcus 2000; Starik & Rands 1995). These can include differences in consumers' willingness to pay for different types of environmental products, environmental nongovernmental organizations' (NGOs) ability to stage protests, and communities' capacity to organize themselves for collective action. These conditions vary within countries and across countries around the world (Rivera 2010). Environmental strategy is also shaped by institutions. Institutions include government regulations and the agencies that enforce them, certification programs managed by industry associations and environmental NGOs, and multisector collaborations among NGOs, governments, and other businesses. These institutions can shape the costs and benefits of a company's environmental improvements.

An environmental strategy can identify opportunities for companies to advance their environmental objectives by engaging with the institutions in their environment. Changing institutions can alter the distribution of environmental improvements' costs and benefits, creating new opportunities and challenges for environmental strategy. A company's environmental strategy might look to lobby governments to increase the stringency of environmental regulations. While stringent regulations may raise a company's costs, it can gain a competitive advantage if the company's competitors face yet higher costs to comply with the same regulations.

An environmental strategy also depends on how the company conducts its business. Companies can have different opportunities for environmental improvements because they make different products, with different production processes, and with different inputs. They may have different (though often overlapping) stakeholders, with different levels of demand for different environmental improvements. Companies can have unique sources of competitive advantage based on their own market and nonmarket strategies and their strategic resources.

What also makes companies different are the people who own them and work for them. Led by its visionary founder, Yvon Chouinard, Patagonia has an impressive history of being at the forefront of business sustainability practices. Ben & Jerry's environmental and social programs reflected the values of the company's founders Ben Cohen and Jerry Greenfield. When Paul Polman became CEO of Unilever in 2009, he touted the company's growing CSR initiatives for their contributions to Unilever's long-term financial goals. Polman said in 2020, "[b]usinesses thrive when they serve all their stakeholders: citizens, employees, suppliers, partners, those who make up the extended value chain. When you make your business relevant to the needs of the communities and societies you serve, then everyone benefits, including shareholders" (Butler 2020).

This book's strategic framework helps companies make choices about how and when to improve their environmental performance. The efficacy of an environmental improvement is likely to depend on circumstances in the company's external environment (its market and nonmarket environment and stakeholders) and characteristics within the company (its competitive strategy, resources, and capabilities). The success of an environmental improvement is also contingent on the company's social context, the behavior of others, and the actors' resources, capabilities, and objectives. An environmental strategy acknowledges trade-offs – no environmental strategy can satisfy all stakeholders while also leaving the company financially viable. At the same time, environmental strategy is an opportunity for finding synergies that enhance the value of the company and its stakeholders.

For scholars looking to answer questions about when companies' sustainability programs will be successful, the book looks to frame research around theoretically grounded research questions and concepts. Early on, central research questions in corporate sustainability focused on whether companies' environmental programs actually improved environmental conditions (Chrun et al. 2016; Starik & Marcus 2000) and whether they produced financial value for the companies enacting them (Barnett et al. 2020; Friede et al. 2015). After years of study, the consensus answer is that environmental programs can be financially beneficial – clearly, there are times when environmental improvements deliver on the promise of the triple bottom line, but this question of whether sustainability pays is misplaced. In fact, it is a somewhat odd question in the first place. In fields like marketing, management information systems, research and development, and operations, scholars rarely ask questions such as "does it pay to allocate resources in this area?" Instead, the important questions in these areas center on what companies must do under specific circumstances to be successful.

Back in 1999, in laying the groundwork for sustainability as a business strategy problem, Forest Reinhardt wrote, "[i]nstead of asking whether it pays to be green, we ought to be asking about the circumstances under which it might pay" (Reinhardt 1999: 1). Later scholars aimed to build on Reinhardt's foundation to identify the drivers and opportunities for environmental strategy (Blackburn 2007; Esty & Winston 2009; Hoffman 2000). How and when should companies allocate resources for product research, marketing, supply chain management, or any other activity? Companies can misspend resources on marketing and operations, just as they can misspend resources on sustainability.

More recently, scholars and business leaders have begun to question whether an environmental strategy in which each company acts on its own can achieve progress, given the magnitude of environmental problems around the world (Geyer 2021). Some call for more collaborations among companies, NGOs, governments, and communities to create new institutions for shared value: the types that balance the costs and benefits of collective action and produce the social and environmental improvements that communities need (Kramer & Pfitzer 2016; Porter & Kramer 2019).

This book builds on insights such as these and aims to advance a comprehensive framework for how companies can design, develop, and implement an environmental strategy. The environmental strategy framework presented in this book allows classifying case studies and larger-sample empirical research into theoretical constructs, which can then lead to integrating findings into a broader, more coherent body of knowledge. The framework helps organize the field's diverse research streams around key questions and analytic dimensions that enhance the cross-fertilization of research findings across studies and disciplines.

A few caveats are in order about the scope of this book's topics. A first is that the book sidesteps the question of whether and how much companies have moral obligations toward the environment. Moral obligations for companies and individuals constitutes an important and complex topic. In 1970, economist Milton Friedman published a famous article in the *New York Times Magazine* titled "The Social Responsibility of Business Is to Increase Its Profits" (Friedman 1970). Some people today agree with Friedman that companies have few if any ethical obligations to do more than comply with the government's laws and regulations as they pursue profits, and some government regulations even impose a fiduciary duty for companies to maximize profits. Other academics and even some business executives argue that companies have a moral obligation to contribute to solving social and environmental problems, even if doing so comes at the expense of profits (Carroll 1999; Hsieh 2017). The ethical questions about whether and how much a company should sacrifice financial gain to produce social and environmental goods are beyond the scope of this book.

Relatedly, there is an open question about whether companies always and only maximize profits and are never willing to sacrifice financial gain on the altar of environmental improvements. In some jurisdictions, companies can be legally chartered as a benefit corporation, which allows them to include social and environmental objectives, along with profits, as their legally recognized goals (Gehman et al. 2019). Patagonia is now chartered as a benefit corporation. It may be true that benefit corporations, and perhaps other companies as well, are willing to accept lower profits in order to produce more environmental and social value. After all, people are sometimes willing to donate money for social and environmental causes, such as when they give money to charities.

This book's premise is that, whatever their moral obligations and however much companies' morals and ethics motivate them to pursue environmental improvements, companies will contribute more environmental goods when they have more incentives to do so. People give more to charity when they have more incentives to do so, whether in the form of tax deductions, social recognition, or other forms of value. This book's aim is to help companies achieve both environmental and financial goals, regardless of how they balance the two, by showing how to identify where companies have more incentives to improve environmental performance. An effective environmental strategy can advance both financial and sustainability objectives, and if a company is willing to sacrifice financial value for environmental gain, the environmental strategy can help identify environmental improvements with the lowest net cost.

The second caveat is that this book largely sidesteps the question of what actions actually improve the environment. Sometimes a practice has clear and unequivocal environmental improvements, such as removing lead from gasoline. Often, however, an environmental improvement comes with trade-offs among its environmental outcomes. Organic food production uses fewer pesticides but is often more resource intensive and thus places more demands on ecosystems. Even seemingly beneficial environmental activities, like recycling (Geyer et al. 2016; Zink & Geyer 2019) and the circular economy (Zink & Geyer 2017), have important trade-offs.

Evaluating environmental performance is important, of course, and there are useful methods for evaluating companies' sustainability practices (Palazzo et al. 2020), some of which are discussed in Chapter 5. For the most part, the discussions in this book assume that a company and its stakeholders hold accurate beliefs about the environmental benefits they are considering – that is, they have properly used the correct methods and reached accurate assessments of the need for environmental improvements, the improvements' trade-offs, and how they can be achieved. The premise in this book is that an environmental problem is "solved" if the problem's stakeholders are fully informed about environmental conditions and accept the status quo. Some might argue that stakeholder consensus does not mean that an environmental problem is truly solved. The solution may not be ecologically optimal or sustainable for the long term. The solution may not satisfy the precautionary principle or other ethical standards. The company may not have contributed its fair share to the improvement. Identifying the "right" levels of environmental improvements and how to achieve them requires bringing together insights from areas such as ecology, industrial ecology, engineering, and environmental ethics. Resolving these types of question requires expertise beyond what this author can offer.

The book is organized as follows. Chapter 2 presents some theoretical background for the book. It opens with a discussion of market failures and environmental problems as negative externalities. Companies' pollution emissions are externalities that damage ecosystems. Stakeholders value healthy ecosystems and want companies to reduce their pollution emissions. The chapter presents a theoretical framework proposed by the economist Ronald Coase. If transaction costs are sufficiently low, the externality producers and the stakeholders can agree to an exchange of value. The stakeholders can provide value to the producers in exchange for pollution reduction. The chapter concludes with a discussion of the transaction costs that can impede the exchanges between companies and their stakeholders.

Chapters 3, 4, and 5 begin the discussion of environmental strategy by presenting a series of challenges to be solved for companies to implement environmental improvements and capture value from them, as discussed: identifying potential environmental improvements and their costs, assessing stakeholder demand, establishing a channel for capturing value from stakeholders, and ensuring the credibility of environmental communications and commitments. Chapter 3 focuses on market strategy and stakeholders and Chapter 4 focuses on nonmarket strategy, stakeholders, and institutions. Chapter 5 continues the discussion by examining the relationship between environmental strategy and companies' strategic resources and capabilities. Environmental improvements and activities can create new sources of competitive advantage or reinforce existing competitive advantages. The chapter concludes by discussing the organization of responsibilities for environmental improvements and environmental strategy within companies.

Chapters 6, 7, and 8 present the theory in specific areas. Each of these chapters opens with a brief case example that illustrates the challenges and potential solutions to win–win environmental improvements, using the framework presented in Chapters 3, 4, and 5. Chapter 6 covers market strategy with an analysis of how companies can successfully market green products. The case example is Stonyfield Farm, a small New England company that was a pioneer in the organic yogurt market and grew into one of the largest organic dairy product companies in the world. Chapter 7 covers employee engagement – how employees react to and engage in companies' environmental programs and initiatives. The case, TD Bank's employee engagement programs, as led by Diana Glassman, shows the challenges and promises of using environmental programs for employee engagement. Chapter 8 examines nonmarket strategy with a focus on how companies interact with environmental NGOs and environmental activists. The case study returns to examine more fully the case of Timberland CEO Jeff Swartz and his response to Greenpeace's Amazon rainforest campaign. Chapter 9 concludes the book with a final case analysis, Nike's "Considered" sustainability initiatives. While Nike's sustainable shoes did not gain transaction in consumer markets, its "Considered Design Principles" became influential in the shoe industry and helped Nike's relations with nonmarket stakeholders.

2 | *Foundations and Background*

A company creates value by making products and services that it sells at prices higher than its costs. The company's costs include materials, labor, production machinery, and overhead: anything it pays for in order to be an ongoing enterprise. A company's goal is to capture as much value as possible through the price it charges to customers, while consumers look to receive greater value from the product than the price they pay. Well-functioning markets benefit both companies and consumers by allowing these exchanges to occur. The buyer and seller both gain from the exchange. Adam Smith described how markets harness private incentives for broader societal good:

Every individual necessarily labours to render the annual revenue of the society as great as he can. He generally, indeed, neither intends to promote the public interest, nor knows how much he is promoting it ... He intends only his own gain, and in this, as in many other cases, is led by an invisible hand to promote an end which was no part of his intention. (Smith 2000: 485)

Smith described exchanges where all the costs and benefits accrue to just the buyer and seller. In practice, sometimes exchanges produce costs and benefits that accrue to other people as well. As mentioned in Chapter 1, as a company produces and sells its products, it also creates environmental harm. All companies have at least some environmental impact, regardless of whether they are creating a product or not. Sometimes a company may want to improve its environmental performance and may even choose to do so of its own accord, without the promise of value from appreciative recipients. Such public-spiritedness is likely to be rare – environmental improvements are costly, and companies face pressures to keep their prices and costs low and to return profits to shareholders to maintain their stock prices.

A company's stakeholders are the people or groups that can affect the company or have preferences about how the company performs (Freeman 2010). Stakeholders include employees, suppliers, shareholders, interest groups, and governments. A subset of a company's stakeholders is its environmental stakeholders. These are the people who interact with the company because of its environmental impacts. When a company reduces its environmental impacts, it creates value when environmental stakeholders appreciate the positive outcomes for the earth's environment and its people. Sometimes people experience these improvements as direct benefits – a fisher can earn a better living if a healthy ocean ecosystem produces more and bigger fish. Other times, stakeholders experience the value indirectly as co-benefits of the environmental improvements. When air pollution declines, conditions for nature and wildlife improve, as does people's health. Sometimes the co-benefits are the emotions stakeholders feel from knowing environmental conditions have improved, even if they do not directly experience them. The opportunity for companies – and the world's ecosystems – is to implement environmental improvements in a way that returns value from the stakeholders that appreciate them. If a company can receive value from its environmental stakeholders, these initiatives do not require public-spiritedness to be implemented, and they are more likely to be implemented as they can bring money back to the company.

Just as consumers bring financial value to a company by paying for products, environmental stakeholders may also provide value to companies for the environmental benefits. Stakeholders use their own resources to influence the company's ability to accomplish its objectives, for better or worse. For example, stakeholders in a community may possess political or legal authority to prevent a company from expanding its operations. Residents may object that a proposed wind farm would obstruct their scenic view and may lobby the government to prevent its construction. Environmental activists may publicly praise a company for its environmental accomplishments. A company and its stakeholders can exchange value and create win–win scenarios that benefit the company, its stakeholders, and the environment, just as in Smith's account of market exchanges where a company sells a product to a consumer.

Understanding these interactions as value exchanges sheds light on how they are formed, what barriers can prevent them from occurring, and what initiatives companies can take on to help the environment in financially sustainable ways. This chapter opens the analysis of how value exchanges between companies and their stakeholders can produce win–win outcomes that resemble the promise of market exchanges. To do so, we start by examining market exchanges and how market failures lie at the root of many of the environmental problems that companies produce. We then show how value exchanges as envisioned by Coase (Coase 1960), akin to buying and selling products, can also be a solution to environmental problems and create win–win outcomes that benefit the triple bottom line. Such exchanges do not occur automatically. They require the exchange partners to overcome several obstacles – finding the partner and assessing needs, negotiating terms of the exchange, delivering value, and ensuring the agreement terms are upheld.

2.1 Markets and Environmental Problems

Environmental problems, such as air pollution, climate change, and overfished fisheries, suggest that markets do not always work to produce triple bottom line outcomes. Markets can fail for many reasons – there are not enough buyers or sellers, no one directly owns the resource that is damaged, and so on – and when failure happens, markets can reduce the overall welfare of society instead of increasing it. Externalities are a common reason that markets fail, and, as we will see, they are at the root of many environmental and pollution problems. An externality is a consequence of an activity that is borne by someone who did not choose to incur it. With a positive externality, the producer pays the costs of making the externality while its benefits spill over to others. The homeowner who pays to install the streetlight receives some benefit from the well-lit sidewalk but does not receive any compensation for all the benefits received by the rest of the people walking on the sidewalk. These types of externalities are underproduced because the producer pays the entire cost of making the externality but receives only a fraction of the benefit. With a negative externality, some of the costs spill over to others, while the benefits accrue only to the producer. When college students throw a party in a residential apartment building, they are producing a negative externality – the students enjoy the benefits of a rocking good time, but the loud music leaves their elderly neighbors sleep deprived. When a company generates pollution as it creates its products, it is also creating negative externalities. The company and its consumers may still experience gains from the sale of the company's products, but the environment and those who experience the pollution are made worse off by the pollution.

From the perspective of society as a whole, the problem with externalities is that the misalignment of costs and benefits changes producers' incentives so that exchanges do not result in win–win outcomes. The homeowner may not derive enough direct benefit from the streetlight to go to the trouble of installing it, even though his benefits combined with his neighbors' benefits are greater than the streetlight's costs. By contrast, if the partying college kids live near many other people, their good time may have been of small value to them compared to the greater suffering among their sleep-deprived neighbors, but they will go ahead with their fun regardless. Many clashes over companies' environmental behavior result from negative externalities being overproduced or positive externalities being underproduced. In this book, we use the phrase "environmental improvement" to refer to situations where a company goes beyond the requirements of government regulations to increase the production of a positive environmental externality or decrease the production of a negative environmental externality.

A similar source of environmental problems stems from how companies and environmental stakeholders can value time differently. Environmental NGOs tend to place more weight on the value of resources in the future. On the other hand, companies tend to place more value on the present, perhaps because their shareholders want money as dividends or because the companies see highly profitable ways to invest the money they have now. Take, for example, two identical forests, one owned by a business and the other by an environmental NGO. The business values the trees because they can be cut down and sold as lumber for a net gain to the business of $1,000. Let us assume the NGO and the business value the trees in this forest at the same amount. The NGO values the trees for the ecosystem services they provide, such as cleaner air, wildlife habitat, and so on. If the forests were allowed to stand, their value would increase over time as the trees grow larger and improve in quality. Let us further assume that the financial value of the sold lumber increases at the same rate as the ecosystem services the NGO values from the forest. In such circumstances, the company would want to cut down the trees and sell them today, while the NGO would prefer to let the trees stand. The reason is not that the NGO values the trees more than the business does. The current and future values of the trees were the same for the company and the NGO. The company preferred to cut down the trees because it had an opportunity to use the proceeds from their sale for some other financially valuable use.

2.2 Solving Environmental Problems

Throughout history, societies have addressed environmental problems in many ways. Sometimes the solution is government-enforced laws and regulations that limit pollution emissions, conserve resources, and protect ecosystems. Sometimes the solution is to define property rights so that market forces can drive improvements. Other times, people can create their own governance institutions to solve environmental problems, as when fishers cooperate to prevent overfishing. Academics and policymakers hotly debate which of these approaches works best. Some approaches work better in some circumstances than in others (Ostrom, Janssen, and Anderies 2007; Ostrom and Cox 2010). When it comes to solving environmental problems, there are no panaceas (Ostrom 2007).

Many solutions to environmental problems use government rules and regulations, such as rules to limit emissions from factory smoke-stacks and noise ordinances in residential neighborhoods. A common regulatory approach is called "command and control": the government issues a rule prescribing how much of a negative externality a company can produce, then monitors and enforces compliance with that rule. Other regulatory approaches look to harness market incentives by charging a price for negative externality production, such as by levying a tax on pollution emissions, which gives polluters an incentive to reduce their emissions, while giving tax breaks for energy-efficient appliances or grants for solar panel research to subsidize the production of positive externalities.

Environmental problems can also be addressed without direct government intervention. Under the right circumstances, people – and, as we will see, companies – can reduce their production of negative externalities by making a bargain with others who would enjoy the benefits of the externalities' reduction. The economist Ronald Coase wrote how people can buy and sell externalities in his famous article "The Problem of Social Cost" (Coase 1960). The idea, now known as the "Coase theorem," is that parties can, if conditions are right, bargain among themselves to account for externalities' effects and allocate resources in ways that make everyone better off. In a "Coasian" scenario, those who would benefit from a positive externality compensate producers for providing that externality; those who would suffer from a negative externality pay for it to be produced less or not at all. A Coasian exchange can also work from the producer's end: the producer of a negative externality could compensate the victims for the damage caused by their activities, assuming that the producer's gains are greater than the damages they cause. An advantage of these solutions is that if conditions are right, the two sides will bargain their way to an efficient level of externality production, and society will see its net benefits maximized.[1]

To understand how a Coasian exchange can work, we can start with a hypothetical example of two people living in a two-story apartment building. Jane is a vegan who lives above Bob, a meat-eater. Bob occasionally likes to barbeque a steak on the grill outside his apartment. The apartment complex has rules permitting tenants to grill as much as they please, even if they live on the first floor and the grill smoke drifts up to the second-floor apartments (a negative externality of the grilling, from Jane's perspective). Suppose Bob decides to grill a steak on a day that Jane happens to be hosting her monthly vegan home-brew and cooking party. Before Bob lights the fire, Jane knocks on his door and offers Bob veggies, hummus, and a growler of home-brewed beer as an inducement not to grill his steak. From a Coasian perspective, this is a win–win outcome because Bob is happier noshing his snacks and beer, and Jane is happier because meat aromas won't invade her party.

The Nature Conservancy (TNC) and California farmers have used a Coasian exchange to create temporary wetlands from rice fields to help migrating birds. Rice farmers were already flooding their fields in January and TNC concluded that keeping some of them flooded for a few extra weeks would give birds a place to stop during their annual migration. During initial conversations with TNC, farmers reacted positively to the idea of receiving payment in return for keeping their fields flooded longer. As one farmer told TNC, "you want us to grow birds, like we grow rice. We know how to do that" (Hallstein & Miller 2014). TNC's program, called BirdReturns, had farmers bid for how

---

[1] Deryugina and colleagues provide modern and real-world examples of Coasian exchanges (Deryugina et al. 2020).

much TNC would need to pay them to keep their fields flooded for a few extra weeks. TNC selected bids with the lowest price that offered the best bird habitat. Over a hundred farmers have participated in BirdReturns, creating over 58,000 acres of temporary bird habitat (The Nature Conservancy n.d.). Through BirdReturns, farmers receive payment for "growing birds," a positive externality that accrued to TNC, its members, and other people who care about birds. For its part, TNC pays a much lower cost than it would if it bought the land outright, and the birds enjoy nice resting spots during their migration.

Coasian exchanges can also occur across international boarders. During the 1990s, the Japanese government used Coasian principles to reduce Japan's exposure to pollutants released by companies burning coal in China and other parts of Asia. Japan's Green Aid Plan spent $500 million to help these companies implement clean coal and efficiency improvements; Chinese companies that did not receive Green Aid Plan funding did not implement improvements (Deryugina et al. 2021).

The logic of a Coasian exchange can also work in situations where the parties assign different values to time, as when the company and the environmental NGO both owned forests. When the company cuts down its forest, the company receives profits from the sale of the wood. The NGO would have preferred the company's forest to remain intact to produce its future ecosystem services. If the NGO placed enough value on the forest and the future environmental benefits it would provide, it might raise the money to purchase the company's forest. This would allow the company to realize its short-term profits while the NGO realizes the forest's longer-term ecosystem benefits. On the other hand, if the company valued cutting down the forest more than the NGO preferred keeping it, the company could pay the NGO for the rights to the forest. The NGO could then use the proceeds to protect the environment elsewhere, perhaps where protection had more ecological value and the financial costs of protecting it were lower.

2.3 Companies, Environmental Impacts, and Stakeholder Exchanges

An *environmental impact* is a "change to the environment, whether adverse or beneficial, wholly or partly resulting from an organization's environmental aspects," according to the best-practice environmental management standard ISO 14001 (Geneva: International Organization for Standardization 2015). Industries that use extensive natural resources, such as agriculture and mining, tend to have large environmental impacts. Large-scale agricultural production can pollute waterways with runoff fertilizer and pesticides. But even apparently benign industries such as banking and consulting have environmental impacts. For example, the electricity that powers offices is often generated by burning fossil fuels, as are the fuels that heat offices, and the airplanes that enable business travel, all of which emits carbon dioxide that contributes to global climate change.

When a timber company cuts down trees on its property to sell, it liquidates an asset and converts it into income when it sells the wood as lumber. If the company does not protect the land, its topsoil might erode and diminish its ability to grow new trees, reducing the asset value of the land. These are all private costs and benefits from tree farming if they affect only the company. A company's environmental impacts are often externalities, as they have impacts that affect others. If the eroded topsoil ends up in a river and impairs its ecosystem, that cost would not be borne by the landowner but would be a negative externality for downstream users. The benefits, or positive externalities, of a sediment-free river and healthy ecosystems – abundant and healthy fish, easy boat navigation, and so on – are available to users beyond the landowners and to those who value healthy natural systems.

Producing a positive environmental benefit, whether by reducing a negative externality or producing a positive externality, is costly. The timber company would lose immediate income when it retains trees to stop erosion. Boiler operators can spend resources for protective equipment and more thorough cleaning to mitigate the risk of accidental discharge and spills of fuel and other chemicals. Companies sometimes have opportunities to purchase and install more energy-efficient equipment that can reduce the amount of pollution associated with their production.

Environmental impacts are opportunities for a company to create win–win exchanges with stakeholders. To make these exchanges happen, the company must identify its stakeholders and their demand for improvements. The company and its stakeholders must overcome the transaction costs that can prevent the exchanges from reaching fruition.

2.3.1 Environmental Stakeholders

A company's *environmental stakeholders* are those who are affected by the company's environmental impacts and are able to express their interest in the company increasing its production of positive environmental externalities (or reducing its negative externalities). Sometimes a company's environmental stakeholders are those who directly experience the harms and benefits of its environmental performance. In 2017, hundreds of Achuar people protested oil production facilities in the Peruvian Amazon. The Achuar are indigenous to the area and have a rich history of preserving their local environment. For forty-three days, the protestors occupied oil fields and shut off road and air strip access, demanding that Petroperú, the state oil company, improve consultation with local communities about the environmental impacts of its oil production (Zaitchik 2020). A company's environmental stakeholders can also include those who want the company to improve its environmental performance, even if its environmental impacts do not directly affect them, such as when European activists boycott companies that purchase palm oil from plantations that destroy local habitats in Indonesia.

Most benefits of the company's environmental improvements accrue to stakeholders outside the company in the form of greater positive externalities or smaller negative externalities. When a company improves its environmental impacts, people may enjoy cleaner air and water, long-term climate change mitigation, more resilient and biodiverse landscapes, or healthier wetlands. A company's environmental externalities are thus opportunities for the company to create and capture value. Value is created when reducing environmental impacts benefits the company's stakeholders. In fact, the same environmental improvement can be valued by multiple stakeholders at the same time. For example, suppose a company improved its production practices to reduce its impacts in the developing world. Consumers who value environmentally beneficial goods may appreciate the environmental features in the company's products while environmental groups may appreciate the protection their local ecosystems. Yet, a mechanism is needed for companies to capture a portion of the value that stakeholders receive from the environmental improvements. Fortunately, Coase provides an answer to how mechanisms can work.

2.3.2 *Transaction Costs and Coasian Exchanges*

Coase showed that the amount of externality production can, under some circumstances, be bought and sold through market exchanges, just like regular products. In theory, these exchanges can make everyone better off and even produce efficient outcomes. The company that reduces its environmental impacts wins because stakeholders provide compensation above the company's cost of making the improvement. The stakeholders win because they received more value in environmental benefits than what they provided to the company.

The discussion so far would make it seem easy to identify and implement a Coasian exchange: simply identify an environmental problem, find the stakeholders who want improvements, and negotiate terms for a deal. But that "under some circumstances" qualifier does not always hold, and the market does not magically create Coasian exchanges. Every market exchange requires buyers and sellers to expend some time, effort, and resources to make an exchange happen: these are what economists call transaction costs. The buyer and seller must be aware of the opportunity to make the exchange and of who their potential partners would be. They must be able to negotiate the quality, quantity, delivery terms, and price of the goods to be exchanged. And they must have confidence that the deal will happen on the terms they negotiated. Any of these things can trip up the potential Coasian exchange.

While every exchange involves transaction costs, some exchanges have more than others. When transaction costs are low, the parties can easily negotiate a deal that makes everyone better off: Jane just needed to walk downstairs with some extra food and beer. High transaction costs can prevent efficient exchanges for the production, or minimization, of externalities: the costs required to make the exchange happen can overwhelm the benefits participants would receive. What if Jane couldn't trust Bob to forgo grilling for the night? Bob might renege on his agreement, deciding that beer and hummus would make tasty appetizers for a grilled steak dinner. Without confidence the deal would be carried out, Jane would be reluctant to make a deal, and both are worse off. Jane endures the smoke from Bob's grill, and while Bob does enjoy the steak, he goes without the snacks and beer he would have enjoyed more. At the same time, it is costly for Bob to establish a reputation as a trustworthy guy since cultivating

Table 2.1 *Transaction cost categories*

Type of transaction cost	Time	Source	Examples
Search and screening	Prior to exchange	Lack of knowledge about exchange opportunities: stakeholders' demand, supply, and quality of goods	Identifying stakeholders and opportunities for pollution reduction, communicating with stakeholders
Bargaining and transfer	During exchange	Ambiguity about rights and obligations in the transaction, the cost of exchanging resources	Negotiation expenses, the cost of transferring goods and value among actors
Monitoring and enforcement	After exchange	Difficulty in discerning adherence to terms of the agreement, problems in enforcing terms	Legal costs, costs of social pressures

trust requires him to pass up benefits to show he genuinely is making sacrifices that would show he merit's Jane's trust.

Understanding the nature and source of transaction costs is an important first step toward mitigating them. Various forms of transaction costs can arise before, during, and after the exchange occurs: the buyer and seller expend resources negotiating terms of the exchange, gathering information about the quality of the products, and enforcing contract terms to ensure neither side reneges on the agreement. Table 2.1 lists three broad categories of transaction costs that can impede market exchanges for externalities.

2.3.2.1 Search and Screening Costs

Buyers and sellers must find partners suitable for the exchange to occur: who is offering products and services, and who wants them. Such information can be crucial for many areas of business strategy. In market strategy, the information needs of a company looking to enter a new market include a rich understanding of the market landscape, the production costs of their products, what potential customers want, and how much they are willing to pay. Potential customers must know about the company's products, quality, and prices and opportunities to obtain them. Search and screening costs are time and resources expended for buyers and sellers to find suitable partners. A low-cost scenario might require expenditures as simple as a company attracting customers through a website. Search and screening costs are an important problem for many companies – they must spend significant resources to market their products to consumers. Online retailers like Amazon and Alibaba reduce search costs for many common household products – rather than traveling to the store, consumers can find products from their home computer.

Searching and screening for potential partners is likewise an important component of a company's sustainability strategy. To make a Coasian exchange happen, the company needs to know quite a bit about its own environmental performance and its potential stakeholder partners. A company needs to understand its environmental impacts and costs for improvements. It needs to know how its stakeholders view its current impact and their demand for different types of improvements. These information challenges can be particularly severe in sustainability domains. A company's environmental impacts can extend far beyond its customers, perhaps deep into the company's supply chain and well outside the stakeholders' view. High search and screening costs can be a barrier to a win–win exchange. Such costs can be reduced when the buyer and seller have more information about the market, its consumers and product offerings, and its prices.

2.3.2.2 Bargaining and Transfer Costs

Most of the purchases people make take place with very little effort spent on bargaining and transferring resources. Consumers can easily see product prices and the means for obtaining them while strolling through their local supermarket. After a few simple clicks online, they can have products delivered to their door. To make such purchases, buyers do not need to spend much effort finding products and their prices, assessing quality, and physically receiving the product. In other cases, buyers and sellers need to spend considerable effort and resources to agree on transaction costs. Buyers might need to physically inspect the product to assess its quality. Transferring ownership may be cumbersome, such as when shipping costs are high.

Bargaining and transfer costs can be particularly challenging for companies and their environmental stakeholders. Exchanges between companies and their environmental stakeholders often occur with nonfinancial resources. Companies provide environmental goods, which often are difficult for stakeholders to assess and are rarely associated with market prices. In some cases, stakeholders provide financial value – such as when consumers pay extra for environmentally friendly products – but very often, stakeholders provide resources that have less clear financial value. Stakeholders may value a company's environmental improvements, and be willing to reward the company for them, but lack a mechanism for easily transferring resources to the company. Environmental stakeholders are often quite diverse and spread across a broad geographic region, making negotiations and resource transfer more difficult and costlier.

Though bargaining and transfer costs may slow or halt a transaction, people can reduce these costs. Money is useful in market economies because it lowers the transaction costs of buying and selling. Think about what would happen if we lived without any money and goods were only bought and sold in barter exchanges. Buyers and sellers would spend a lot of time figuring out value and haggling about the amount and quality of goods to be sold. A baker would need to figure out how many loaves to offer for a basket of vegetables, a new oven, and a chocolate gift for her wife. A dollar provides the evaluative yardstick for comparing the value of different goods and products. Money also lowers transfer costs. It is a lot easier for our baker to bring her wallet to the oven store than a truckload of bread loaves. As with search costs, Amazon and Alibaba's online marketplaces also reduce transfer costs – the companies ship the products to consumers' homes rather than requiring travel to the store.

2.3.2.3 Monitoring, Enforcement, and the Holdup Problem

A final set of transaction costs stems from the fact that parties to a deal may have the opportunity to back out of their commitments.[2] This can happen in several ways. A company might claim to have produced an environmental benefit without having actually done so.

---

[2] This section draws on (King 2007) for insights and examples on transactions costs and the holdup problem in environmental agreements.

It is often difficult for stakeholders to assess the quality of the environmental goods that companies create, leaving them reluctant to reward companies for environmental improvements. Likewise, even when the companies and stakeholders both have relatively complete information about the exchanges, they may have concerns that the other side will follow through and fulfill the full terms of the exchange to which they agreed.

An important transaction cost obstacle to Coasian exchanges occurs when those who would compensate a company for producing an environmental good are unable to evaluate its quality. We can call this the "green lemons" problem because it is an example of the scenario that George Akerlof presented in his famous paper "The Market for Lemons," for which he was awarded a Nobel Prize in economics (Akerlof 1970). In a lemons market, the quality of goods ranges from low to high, and sellers know more about the quality of a good than do buyers. Fearing they will receive a low-quality good if they paid for a higher-quality one, consumers refuse to pay anything but rock-bottom prices. Without confidence that buyers would pay for higher-quality goods, sellers end up producing only lower-quality goods. If consumers were fully informed, those who want the higher quality would pay higher prices, fully confident they were getting what they paid for. Once again, Amazon and Alibaba provide examples of ways to lower monitoring and enforcement costs in consumer product markets. Consumer reviews posted on the website provide information about how other people have experienced the product. Because negative reviews can harm sales, sellers have incentives to make sure their offerings meet customers' expectations.

The green lemons problem exists because stakeholders are rarely in a position to directly evaluate the amount and quality of a company's environmental performance, especially since many companies have far-flung, complex, and difficult-to-observe environmental impacts. Anyone can tell how a banana will taste just by looking at it: bright yellow skin with just a few brown spots indicates its precise ripeness. But it is not easy to tell whether that banana has been sustainably produced; ripe or not, an organic banana looks the same as any other. Companies collectively release thousands of pollutants into the air, water, and land, each of which can trigger local, regional, and global consequences of widely varying magnitudes, and all of which can be difficult to measure, aggregate, and compare. Many types of environmental impacts are geographically distant from most stakeholders. Pollution emissions by overseas suppliers are distant from local consumers. Even proximate production processes are often hidden from stakeholders' view or are visible but difficult to measure – such as how much pollution is being emitted from a nearby factory's smokestack or effluent pipe.

People know that environmental goods are costly to produce and that companies' pursuit of profits leads them to cut costs where they can. Any company can claim to be sustainable, but without the reassurance that the environmental externalities are genuine, people may suspect the company is engaging in greenwashing – falsely claiming to have produced an environmental benefit (Delmas & Burbano 2011). A company might greenwash by highlighting the narrow environmental improvements it produces while failing to mention the larger environmental problems it contributes to. As a result, companies often face stakeholder skepticism about their environmental performance claims, including whether their claimed investments are merely symbolic and how much environmental performance improvement actually resulted. Stakeholders are unlikely to be willing to reward a firm that claims to act sustainably unless they are confident those claims are true. For most companies, establishing credibility for their environmental quality claims can be quite challenging. And, the credibility challenge can be especially daunting for companies in industries that consumers think of as "dirty" or "polluting," for companies that are producing green products for the first time, or for companies whose products' green features do not provide obvious, immediate, and direct consumer benefits.

A holdup problem occurs when one party spends resources to make an exchange happen, and the other party has the opportunity to not follow up on her end of the deal. The holdup problem can arise when the exchange of resources occurs at different times. The first mover makes an initial payment or investment for the deal, while the other party's payment in return happens later. The first mover may be reluctant to make the up-front payment without insurance that the return payment will happen. The parties in the exchange need to be confident the other side will follow through on his end of the deal. In market exchanges, contract law usually prevents the holdup problem: our auto mechanic is willing to fix our car because she knows we will pay her once the repairs are complete. Consumers buy advance tickets to a theater production because they know they will receive a refund if the show does not go on. In many cases, public law helps solve holdup problems. Because we are legally obligated to make payment once repairs are complete, our mechanic can confidently work on our car.

A company may be reluctant to make its environmental improvements without confidence the stakeholders' rewards will be forthcoming. Unlike market transactions where public law usually requires parties to uphold their end of the deal, such as paying for car repairs or refunding theater tickets, many of the exchanges between companies and their stakeholders lack the backing of public law. Consider again the timber company that can prevent silt runoff from damaging a river's ecosystem. Suppose the company and the association representing local anglers made an agreement. The company would make an up-front investment to prevent soil runoff, maybe changing its harvest schedule or improving drainage to prevent runoff from its roads. In exchange, the angler association would, over time, provide value back to the company, perhaps by helping to pay for several years' backwoods road maintenance. The holdup problem arises if the angler association has an incentive to back out of its end of the deal: once the timber company makes an up-front drainage investment, the association may decide that it can enjoy the benefits of fishing in a sediment-free river without paying back the company.

Absent the threat of legal sanction, what would stop a restaurant diner from refusing to pay for her meal? Why would a company not deceive customers by swapping in cheaper materials for its products? Along with public law, holdup and lemons problems can likewise be solved through costly signals that make each side's commitments credible to the other. "Costly signaling" can increase credibility. A signal is costly when the sender bears a cost should the receiver find out the message is untrue (Spence 1973). An example of a costly signal is when a company pays for an independent audit of its environmental performance, which both costs money and increases risks that the auditor will return with a negative verdict. Such audits are generally more credible than if the company simply released its own internal review of its environmental performance. Another way to address these problems can occur when participants see value in the prospect of future interactions and exchanges. A company may refrain from exploiting its advantage today because it would lose out on tomorrow's gainful interactions should its malfeasance become known.

2.4 Conclusion

Understanding why companies produce environmental harms is an important first step toward mitigating the problem. In some cases, a company might be misinformed about the problem it is causing. Psychological biases and cognitive limitations may prevent people in companies from fully perceiving environmental impacts, which tend to occur outside the company and distant from the areas where most business managers focus their attention. Or perhaps the right information is within the company, but it is not shared with those empowered to make decisions, as we discuss in Chapter 5.

This chapter discusses how externalities provide insights into why businesses make the environmental decisions that they do. The source of environmental problems can often be found in misaligned costs and benefits and the difference in how stakeholders and companies value environmental goods. Companies produce environmental harm when they purchase inputs, produce products and services, and deliver them to customers. People experience these environmental consequences as externalities, whether as a direct harm to their health or well-being or as a damage to something they value.

Win–win Coasian exchanges can occur, and not just between businesses and their stakeholders. In fact, we often engage in them ourselves. When we throw a party, our neighbors might not be first on our invite list, and we may even be disinclined to invite them at all. But, as we all know, a neighborly invitation can smooth feathers that would be ruffled when we end up dancing through the night to loud music. Or perhaps, we offer our neighbors a small gift – a bottle of wine or some cookies – as a goodwill gesture for enduring the inconvenience of our party. With a Coasian and transaction cost theoretical framing, we can see why these exchanges occur. Our raucous good time will create externalities: loud music that would disrupt our neighbors' enjoyment of a quiet night. We can also see the obstacles that can prevent a resolution to this problem – it helps to know something about our neighbors: how much noise annoys them, how much they like wine and cake, and so on. We need to take the time to let them know about our party and bring them a cake. And, we would want to know that our neighbors, satiated with cake or wine, would feel enough goodwill toward us that they will refrain from filing a noise complaint to shut down our party.

A company can create value through its environmental improvements – reducing the costs of its stakeholders' experience – such as lower pollution emissions, improved ecosystems, and expanded wildlife habitats. A company that improves its environmental performance creates value for its stakeholders, thus setting the stage for the type of Coasian exchange described in this chapter: the company produces an environmental good and receives rewards from stakeholders who value these improvements. Such exchanges can increase a company's incentives to implement environmental improvements.

Creating a Coasian exchange requires overcoming transaction costs. The externality producer and recipient must engage in the activities necessary to bring any market exchange to fruition. There may be search and screening obstacles: the company may lack knowledge about how it can produce and supply environmental goods and how much stakeholders would demand those goods. There may be bargaining and transfer obstacles: a portion of the value stakeholders receive from the environmental improvements must be translated back into value to the company. And finally, there may be monitoring and enforcement obstacles: the company and its stakeholders need assurance that all will uphold their obligations in the exchange.

As we will see in the remainder of this book, the transaction costs for environmental problems and improvements are likely to be significantly more challenging than for market exchanges for regular goods and services. For environmental problems, search and screening costs are likely to be higher because the producer and recipient may not be geographically proximate and may not have other venues for interacting with each other, such as a grocery store or other market venue. Bargaining and transfer costs are likely to be higher: there may not be clear exemplar contract terms because exchanges for environmental goods are more rare than for market products. Finally, environmental improvements may also have higher monitoring and enforcement costs than other products because stakeholders are rarely able to evaluate the quality of a company's environmental improvement prior to the exchange occurring. An environmental strategy helps companies identify these obstacles and the opportunities for improving their environmental performance. Overcoming the obstacles can help companies capture value from their environmental improvements through Coasian exchanges with stakeholders.

3 *Environmental Strategy Choices and Challenges*

A company's environmental externalities are an opportunities to create and capture value. As we saw in Chapter 2, Coase provided the theoretical foundation for how exchanges between companies and their stakeholders can lead to environmental improvements to the benefit of all (Coase 1960). Coase also cautioned that transaction costs could prevent these win–win exchanges from happening. For an exchange to occur and fulfill its win–win promise, potential partners must find each other, negotiate terms, exchange resources, and ensure the deal's terms have been met. This chapter uses Coase's ideas to develop a framework to help companies develop an environmental strategy that guides them toward implementing financially sustainable environmental improvements. The framework identifies the key challenges companies must overcome for their environmental strategy to succeed. A strategy helps guide choices – companies must choose which environmental improvements to pursue, how to structure exchanges with stakeholders, and how to assure fidelity to agreement terms.

The chapter follows the format of the discussion in Chapter 2. It begins with search and screening problems. What are the company's environmental impacts, and how much will it cost to achieve environmental improvements? How much do stakeholders value these improvements? These questions help identify conditions where there may be a way for the company and its stakeholders to exchange value. To make these exchanges occur, what channels are available for exchanging resources around environmental improvements? Finally, there needs to be sufficient credibility to ensure the company's environmental improvements are genuine and that participants will deliver the agreement's terms: can the company stakeholders ensure the credibility of its environmental improvements and commitments? Can the company have confidence that stakeholders will do the same? Finally, the chapter ends with a discussion of market and nonmarket strategies to capture value and how environmental strategy can fit with each.

3.1 Search and Screening: Identifying Environmental Improvements, Costs, and Stakeholders

Developing an environmental strategy begins with identifying opportunities to make environmental improvements and screening them to identify the extent to which they create value for stakeholders. The goal is a comprehensive understanding of the company's environmental impacts – what environmental improvements the company can produce, how much it will cost to produce them, and how much stakeholders will value those improvements. Undertaking these activities are part of the search and screening costs that are important to bringing Coasian exchanges to fruition.

3.1.1 Identifying Supply: Environmental Impacts, Improvements, and Costs

To develop an environmental strategy, a company needs to assess its current and potential environmental impacts from a broad perspective by looking across its processes, from procuring inputs through production, and to how its products function and are disposed of at the end of their life. Comprehensiveness is critical: environmental impact evaluations often focus quite narrowly on one or two direct environmental impacts, such as a company's pollution emissions or on outcomes that are currently most salient to stakeholders. An assessment that does not systematically identify all environmental harms can easily overlook important problems, particularly those that are of potential concern to stakeholders even if they are not currently salient. Many people today, for instance, believe that climate change is the most important environmental problem, but their priorities may shift if they see their local environment threatened by a new factory moving into their neighborhood.

Environmental impact evaluations can also end up being unduly narrow because they assume that a few outcomes proxy the overall environmental impact of a company or its products. For example, companies often justify their "buy local" policies on climate mitigation grounds: products are seen to have a smaller climate change impact when they travel shorter distances. But focusing just on "miles traveled" in product distribution can be quite misleading. "Miles traveled" is only one component of a product's climate impact. Production processes for the same product can have very different climate impacts in different geographic locations. A product may travel many miles to reach consumers, which does have some environmental impact. But even with all those miles, it may be a better environmental option if production at the distant locale had a much lower climate impact. A good example of this can be seen in the case of lamb produced in New Zealand and Great Britain. It turns out that lamb flown by airplane from New Zealand to Great Britain has a lower overall carbon footprint than meat produced and consumed locally in Great Britain. New Zealand sheep graze on mountainside pastures during production while English sheep are fed hay grown on separate fields. New Zealand lamb has a smaller greenhouse gas footprint than British lamb because the difference in environmental impacts during production processes outweighs those in transportation (Edwards-Jones 2010).

The importance of environmental impacts can change over time in response to shifts in external conditions, stakeholder preferences, and scientific understanding. An environmental impact can be more severe as others engage in similar activities. For instance, a lightly fished fishery can easily replenish itself, but the fishery can collapse if the fishers' harvest becomes too large. Scientists may discover harms from practices previously thought to be benign. For a long time, synthetic fleece was generally considered environmentally benign once produced and made into clothing. Today, there is growing evidence that microfibers released from washing synthetic cloth can end up harming life in rivers and oceans (Mishra et al. 2019). Patagonia has recognized the microfiber problem and provides consumers with a garment-washing bag that catches microfibers before they reach waterways (Patagonia n.d.).

Once a company inventories its environmental aspects and impacts, the next step is to identify how it can mitigate them. There are many ways a company can improve its environmental impacts – replacing toxic inputs with more benign ones, cleaning emissions before releasing them into the air and waterways, improving production efficiencies, and on and on. The practicality of any improvements is likely to depend on the company's particular circumstances, the availability of alternatives, and, most importantly, the costs. Assessing the short-run cost of environmental improvements tends to be a relatively simple matter. Quite often, it is easy to obtain quotes to learn how much such improvements cost. For example, suppose a food-processing company seeks to switch its feedstock from conventionally grown to organic vegetables. Vendors can provide accurate estimates of the costs to purchase and install energy-efficient equipment or less environmentally harmful materials. Over longer time horizons, forecasting cost savings is more complex: market prices can change with weather conditions, shifting consumer demand and suppliers entering or leaving production.

In some cases, reducing environmental impacts can generate direct cost savings, thereby creating immediate financial returns (Porter & van der Linde 1995). Investments in energy efficiency can sometimes lower a facility's annual operating costs enough to pay back the initial outlays within just a few months or years. Success in finding such cost savings is likely to depend on the company's particular circumstances (Reinhardt 1999). There is considerable debate among academics about the extent of these self-funding environmental opportunities and whether government regulations can spur companies to adopt more of them (Cohen & Tubb 2018). If companies are failing to invest in value-enhancing environmental initiatives, it may be because decision makers within the company do not have the information or authority to implement the improvements.

Whatever the cost savings or other immediate financial returns from environmental investments, companies are more likely to do more if they have ways to capture additional value from them. Suppose a company is considering investing in a wind farm that would produce carbon-free electricity, replacing the public utility electricity produced by burning fossil fuels. Without capturing some economic value to offset this investment, the company would be at a disadvantage relative to its competitors if relying on wind power raised its electricity cost. Raising prices to offset the higher cost of wind power runs the risk of seeing sales diverted to a cheaper but less environmentally scrupulous competitor. Such an investment would create value for society, but the company needs to find compensating benefits to justify making the investment. In such circumstances, which are quite common, companies need other value sources to economically justify environmental improvements.

Even if immediate financial returns prove uneconomical and stakeholder demands appear low, there may still be reason to assess environmental impacts and costs. Circumstances may change, such as when a sudden event changes stakeholder demands for environmental improvements. A company may also find opportunities to improve its environmental performance at a lower cost than its competitors. A company with such a cost advantage may look for ways to compel its competitors to adopt the improvement, such as by stoking stakeholder pressures for the improvement, lobbying for government regulations, or seeking an industry self-regulatory standard (Rugman & Verbeke 1998).

3.1.2 Identifying Demand: Environmental Stakeholder Analysis

The financial value of a company's environmental improvements lies in how it meets its environmental stakeholders' demands. While there are many definitions of "stakeholder," this book takes a broad definition and refers to environmental stakeholders as any group or individual that has an interest in a company's environmental performance and can exert influence on it (Miles 2017). Market stakeholders, such as consumers, lenders, and investors, engage with companies through financial exchanges, while nonmarket stakeholders, such as governments and NGOs, engage companies in other ways, such as through enforcing environmental regulations or engaging in social protests. A stakeholder analysis identifies the individuals and groups who are affected by the companies' environmental impacts (Bryson 2004, 2018; Freeman 2010). An environmental stakeholder analysis asks who the environmental stakeholders are; how much they value environmental improvements; and how much power, legitimacy, and urgency they hold (Cummings & Doh 2000; Frooman 1999; Mitchell et al. 1997; Reed et al. 2009). Table 3.1 lists some common factors that can increase stakeholder influence, which are further discussed later in the chapter.

The first step in stakeholder analysis identifies a company's current and potential environmental stakeholders. Stakeholder analyses require a broad scope to identify the full range of people who might respond to a company's environmental improvements and how they may act on their responses. Stakeholders can receive direct and indirect benefits from an environmental improvement. Direct benefits are the value stakeholders receive from alleviating the environmental harm. Important stakeholders are likely to include those who most directly experience benefits from the improvement. Residents living next to an oil-extraction facility may care deeply about its pollution emissions or its potential for toxic chemical spills because they directly experience its environmental consequences through damage to their

Table 3.1 *Sources of stakeholder influence*

Source	Examples
Number of stakeholders	Size of green consumer market segments
	Number of people experiencing environmental improvement
Amount of demand	Amount of environmental harm experienced by stakeholders
	Co-benefits of environmental improvements
	Environmental improvement yields nonrivalrous benefits
Stakeholder access to resources of influence	Access to media channels
	Ability to influence government
	Availability and strength of supportive allies
Ability to organize collectively	Stakeholders have experience in collective organization
	Access to allies and institutions that can facilitate collective organization

property or harm to their health. Stakeholders can receive co-benefits from an environmental improvement even when they do not experience any of its direct benefits (Delmas & Colgan 2018).

Co-benefits can be tangible or financial, such as when an energy-efficient appliance lowers a consumer's utility bills. Co-benefits also can stem from social sources, such as when a committed environmentalist feels solidarity with peers while participating in an environmental protest. Stakeholders can experience co-benefits as positive emotions, such as when stakeholders reinforce their moral values or sense of self-identity by taking positive environmental action. Some people support charitable causes such as environmental protection or providing healthcare to the poor because doing so supports their personal moral values. Economists sometimes call this source of reward the *warm glow* (Andreoni 1990). Warm glow stakeholders might value environmental improvements that improve the odds that wildlife habitats are left pristine, even if they never visit those habitats.

Stakeholders can also have latent environmental demands; they do not express their demands until they become aware of an environmental harm. Companies need to consider not just how stakeholders will value environmental improvements, but also how stakeholders react to current and future environmental harms. For instance, Exxon faced multiple boycotts after its *Exxon Valdez* tanker hit a reef and spilled millions of gallons of oil into Alaska's Prince William Sound; thousands of customers returned their Exxon credit cards (Williams & Treadaway 1992). Even though such customers had previously been loyal despite the ecological risks posed by Exxon's oil business, they responded when those risks were borne out. There does not have to be a sudden catastrophe like an oil spill to spark new interest. Accumulating news reports or stakeholder action about ongoing, chronic pollution emissions can trigger uproar and boycotts, such as periodic storms over pesticide contamination in food and the environment (Tompkins 2016). Stakeholders may appear, at any given time, to have little willingness to pay for environmental improvement, but their intensity of interest can surge once their concerns are activated.

Different stakeholders can receive value from the same environmental improvement. In this sense, the benefits of a company's environmental improvement are nonrivalrous for its stakeholders. Nonrivalrous means that once one stakeholder receives a benefit, it is still available for other stakeholders to receive as well (Ostrom 1990: 19). Suppose a company decides to sell a version of one of its standard products, enhanced with some environmental improvement feature. Environmentally conscious consumers pay a price premium for the product because they appreciate this new feature. Meanwhile, the companies' employees may feel more committed to their work because producing the "green" product aligns with their own moral values. Both the employees and the consumers have "consumed" (or received enjoyment from) the products' environmental features without interfering with the other stakeholder's benefits from the same environmental features. In this sense, an environmental improvement is not like most physical goods or services where consumption is rivalrous: once a consumer buys a product, it is no longer available to others to purchase. Two people cannot buy and eat the same banana. Instead, an environmental good is more like a streaming movie service, like Netflix, or watching a basketball game on TV; one consumer's enjoyment of the good does not diminish other consumers' enjoyment of the same good.

Stakeholder analysis is akin to the market segmentation and targeting analyses conducted by a typical marketing department: the goal is to identify a clear stakeholder segment toward which the company can target its environmental improvements as a value proposition. In developing a market strategy, companies usually look to potential customers' financial resources and willingness to pay for products and features. For an environmental stakeholder, a financial resource is simply the amount of money a stakeholder would expend for an environmental benefit, analogous to a consumer's willingness to pay for a product. The amount of financial and nonfinancial resources can depend on the size of the stakeholder group who experience the company's environmental improvements or harm. Stakeholders can, without being individually powerful, gain clout through their large numbers. Millions of people have expressed their preference for organic food, with sales in the USA topping $55 billion in 2019 (Organic Trade Association 2019). Worldwide, people have expressed their preference for organic food with worldwide sales of organic foods topping $120 billion (Shahbandeh 2022). Even though no one consumer of organic groceries typically buys enough to motivate a company to shift into organic production techniques, the combined weight of large numbers of grocery shoppers willing to pay for such foods can make it worthwhile for corporations to pursue the market. Sometimes the stakeholders can be smaller in number but with intense preferences. A small group of highly motivated activists can obstruct a company's operations by denying access to resources, such as by preventing them from using local water supplies.

Stakeholder analyses can be more complicated than market analyses. In environmental strategy, money is not the only important resource stakeholders have for influencing companies. Stakeholders can also have nonfinancial resources they can deploy to affect a company. For example, stakeholders may have access to political power that can influence the regulations and enforcement a company faces. They can demand that a company face more stringent environmental regulations, thus raising the company's costs relative to its competitors. Or stakeholders may be able to garner media attention to publicize a company's harmful environmental impacts. Stakeholders can also have resources that help a company capture value from its environmental improvements. For example, an environmental NGO may have expertise about how to achieve pollution reductions at a lower cost. A partnership with the environmental NGO, in this case, may be beneficial for the company.

Stakeholders can have more influence when they are able to organize themselves and work together as a group. Organized stakeholders can exert more influence. A consumer boycott will be more influential if those customers all coordinate to stop buying the company's goods at the same time and make it clear that they share widespread unhappiness about the company's environmental performance. Stakeholders' ability to engage in this sort of "collective action" tends to depend on circumstances, such as how easy it is to identify others with the same interest, how many other interests they have in common, and how frequently they interact with one another for other reasons (Olson 2009). Stakeholders' ability to organize is one reason why more concentrated environmental harms frequently face more concerted stakeholder opposition than when the harm is felt over a more diffuse area. When a fracking company threatens to pollute a town's water supply – even in a relatively conservative place where you might not expect much environmentalism – opposition is often fierce: the neighbors are better able to find each other, organize in face-to-face conversations, rely on preexisting local institutions to help arrange protests against the company, and identify and stigmatize people who fail to support the protest (Auyero et al. 2019).

3.2 Bargaining and Transfer: Channels for Exchanging Value

After establishing how much stakeholders value environmental improvements, the next step is to identify how the company captures value from its environmental improvements. Even if a company identifies stakeholders who have strong demand for a particular environmental improvement and are willing to pay some resources to receive it, there may not be a cost-effective means for transferring the value from the appreciative stakeholders to the company. Stakeholders need to know what environmental improvements the company is making. There is no centralized "market" where businesses advertise their potential environmental improvements and the prices they would want stakeholders to pay for them.

The collective goods nature of the environmental improvements adds a further complication to the challenge of organizing the exchange:

the benefits of the company's environmental improvements may be so thinly spread out across so many stakeholders that there is not an economical way for the company to receive value from each individual stakeholder. Mitigating climate change is an important example of this – the mitigation efforts of even the largest and most aggressive companies end up as only a relatively small piece of the climate change solution. And the benefits of addressing climate change will be spread out all over the planet and well into the future as people experience fewer extreme weather events, more temperate climates, and so on. Given the global reach of the causes and consequences of climate change, there can be very high costs to executing a direct exchange value between those mitigating climate change and those receiving its benefits.

A channel is a mechanism that facilitates value exchanges between a company and its stakeholders. A channel lowers costs by clarifying the terms of the exchange – what value will be transferred, who will be paying, and how the company will receive this value. In a market channel, the company receives direct financial value from market stakeholders in exchange for its environmental improvements. Market stakeholders engage financially with the company. Consumers pay money for goods and services. Investors purchase equity stakes in companies. Insurers sell contracts to provide financial compensation if a negative event occurs. In cases such as these, market stakeholders provide financial value to companies for their superior environmental performance. For example, an insurance company can offer lower prices to recognize the lower risk associated with an environmentally strong company (Koh et al. 2014). How do companies capture value from market stakeholders? What kind of channels help companies do so?

3.2.1 Market Channels

3.2.1.1 Environmental Products and Services

Some consumers prefer environmentally superior products such as organic food and energy-efficient appliances. They may be willing to pay extra for such a product or simply prefer buying the product over a product that does not have the environmental feature but is otherwise identical. Consumers' "green demand" can come in different varieties that affect the types of environmental products they are willing to purchase. Some consumers are willing to pay a price premium when they believe that their purchases help them live in accordance with their moral beliefs (Rivera 2002; Delmas & Colgan 2018). In such cases, the price supplement they pay for a green product is akin to making a charitable donation; in return for financially supporting a cause the consumer believes in, they receive a warm glow of emotional satisfaction. In other cases, consumer demand for a green product's environmental features stems from the direct value it provides to the consumer. Organic foods, for example, offer consumers several types of benefits, the warm glow value that their consumption is resulting in fewer pesticides being released into the environment, health benefits of eating food without pesticides, and perhaps better taste. Some environmental features create value for consumers by improving how they feel about themselves, such as by reinforcing their self-image or their public reputation of being environmentally aware. For example, surveys indicate that the desire to project a green image is a critical factor that leads some consumers to purchase hybrid vehicles (Chua et al. 2010).

Conversely, negative environmental performance can tarnish a company's brand, hurting its relations with customers and ultimately its financial performance. Companies' environmental scandals provide clear examples. In September 2015, the German car company Volkswagen was found to have been cheating on its US Environmental Protection Agency (EPA) tailpipe pollution emissions testing, leading to a major scandal that cost the car manufacturer an estimated $18 billion. The public relations fallout was so severe that Volkswagen CEO Matthias Mueller found himself saying: "We are not a criminal brand or group" (Bomey & Snavely 2016). Similarly, British Petroleum's (BP) disastrous 2010 oil spill in the Gulf of Mexico was still hurting the company's brand three years later, despite the company spending over $100 million on post-disaster advertising (Swanson 2013). Consumers who had previously seen advertisements from BP's "Beyond Petroleum" campaign, which touted the company's commitment to renewable energy, were more likely to avoid purchasing gas from the company after the spill. Interestingly, an existing positive reputation can insulate companies from the fallout from environmental scandals. Companies with stronger social corporate responsibility practices, including better environmental performance, experience smaller declines in their stock prices following product recalls (Klein & Dawar 2004; Minor & Morgan 2011).

3.2.1.2 Financial Channels: Investors, Lenders, and Insurers

Lenders and insurers also use companies' environmental performance when setting the prices they charge. Companies with weaker environmental performance face higher insurance and financial borrowing costs (Cheng et al. 2014). In fact, environmental risks for some companies can be so high that insurers may not want to issue policies at all. As one insurance executive describes his company's reasoning for moving away from the environmental insurance business: "We're foregoing premium income [by not writing environmental risk policies], but the loss from accidents, spills and so on would not be tolerable. Even at a higher premium, we wouldn't want the business" (Hoffman 2000: 74).

Sometimes, companies can extract value from investors with stronger environmental preferences. Some investors prefer stocks of companies whose performance reflects their own ethical values, and some investors view companies with better environmental and CSR records as an indicator of lower financial risk and even as evidence of better overall management (Amel-Zadeh & Serafeim 2018). There is some evidence that strong social and environmental performance indicates that a company has yielded better financial returns down the road (Chatterji et al. 2009). Several rating companies, like Sustainalytics and MSCI, evaluate companies' environmental and social performance to enable investors to select those with better records. Some large investment companies, including Blackrock, have announced that they are evaluating environmental, social, and governance (ESG) factors in all their investment decisions (Blackrock 2021).

3.2.1.3 Human Resources

Companies can use their environmental programs as a human resource program as a way to boost productivity through better employee recruitment, motivation, and retention. Some job applicants are more attracted to companies with positive environmental reputations (Jones et al. 2014), and some employees are willing to accept a lower salary to work at a company they perceive to be environmentally responsible (Burbano 2016). Learning about a company's environmental contributions and programs can improve employees' workplace commitment and may even reduce turnover, bringing value to the company by reducing the cost of recruitment and training (Bode et al. 2015). Employees are more motivated at work and even take on extra work assignments when they learn that their employer shares their environmental concerns (Burbano 2019). In surveys, millennials are especially likely to report that they consider a company's social and environmental commitments when deciding where to work (Cone Communications 2016). Environmental improvements can thus help a company capture value by lowering labor costs and increasing productivity, but they also risk employee scorn should they turn out to be another form of greenwashing. Chapter 7 discusses employees and sustainability in more detail.

3.3 Monitoring and Enforcement: Mechanisms for Credibility

Once a company has identified its environmental improvements, the costs of these improvements, the stakeholders willing to pay for them, and the mechanism for the exchanging value, the final challenges for environmental strategy center on solving the information and holdup problems. The information problem, or green lemons problem as it was introduced in Chapter 2, exists because companies' environmental improvements are difficult for outsiders to observe and evaluate directly, and consequently stakeholders are reluctant to bestow rewards on companies claiming improved environmental performance. The holdup problem exists because of the asynchronicity of value exchanges – the party that gives value first is at risk of not receiving value in return.

A company needs to assure stakeholders that it will live up to its promises and produce genuine environmental improvements. In some cases, effective public law improves credibility – if the company misrepresents its environmental performance it can face charges and potential punishment. For example, the US Federal Trade Commission's (FTC) "Green Guides" are formal regulations in place since 1992 that aim to ensure that companies do not engage in deceptive environmental marketing (US Federal Trade Commission 2010). The regulations define terms such as "recyclable" and "renewable," and prohibit companies from making "general environmental benefit" claims without precisely specifying the environmental benefit. In 2017, the FTC found that Moonlight Slumber, a mattress company, had deceived consumers with its environmental marketing. The FTC concluded that Moonlight Slumber advertisements displaying a "Green Safety Shield" logo misleadingly suggested that the mattresses had received a third-party certification, and consequently prohibited Moonlight Slumber from using the logo (US Federal Trade Commission 2017).

Table 3.2 *Mechanisms for environmental credibility*

Mechanism	Examples
Measurement and reporting	Participation in a formal disclosure program, such as Carbon Disclosure Project
	Reporting "raw" data on pollution resource consumption
Company brands and culture	Brand message is consistent with environmental message (product quality = environmental quality)
	Company culture that cares for its employees also cares for the environment
Certification programs	United States Department of Agriculture (USDA) Organic Labeling
	ISO 14001
	Fair Trade Certified

Most often environmental exchanges between companies and stakeholders are informal agreements, based on promises and expectations that are not enforceable through formal legal structures. The company promises its stakeholders that it will "do the right thing," with the expectation of receiving stakeholder rewards in return. In such informal contracts, the punishment and rewards for honoring the agreement stem not from the government's rulings and sanctions but rather from the rewards or sanctions bestowed by stakeholders for adhering to or violating the agreement. These stakeholder rewards may be increased sales, customer loyalty, or motivated and engaged employees. The sanctions stem from the loss of those positive interactions and perhaps even additional costs in the form of boycotts, bad publicity, or other forms of protest. In 1989, Walmart began selling products labeled as "environmentally friendly" by using a green tag system on its store shelves. While the products' environmental claims may have survived close legal scrutiny, they did not meet customer and stakeholder expectations for sustainability. Walmart received a maelstrom of bad publicity when word got out that the only sustainable feature of its "green label" paper towels was the recycled content in the towels' inner cardboard tube (Plambeck & Denend 2008). Table 3.2 lists some examples of costly signal mechanisms through which companies can credibility communicate their environmental improvements. These mechanisms are discussed further later in the chapter.

3.3.1 Measurement and Reporting

While a company's unilateral declarations often receive stakeholder skepticism, there are ways companies can increase the credibility of their environmental messaging, even without relying on third-party endorsements and certifications. Measuring and reporting environmental performance, particularly with quantitative metrics, can improve the credibility of a company's environmental reporting. Quantitative measures facilitate comparisons; stakeholders can evaluate the company against its peers, its own past performance, or against an industry standard of best practices. For some salient environmental issues, reporting standards codify how companies should measure, document, and report their environmental performance. CDP (formerly known as the Carbon Disclosure Project) is a nonprofit that issues standards for companies to report their environmental performance, most prominently greenhouse gas emissions. Public disclosure standards may not be perfectly credible – there is evidence that companies manipulate their voluntary reporting in CDP their disclosures (Callery & Perkins 2020). Misreporting is perhaps not surprising given that many of these programs lack credible mechanisms to monitor and sanction company's self-reported claims (Potoski and Prakash 2013). Companies can increase credibility through transparent reporting processes, in which stakeholders observe and perhaps even contribute to the process of collecting, distilling, and reporting environmental data and performance (Blackburn 2007).

3.3.2 Company Brands and Culture

A company's brand and culture can be important resources for improving the credibility of its environmental messaging and commitments. Company brands and culture are costly signals (Rao et al. 1999). A company receives value when stakeholders use its culture or brand to infer that the company will behave favorably in the future. If a company is found to behave in violation of its brand or culture, stakeholders may no longer engage in favorable ways. As many scholars have noted, organizational culture is a particularly challenging topic for analysis (Barney 1986; Fiol 1991; O'Reilly 1989). Culture defies easy definition and categorization, though there is no disputing its importance for organizational and economic performance. While there are different ways of defining company culture, we use a fairly simple and general definition. A company's culture is the set of norms and values that are widely shared and strongly held throughout the organization (Barney 1986; Fiol 1991; O'Reilly 1989).

A company's culture can also provide stakeholders with credible assurance that the company will live up to its promises. A culture provides information about how the organization is behaving today and how it will behave in the future. Ben & Jerry's, the now-iconic ice cream company, was founded in 1979 by a couple of idealistic hippies in Burlington, Vermont. As the company grew, it remained true to the values of its founders – the importance of social and environmental causes, treating employees well, and producing high-quality ice cream. Based on its brand reputation, Ben & Jerry's customers wouldn't be surprised to know that the company is working with dairy farmers to improve their agricultural practices, and many would even expect the company be doing so. The Ben & Jerry's brand conveys the company's strong tradition of social and environmental activism, which can reinforce warm glow purchasing among consumers who share those concerns and who wish to align their purchasing practices with their own moral values.

A brand signals to consumers distinct features about the company and its products. It positions products in consumers' minds, signaling to consumers the product's difficult-to-observe qualities, the product's impact on consumers' emotional states, and even its impact on consumers' sense of identity. Brands that perform these functions well can increase consumer willingness to pay. Without a credible brand, a company might need to offer a money-back guarantee or rely on other costly measures to assure customers about its products' quality. Over time, a company can spend resources to build a favorable brand image in consumers' minds, conveying confidence that the product will meet their expectations. Brands can also convey emotional messages about products.

Failing to live up to the promise of its brand or culture can be costly to a company. Customers and other stakeholders may doubt the credibility of its claims about product quality and will avoid purchasing from or otherwise rewarding the violating company. The violation may even undermine credibility beyond the broken promise – stakeholders may no longer believe the company's branding claims in other areas, such as about the quality and performance of other products or how well it treats its employees. Volkswagen experienced a precipitous decline in sales and share price after its 2015 emissions scandal (Bachmann et al. 2019). A violation of stakeholder trust may even trigger outrage and attempts to punish the company in retribution, as we saw with Greenpeace activists' reactions to learning about Timberland's supply chain practices in the Amazon.

3.3.3 Certifications

Third-party endorsements and certification can add credibility to firms' environmental communications, particularly when the endorser itself has credibility with the company's targeted stakeholders (Aragón-Correa et al. 2020; Potoski & Prakash 2005; Rivera & De Leon 2004). A certification signifies that an authorized third-party organization has attested that a company, process, product, building, or report has met the requirements of an environmental standard. Consumers, producers, and regulators can all benefit from environmental certifications administered by a reputable party. Because the third-party certifier has no direct stake in the sale of the certified goods, customers may be more confident that the product has the promised environmental characteristics. This can both provide peace of mind to customers and induce them to engage in more transactions – which in turn increases sales and profits for the producer. Regulators, meanwhile, need not expend so many resources scrutinizing a firm that has been audited by a credible outside agency, allowing them to more efficiently direct their focus on firms and practices where attention is actually needed. Many consultancies and accounting firms offer an assurance service that validates and endorses companies' environmental or sustainability reports. For example, Coca-Cola's water use was audited by LimnoTech and Deloitte, and its water sustainability initiatives were conducted in association with TNC, a well-respected environmental NGO (Isidore 2016). An independent third-party auditor has its own reputation to protect, so stakeholders can be more confident that Coca-Cola's claims are true because the third party would otherwise seriously jeopardize its reputation.

There are hundreds, if not thousands, of environmental standards to which companies can become certified, covering the range of environmental impacts across a product's life cycle: the environmental quality of raw materials, pollution minimization during production, energy efficiency during use, and how the product can be recycled. For example, real estate developers and owners can credibly communicate to potential buyers and renters that their buildings were constructed using environmentally preferable practices by becoming certified to the LEED, a set of standards for environmentally friendly building construction created by the US Green Building Council. The LEED standards reference other third-party environmental standards such as the Forest Stewardship Council's certified wood.

3.4 Market Environmental Strategies

A company that achieves a competitive advantage faces pressures from suppliers, customers, stakeholders, substitutes, potential entrants, complementors, and industry competitors, who want to get the value for themselves. Competitors might aim to offer a similar product at a lower price or a superior product at similar prices. The incumbent company would be forced to lower its prices or pay the costs to improve quality, resulting in lower profits. The competitors might follow suit with price cuts or quality improvements of their own, resulting in a competitive cycle that, as Adam Smith's invisible hand suggests, benefits consumers but makes companies' profits difficult to sustain. A competitive advantage is financially sustainable when, for one reason or another, it is difficult for competitors to mimic and the company enjoys freedom from pressures to lower prices or improve quality. A strategy can proactively seek out opportunities for advantage or reactively respond to external threats in a changing environment (Oliver & Holzinger 2008). The opportunities may be particularly important for competitive advantage (McWilliams et al. 2002; McWilliams & Siegel 2011). A first mover in the nonmarket arena may acquire scarce resources on more favorable terms. For example, a company's CSR innovation may be more positively received among stakeholders because they see it as more sincere and credible.

The business strategy literature is rich in the diversity of perspectives it offers on how and when companies can establish and maintain sustainable competitive advantage. The market strategy perspective emphasizes the position of a company and its products within industries and markets (Porter 2008). The nonmarket perspective focuses on how a company can achieve sustainable competitive advantage through interactions with nonmarket institutions and stakeholders (Baron & Diermeier 2007; Dorobantu et al. 2017b). While these perspectives differ in their focus, they are not incompatible; they often point to the same sources as potential causes of competitive advantage. A company's nonmarket strategy can create a market advantage, such as when its lobbying efforts create patent protections or raise its competitors' costs.

The following discussion examines the relationships between market strategy and environmental strategy. Environmental initiatives that create financial value can be vulnerable to competitive pressures. A competitor might mimic an environmental strategy that gains favor with nonmarket strategy, granting the company equally favorable access to important resources. The remainder of this chapter presents market perspectives on competitive strategy and discusses how environmental strategy can fit within a market strategy.

When a company finds opportunities to increase the wedge between its costs and customers' willingness to pay in a manner that is insulated from competitors' imitation, it ensures sustained financial returns. Perhaps the most famous perspective on market strategy is Michael Porter's Five Forces Framework (Porter 2008), which showed that competitive advantage can be influenced by factors within a company's industry:

- entry barriers, such government regulations that favor larger, more established incumbent companies, or difficult licensing requirements;
- supplier bargaining power, such as resources controlled by a single seller;
- customer bargaining power;
- threat of substitutes for the industry's products;
- rivalry among incumbents.

A competitive advantage can also stem from how the company's products are positioned in their markets. A product differentiation strategy aims to position the company's products to fit the tastes of narrower customer segments who are willing to pay more for the features they want (Pankaj & Rivkin 2014). A company can achieve sustained competitive advantage when competitors face obstacles to mimicking the company's unique product features. Such obstacles can come when customers face higher costs in switching to other products. Consumers may latch on to the first product on the market and be reluctant to try follow-on products, perhaps because they become comfortable with its familiar taste or other qualities become appealing. Intellectual property protections, such as patents and trademarks, can convey competitive advantage by preventing competitors from mimicking sources of the owner's success. A company's brand can be a source of competitive advantage. Brands take time and effort to become established among consumers, and because they are often difficult for competitors to create, they can be a source of competitive advantage.

Environmental strategies can reinforce competitive advantage by increasing customers' willingness to pay or lowering costs. Environmental product differentiation is a strategy of creating a product that is differentiated by being "greener" than competitors' offerings in ways that are difficult for competitors to mimic. Stonyfield's organic yogurt was among the first to reach supermarkets' shelves back in the early 2000s, gaining a first-mover advantage among consumers who liked the yogurt enough to make it a regular purchase and did not want to go the trouble of sampling other organic options as they came on the market. Chapter 6 expands on both the challenges of environmental product strategies and how Stonyfield grappled with them.

A low-cost strategy aims to meet the minimum product needs of a large market segment by offering a product with the lowest price. Differentiating such a product with an environmental feature often raises production costs without generating any more willingness to pay among the targeted broad market segment. But a creative environmental strategy can still synergize with a low-cost product strategy. An environmental improvement can lower production costs by reducing input needs or improving efficiencies (Porter & van der Linde 1995).

Market-focused approaches to business strategy, such as what Porter (2008) proposes, start by looking at the external competitive environment – the industry and its entry barriers, the level of competition among incumbents, and so on. The company acquires inputs and produces products to fill a market niche where it can enjoy profits while buffered from competitive pressures. An environmental strategy can reinforce competitive strategy by increasing willingness to pay or lowering costs, while at the same time creating value for nonmarket stakeholders.

3.5 Conclusion

An environmental strategy answers the question: how can a company develop and implement environmental improvements in ways that capture value in return? The framework laid out in this chapter helps guide choices about how environmental improvements can produce value: where costs are low and stakeholder demand is high, where mechanisms allow for the transfer of value, and where the company can credibly assure stakeholders. The choices laid out in the chapter depend on factors external to the company: how its actions influence the environment and its environmental stakeholders and how it can shape interactions with its stakeholders for mutual gain. An environmental strategy needs to fit with the company's competitive strategy, where and how it should compete in the marketplace, and how it interacts with its nonmarket stakeholders.

An effective environmental strategy can help ensure that the value the company receives from its environmental improvements is sustainable over the long run. Some environmental strategies create a new source of competitive advantage by allowing companies to generate financial and nonfinancial value in ways that are difficult for other companies to mimic. Perhaps more often, an environmental strategy extends an existing competitive advantage in a new direction. Whether as a source of new competitive advantage or by reinforcing existing ones, a company should aim for congruence between its environmental strategy and its broader strategic portfolio. The environmental strategy makes the competitive strategy more effective, and the desire for competitiveness motivates the environmentally conscious choice. A company's choices should be based not just on external factors but on internal ones as well. An environmental strategy should synergize with the company's strategic resources, including the capabilities and expertise of its workforce, a topic we address in Chapter 7.

4 | *Nonmarket Strategy*

The discussion and framework presented so far in this book have examined how companies capture a portion of the value from environmental improvements through market channels: the company creates the environmental good in anticipation of financial rewards from customers and other market stakeholders. While many companies have been paying closer attention to their environmental performance, and some have made dramatic improvements, stubbornly persistent and important environmental problems remain. Many companies' social and environmental performance has not kept pace with rising pressure for greater contributions to social and environmental improvements. Back 2011, the business scholars Michael Porter and Mark Kramer wrote, "the more business has begun to embrace corporate responsibility, the more it has been blamed for society's failures" (Porter and Kramer 2011: 4). Companies were not meeting stakeholder expectations because a single company, acting on its own, often faces risks in putting itself at a competitive disadvantage relative to the companies that eschew making the improvements. Meanwhile, expectations for companies' environmental performance have continued to rise.

For many academic and business leaders, if companies are to meet rising stakeholder demand for social and environmental performance, they will do so through a nonmarket strategy rather than a market strategy. Common nonmarket stakeholder groups include communities that surround a company's establishments, environmental NGOs, and government agencies. Nonmarket stakeholders are an important consideration because they can influence a company's financial performance in important ways, such as by affecting the perceptions of customers and investors about the attractiveness (or unattractiveness) of a company's products and future prospects. Porter and Kramer propose that companies' nonmarket strategies focus on shared value, which they define as "policies and operating practices that enhance the competitiveness of a company while simultaneously advancing the economic and social conditions in the communities in which it operates. Shared value creation focuses on identifying and expanding the connections between societal and economic progress" (Porter and Kramer 2011: 4).

The "shared value" term caught on among business leaders. Nestlé's chairman and CEO, Paul Bulcke, introduced his company's 2013 sustainability report (Nestlé 2013) by highlighting the role of shared value in Nestlé's social and environmental programs. Bulcke wrote:

We believe that we can create value for our shareholders and society by doing business in ways that specifically help address global and local issues in the areas of nutrition, water and rural development. This is what we mean when we speak about Creating Shared Value (CSV). We proactively identify opportunities to link our core business activities to action on related social issues.

Other companies, like Walmart, Campbell's, Eli Lilly, and Pearson frame their social responsibility programs in shared value terms.

Beyond stakeholders, nonmarket strategy occurs in an institutional context that shapes how companies interact with stakeholders and the benefits and costs of their environmental improvements. Institutions are the rules and norms that people create and follow to structure their social interaction (Ostrom 1990). Rules are more formal codes of conduct promulgated by legitimate organizations, such as governments and industry associations. Norms are informal codes of conduct in the absence of formal authority, such as when neighbors agree to collect each other's mail while the other is on vacation. There are many different types of institutions. Governments, NGOs, and companies are all institutions that organize social interactions on a large scale. The terms of a company's social license to operate are an example of an informal set of norms about the company's behavior toward the environment and its stakeholders.

In a broad sense, every environmental problem could be addressed through an institution of some form. In simple terms, institutions can mitigate collective action problems by channeling costs and benefits so that individuals have incentives to behave in ways that promote collective goods, such as environmental improvements. The institutional context is also important for environmental strategy because it shapes how companies engage with stakeholders and the costs and benefits of the environmental improvements companies may implement. Governments can use tax policy to incentivize pollution reductions and regulations to limit pollution emissions and access to resources. Institutions can also influence environmental strategy by shaping interactions between companies and stakeholders. Fraud laws constrain companies from overtly lying about their environmental performance, allowing activists to more accurately identify those that deserve praise or scorn. Nongovernmental institutions can also influence costs and benefits. Industry associations lobby governments for policy change and create their own nongovernmental institutions seeking to regulate their members' behavior. Other institutions are the product of broader collaborations among companies, NGOs, governments, and communities.

Companies face choices about how to interact with nonmarket stakeholders and when to engage in efforts toward institutional change. Sometimes a company faces protests from activists and environmental NGOs and sometimes a company has the opportunity for collaboration with governments, communities, NGOs, and other companies. Chapter 3 discusses environmental strategy for making choices about how to engage with market stakeholders. This chapter presents a framework to help guide companies' choices about how and when to engage with institutions and seek institutional change.

4.1 Stakeholders and Institutions

To understand nonmarket strategy, it is useful to begin with a brief review of the different types of nonmarket stakeholders, how they engage with companies, and the nonmarket institutions that structure their engagements. When companies engage with nonmarket stakeholders, the transfer of value often occurs not through financial terms but through other types of values that influence a company's financial position: the company produces nonfinancial value through its environmental improvement and receives in return nonfinancial value from stakeholders. On the positive side, nonmarket channels such as recognition awards or public praise can provide incentives for companies to improve their environmental performance. On the negative side, nonmarket stakeholders can impede companies' regular operations, making it more costly to produce and sell products.

A sometimes overlooked distinction between market and nonmarket stakeholders and institutions is the degree to which companies

Table 4.1 *Nonmarket stakeholders*

Mechanism	Examples
Governments	Environmental protection agencies
	City councils
	Courts
People and communities	Local residents
	Neighborhood groups
Environmental NGOs	Greenpeace
	World Wildlife Fund
	Local environmental groups
Competitors	Other companies in the same industry, selling similar products, or seeking access to the same resources
	Industry associations
Collaborations	Marine Stewardship Council
	International Organization for Standardization

can choose whether to engage with them. Companies have more discretion in choosing how to interact with market stakeholders and institutions. So long as they comply with the law, companies can decide whether to sell products; they can choose among competing suppliers and hire and release employees. Nonmarket stakeholders, on the other hand, are self-legitimizing: they can choose whether to engage companies, and their leverage depends on the clout they can marshal for influence. The citizens of a town in which a factory is based are nonmarket stakeholders if they perceive their health to be impaired by its emissions. These stakeholders can hold protests to disrupt the factory's operations or lobby the government to revoke its permits. The following discussion briefly describes some important stakeholder types and the institutions through which they engage with companies. Table 4.1 lists some categories and examples of nonmarket stakeholders, which are discussed further later in the chapter.

4.1.1 Governments

Governmental environmental agencies develop and enforce regulations. In more democratic countries, governments aggregate citizens' preferences for environmental regulations and translate them into polices to regulate companies' environmental performance (Prakash & Kollman 2004). Government policies can come in many different forms. Some are command-and-control regulations where the government issues policy standards to limit how much pollution actors can release into the environment, establishes a monitoring system to detect violations, and sanctions those found to be violating the standards. Emissions permits and taxes require companies to pay a fee for each unit of pollution they emit. Information-disclosure regulations, such as the US EPA's Toxic Release Inventory, require companies to report their pollution emissions.

Governments monitor companies to verify if they are complying with policies and regulations. When a company fails to comply with a rule, regulators can enforce compliance and penalize violators with fines and penalties. With severe noncompliance, a regulator may even withdraw operating permits and force the closure of a firm's facilities until the company demonstrates it is capable of operating in compliance. A superior record of environmental performance may lead regulators to provide faster permit processing, less onerous inspections, and even lower fines and sanctions as regulators interpret stronger environmental performance as evidence of good-faith efforts to comply with rules (Potoski & Prakash 2004). In 1984, Toyota Motor Company and General Motors (GM) formed an alliance in which Toyota assumed management of a GM facility in Fremont, CA. The goal was for Toyota to learn how to manufacture cars in the USA and for GM to learn about Toyota's lean production methods. When Toyota's managers discovered a chemical leak in the plant's painting facility, they immediately reported it to the EPA, much to the surprise of the plant staff who had been used to GM's more limited reporting approach. When the EPA quickly granted Toyota's air pollution permit request for a new truck production facility three years later, one observer believed the EPA's quick and favorable response was due to Toyota's history of transparency in reporting its own chemical spills (Werbach 2009).

Governments' environmental policies can differ in important ways (United Nations Environment Programme 2019). Air pollution regulations in the United States mandate the technologies companies use to control pollution rather than the amounts they can emit. Other governments use regulations that directly specify emissions limits. Beyond the means of limiting pollution, government policies can also vary by their stringency: the amount of environmental performance companies are required to achieve. Finally, some governments may do little to monitor companies' compliance or enforce policies when they detect noncompliance. While the number and stringency of environmental regulations has increased, implementation and enforcement can be uneven around the world.

4.1.2 People and Communities

The general public can sometimes be an important stakeholder group. Ordinary people's influence can be easily overlooked because they do not always express their preferences in a clear and precise manner. Prominent institutions have clear paths for influencing companies. Governments write environmental laws and policies to express their expectations for companies' environmental performance. Environmental NGOs issue threats and articulate their demands in environmental protests. Many people may care about a company's environmental impact and, if they see that the company's performance falls well below their expectations, they may take action in pursuit of improvements. Conflict over scarce resources, or a company's high-visibility spills and accidents, can lead people to become angry enough to express their views and take actions to address them.

The challenge for a company is that it may be difficult recognize stakeholder expectations when, for the most part, they are held silently until people become angry. The company is left reacting to scandals rather than finding ways for proactive engagement. One way to avoid such problems is to treat stakeholders' expectations as a "social license to operate." A legal license gives the licensee legal permission to perform some specified activity, such as operating a heavy truck or selling a credentialed professional service. A social license to operate is similar, but stakeholders, not the government, set and enforce the license terms. When a company has a social license to operate, it enjoys good standing with important nonmarket stakeholders, such as citizens and groups in its local community and environmental groups and activists. The stakeholders accept the company's environmental activities and allow it to perform its routine operations. However, if people believe a company has violated the terms of its social license to operate, they may engage in protests, express their anger through media outlets, or pressure governments for intervention.

Over the past couple of decades, air pollution has been one of the most visible environmental issues and often leads to social activism and protest. Hangzhou is a large city in China's Zhejiang Province. In the early 2000s, Hangzhou was home to many chemical plants, paper mills, and pharmaceutical factories. Pollution from these facilities created severe air quality problems throughout the city. Despite filing over 1,000 complaints to their local government, Hangzhou's residents continued to endure unclean air, poor health, and bad smells. Hangzhou's middle class was large and able to organize itself to form an organization to curb local air pollution. In 2008, residents created Protest Against Air Pollution (PAAP), a community group that worked to identify the sources of local air pollution. PAAP found two companies who were large pollution emitters, Hangzhou Aidiya Arts & Crafts, a chemical producer, and Hangzhou Blue PeaFowl Chemical Fiber, a chemical plant. PAAP presented its findings to the Hangzhou Environmental Protection Bureau (EPB). The EPB used PAAP's findings and together they took on the city's major sources of air pollution. Within a month, the EPB shut down the Hangzhou Aidiya Arts & Crafts Company after it turned out the company had been operating without a permit for pollution emissions (Shen 2015).

The importance of a social license to operate can vary across locations where companies do business, based on the strength of stakeholders' demand, their capacity to express them, and their access to leverage over companies. Wealthier and better educated communities, for example, tend to have stronger demands for environmental protection and are better able to express their environmental demands. Communities can have more influence when they are better able to organize themselves toward a collective voice and collective action. People who can attract the attention of media and NGOs beyond their community can have more leverage.

4.1.3 Environmental NGOs

Among the most important nonmarket stakeholders are environmentally focused NGOs and activists. These stakeholders bring their passion and knowledge about environmental causes to shine a light on perceived environmental failures, and they can also help companies find solutions. Some environmental NGOs use tactics that seek to "punish" firms they see as harming the environment, such as by organizing consumer campaigns and boycotts that bring to light companies' environmental harms. Greenpeace is a global environmental group that often uses colorful publicity campaigns and leads boycotts targeting companies it sees as causing environmental harm. A 2010 Greenpeace campaign accused Nestlé of buying palm oil for its KitKat bars from sources that harmed indigenous Indonesian forests and threatened orangutan habitats. The Greenpeace campaign included a graphic campaign video that ended with a bloody orangutan finger lying next to a KitKat wrapper (Greenpeace International n.d.-a).

NGO tactics can also use direct action to disrupt companies' operations, denying them access to important resources while also attracting attention to an environmental cause. For example, Earth First!'s direct action campaigns have included its members "spiking" trees by inserting nails to impede logging operations and bring attention to companies' logging practices. Greenpeace activists chained themselves to the front doors of Kimberly-Clark's headquarters and held sit-ins in its offices to protest its logging practices. Greenpeace has also used its boats to disrupt whaling operations as part of its campaign for a worldwide ban on commercial whaling.

NGOs can also provide positive incentives for companies to improve their environmental performance. Environmental groups can use their reputation to help firms that are committed to reducing environmental harm. A reputable NGO that publicly praises a company's environmental improvements can be a powerful signal to the company's stakeholders; the environmental group has its reputation to protect and has a lot to lose if it is perceived to be colluding with a firm that is not committed to environmental improvement. Some environmental NGOs have provided positive publicity and endorsements to reward companies for environmental improvements. After McDonald's agreed to Greenpeace's demands that it reduce deforestation practices in its supply chain, Greenpeace issued a press release stating that McDonald's was taking "historic action" and posted an image on its website of Ronald McDonald hugging a tree (Greenpeace International n.d.-b).

The strengths of environmental groups can be very different in different locations where companies do business. People can more effectively organize into groups in places where they have resources that support collective action, such as freedom of association, access to media and information distribution channels, and channels to influence governments. Environmental groups in the developed world are often better funded, more professional, and better supported than those in the developing world. Chapter 8 discusses environmental groups and their tactics in more detail.

4.1.4 Companies

While other companies may not come to mind as environmental stakeholders, they can have an interest in a company's environmental performance and they can be influential in important ways. Companies' interest stems from the fact that one company's environmental performance can have important consequences for its competitors. Companies may be competing for scarce resources or common-pool resources whose quality can decline if overconsumed. Open-access fisheries can end up in a tragedy of the commons; when one fisher catches a fish, it is no longer available for others to consume, and catching too many fish can harm the long-term health and productivity of the fishery. Overfishing threatens the long-term health of many global fisheries (Memarzadeh et al. 2019).

Companies can also be each other's stakeholders because they are in collective action situations. Environmental regulations may apply to all companies in an industry, giving them a collective interest in lobbying the government's policy process. One company's environmental mishap may spur governments toward more onerous regulations for other companies. The Seveso Directive is an EU law governing the handling of hazardous substances by industrial facilities. The EU enacted the law in the aftermath of a major release of toxic chemicals occurred at a facility located near Seveso, Italy and owned by Industrie Chimiche Meda Società Azionaria. The spill caused immediate illnesses among hundreds of people and killed thousands of animals.

At the same time, different companies can experience different costs and benefits from regulations, giving them competing lobbying incentives. Companies are also interested in each other's environmental performance when they are bound by a collective reputation. A collective reputation exists as a stereotype in the minds of stakeholders that characterizes how a group of companies preform on difficult-to-observe qualities. Stakeholders can sometimes see that environmental conditions are deteriorating, but are not able to identify which companies are more responsible than others. Companies in such circumstances may find themselves "tarred by the same brush." Unable to identify which companies are performing better than others, stakeholders create a mental stereotype based on the observable and unobservable qualities they believe are representative of the group members. The stakeholders may use this stereotype to make assessments where they lack direction information about individual companies.

Competitors' environmental performance can threaten a company's social license to operate, even if stakeholders can readily observe that it is performing better than its peers. The cumulative environmental harm from all companies may be greater than what stakeholders are willing to accept. When environmental problems are seen to be sufficiently severe, stakeholders may threaten to block all companies' access to important inputs or markets, regardless of how much each contributed to the problem. As we will see in Chapter 8, Timberland's contribution to Amazon rainforest deterioration was probably small and perhaps even significantly less than other shoe and apparel companies. But it was nonetheless a target of Greenpeace's campaign.

Industry associations are NGOs that represent the common interests of the owners and managers of firms in an industry: a desire to avoid what they see as regulations that would harm their industry as whole, to sustain or increase subsidies, or to protect or improve their industry's collective reputation. To pursue these aims, some industry associations have created voluntary regulatory standards that ask their members to adopt environmentally beneficial practices, such as when the Chemical Manufacturers Association (now the International Council of Chemical Associations) established its Responsible Care program in 1985 after thousands of people died from a toxic gas leak at a Union Carbide facility in Bhopal, India. As with government regulations, the competitive implications of these industry standards can vary across companies (Shah & Rivera 2013). Responsible Care, for example, requires participants to establish an environmental management system for their operations. The cost of such requirements is generally lower for larger companies and those with more management system experience (Darnall & Edwards 2006). As we discuss further in the discussion of collaborative institutions, industry associations can be venues for competition among group members, even though their stated function is to achieve collective action across the whole group.

4.2 Institutions and Nonmarket Strategy

This section investigates how companies can develop a nonmarket environmental strategy for engaging their institutional context. The aim is to identify how companies can engage with institutions so that they to generate environmental improvements while contributing to the company's financial goals. Governments, NGOs, industry associations, and the social license to operate are all important types of institutions that can influence nonmarket environmental strategy. Porter and Kramer's call for collaboration among companies, NGOs, governments, and communities are in essence calls for more effective institutions to create shared value and improve collective impact.

A company considering participating or modifying an institution as part of its environmental strategy needs to consider the value it would receive for its efforts. Companies face strategic choices about how to engage with the institutions in their environment. If a company is to spend resources to engage institutions, how can it find ways to capture a portion of the value the institution creates? A first set of choices is about participating in institutions. While a company may not have a choice about complying with public law (at least in legal and moral senses), it does have choices about whether and how to engage with governments and other stakeholders. A company can seek an environmental certification for its green product. A company might seek to join a multistakeholder collaboration to produce shared value. And as we discuss in Chapter 8, a company can also decide how to respond to NGO protests and stakeholder conflict.

A second set of choices is about choosing how to influence its institutional environment. Changing institutional practices can affect a company's financial performance and the value it receives from producing environmental improvement. A company faces choices about whether to influence public laws and regulations, such as by lobbying a government legislature or supporting a publicity campaign to support an environmental issue. A company can also choose whether to seek influence with nongovernmental institutions. A company might seek to change the code of conduct established by an industry association. Or a company might seek to influence the terms of an NGO's environmental certification.

These strategic choices are shaped by the characteristics of the institutions themselves, including the resources they hold, their rules, and how they allocate value among stakeholders. One important distinction is between government and nongovernmental institutions. Governments can exert legal authority over social behavior. People, companies, and organizations do not choose whether the law applies to them. Outside of governments lies the realm of voluntary institutions, such as industry associations, NGOs, and collaborations among them, with whom companies can engage with more discretion.

The institutions described earlier aim to contribute to environmental improvements in one way or the other. Institutions like government regulations and the social license to operate aim to constrain companies so that they reduce their environmental harms. Certifications provide incentives to companies that improve their environmental performance. Institutions can create value for stakeholders, redistribute value among stakeholders, and influence how stakeholders interact with each other. Institutions are of course not free; there are costs to creating, managing, and changing an institution. The discussion that follows describes the different ways that institutions can contribute to environmental improvements.

Direct provision of environmental goods. Some institutions directly improve environmental conditions by producing goods and services that enhance ecosystem performance. Governments maintain parks and national forests, collect garbage, and manage recycling programs. As discussed in Chapter 8, some NGOs produce environmental goods by planting trees or by purchasing and managing land in ecologically sensitive areas. Companies produce environmental goods when they reduce their pollution emissions or use fewer environmentally damaging resources.

Indirect provision of environmental goods: incentives. Sometimes, institutions provide positive incentives directly to those that produce environmental goods. Such payments are sometimes called "selective incentives" (Ostrom 1990) because they are given only to those who contribute to the production of a collective good. The US federal government provided $7,500 tax incentives to the first 250,000 consumers that purchased new editions of electric powered cars and trucks. Selective incentives can also come in nonfinancial forms, such as when NGOs enhance a company's brand by praising its superior environmental performance.

Institutions can also indirectly produce environmental improvements by establishing procedures for identifying and sanctioning behaviors that harm the environment. Government agencies, industry associations, and other NGOs can promulgate standards for companies' environmental performance and seek sanctions against those who violate them. Liability laws also provide incentives for companies to mitigate environmental harms – a company causing environmental harm can face large fines penalties. BP paid the US Department of Justice $4.5 billion to settle cases stemming from its Deepwater Horizon oil spill in the Gulf of Mexico. Of course, governments have the authority to issue laws and regulations that compel companies' behavior. In some parts of the world, participation in an industry association is voluntary, and in others it is mandatory. The social license operates similarly, though its standards and enforcement mechanisms are informal and their enforcement depends on how much influence civil society stakeholders can muster to sanction violators. Environmental NGOs and social movements can sanction companies with poor environmental performance through protests and boycotts.

Indirection provision of environmental goods: reducing transaction costs. Institutions can also improve collective action by reducing transaction costs to facilitate mutually beneficial exchanges among actors. Recall that environmental problems can be mitigated through Coasian exchanges – the recipients of environmental harms compensate producers for harm reduction. Transaction costs can impede Coasian exchanges and collective action that improve environmental conditions. Many certification programs reduce transaction costs by mitigating the green lemons problem. An effective certification provides credible information about which companies have improved their environmental performance, allowing stakeholders to bestow their rewards more confidently, which in turn provides companies with incentives to improve their environmental performance (Prakash & Potoski 2006). A certification program can also incorporate effective commitment devices that mitigate potential holdup problems between a company and its stakeholders. Stakeholders can be more confident the company will continue its environmental performance if the certification program imposes sanctions for noncompliance with its standards.

Institutions can also reduce transaction costs by facilitating coordinated action that leads to environmental improvements. In the USA, the plastics industry created the labeling systems – three arrows in a triangle with a number in the middle – to indicate which types of plastics can be co-mingled for recycling. The labeling system lowers the costs of recycling because plastics can be more easily sorted prior to disposal and the recyclers have lower costs for decontaminating their inflow streams.

The costs to create an institution include organizing participants and creating the institutions' structures, procedures, and rules so that participants view the institution as legitimate and will therefore be willing to participate in its operations. Once created, an institution also requires resources for its operation and maintenance, such as monitoring and enforcing the institution's rules, updating policies and procedures, and ensuring legitimacy with stakeholders. Changing an institution's rules and procedures likewise requires time and effort. Decision makers may need to persuaded of the need and direction for change. New rules need to be written, implemented, and enforced. Stakeholders need to be informed about the new rules and their impacts.

4.2.1 Engaging Environmental Institutions

The foundations of nonmarket strategy lie in recognizing the distribution of institutional costs and benefits. These costs and benefits can vary across companies and institutions – the same institution can yield different costs and benefits for different companies, which shapes their incentives for engaging them. What follows is a brief discussion of how companies experience costs and benefits from institutions.

Institutions can impose different types of costs on companies. Sometimes the costs are imposed directly on companies. Governments spread costs across taxpayers, impose regulations on a few companies, and charge fees for using environmental resources. Voluntary associations can charge membership fees and create their own standards for members' behavior. Institutions can also impose costs through their standards for companies' behavior, particularly when the institution aims for indirect provision of environmental improvement. A company receiving an environmental certification may experience costs in complying with the certification's standards and, for some certifications, paying for an external audit and verification of its compliance with the standards.

When a company bears these institutional costs, it might have an incentive to seek to change institutions to pass those costs on to others, while continuing to enjoy the institution's benefits. Companies can experience an institution's costs in different ways. The same institutional feature may impose much larger costs on some companies than others. Many institutions aim to impose rules and regulations to govern the environmental behavior of a group of companies. Such rules can take the form of government regulations, a social license to operate, or an environmental certification. A cost advantage occurs when some companies experience higher costs than others. The costs of switching to new practices can differ because companies employ different production processes, use different technologies and raw materials, and have different types of human capital and resources. Regulations that impose high fixed costs, for example, can favor larger companies that spread those costs across more units of output. Air pollution control devices (such as smokestack "scrubbers") incur capital and operating costs that exhibit economies of scale and therefore provide a comparative advantage for larger operations. A tax on production inputs, such as a gasoline tax, favors companies with more efficient production processes. Companies that can improve their environmental performance at a lower cost can benefit from more stringent regulations as their competitors face higher costs to meet the same more demanding regulatory standards (Rugman & Verbeke 1998).

Companies' incentives to engage with an institution can also depend on how it allocates benefits. Some institutions provide benefits that can be targeted to specific recipients: what are sometimes called selective incentives. A good environmental certification program only recognizes those companies that have achieved the superior environmental performance its standards require. An environmental certification is a valuable resource to companies – a certified company can more credibly communicate its superior environmental performance relative to its uncertified peers. Selective incentives increase companies' willingness to participate in, and contribute value to, an institution.

4.2.2 Collaborating and Institutions

Some institutions are the product of interactions among groups of stakeholders. Sometimes the stakeholder interactions are competitive, as different groups look to adapt an institution to suit its own needs. Other times, institutions are the result of collaboration and cooperation among diverse stakeholders. Porter and Kramer (2011) see such collaborative institutions as pursuing "collective impact." They wrote:

[C]ollective impact is based on the idea that social problems arise from and persist because of a complex combination of actions and omissions by players in all sectors – and therefore can be solved only by the coordinated efforts of those players, from businesses to government agencies, charitable organizations, and members of affected populations ... To advance shared value efforts, therefore, businesses must foster and participate in multisector coalitions – and for that they need a new framework. (Porter and Kramer 2016: 3)

Porter and Kramer's prescription for shared value and collective impact is a welcome addition to the portfolio of approaches for addressing the challenging environmental and social problems facing society. When environmental problems persist in the face of companies' individual and bilateral efforts, nonmarket strategy can help find a path to how companies can engage institutions to create positive synergies among stakeholders and improve environmental conditions.

A company can have a strong incentive to engage with an institution when it receives some of the resulting benefits. For example, during the 1980s, scientists found that chlorofluorocarbons (CFCs) were leaking into the atmosphere and contributing to the depletion of the world's ozone layer. At the time, DuPont was a leading CFC producer that lobbied against laws and treaties banning the chemicals. After investing considerable effort to develop more environmentally benign CFC alternatives, DuPont switched its position and lobbied in favor of the Montreal Protocol, the international treaty that banned CFCs. Competitive advantage can explain DuPont's shift: if CFCs were banned, it would be in a unique position to offer alternatives (Barrett 1991).

More often, a company may find itself in a situation where it may want some institutional change that would lead to environmental improvements, but faces costs that are too large for it to bring about the change on its own. The company would pay the full costs of bringing about the change while the benefits would accrue to other stakeholders. Such circumstances are ripe for collective action, where those who receive benefits work together as a coalition to share the costs for achieving the institutional change.

Lobbying by a group of chemical companies in support of the US EPA's Toxic Release Inventory (TRI) provides an example of a coalition collaborating for institutional change. In the 1980s, the chemical manufacturing industry in the United States industry had a poor collective reputation. Companies in the US chemical industry had become known for being highly polluting at a time when the public wanted a cleaner environment. In 1985, the US Congress considered a new environmental law, the Emergency Planning and Community Right-to-Know Act (EPCRA), which included authorization for the TRI (Hanson 1985). Through the TRI, the US EPA would make publicly available detailed information about how much pollutants large facilities – and their parent companies – were releasing into the atmosphere and waterways, allowing anyone to find out which companies were polluting more than others. Three major chemical companies – DuPont, Union Carbide, and American Cyanamid – publicly endorsed the TRI's public disclosure requirements, writing: "We believe the types of programs [listed in the EPCRA] are an important element of our safety, health and environmental effort" (Waxman 1985). Other chemical companies, including Dow Chemical, Exxon Chemical, and Monsanto, publicly opposed the TRI. During congressional hearings on the EPCRA, these companies sought to limit the scope of the TRI, arguing that mandatory reporting should be required for only the ten most toxic chemicals. Harold Corbet, CEO of Monsanto, further testified that "the safety record of the chemical industry comes, in large part, from self-improvement ... it did not come as a result of regulation" (Waxman 1985).

The TRI became public policy, and the first report of companies' pollution emissions was made public on June 19, 1989. The TRI data showed that firms who lobbied against the TRI, such as Dow Chemical, Exxon Chemical, and Monsanto, were among the highest polluters. Companies that had lobbied in support of the TRI, such as DuPont, Union Carbide, and American Cyanamid, had lower pollution emissions than their peers. Wall Street noticed; the high-polluting companies saw their stock prices decline, and the stock prices of cleaner companies rose (Hamilton 1995).

Collaboration can be easier to achieve among a smaller number of participants, such as when only a few stakeholders would receive the vast majority of value from an institutional change. Voluntary institutions can be an attractive path that addresses social and environmental problems where government action falls short. Those most directly involved in producing the problem and experiencing the benefits of solutions may collectively have the strongest incentives to produce a collaborative, or shared value, institution. For example, the Marine Stewardship Council (MSC) was created through collaboration among Walmart, Unilever, and the World Wildlife Fund (Gulbrandsen 2009). The MSC created a voluntary certification that aimed to ensure the long-term sustainability of larger international fisheries. Fishery managers could receive MSC certification by ensuring that the fishery had effective rules to prevent overfishing.

4.2.2.1 Nonmarket Strategy Case: Huawei Technologies and the Joint Auditing Cooperative

To illustrate the promise and challenges of nonmarket strategy, this section presents a brief case study of Huawei Technologies and the Joint Auditing Cooperation (JAC). By 2010, Huawei Technologies had become a major supplier to developed country telecommunication companies and was confronted with questions about how to work with them to respond to stakeholder pressures for improved environmental and social responsibility in the telecommunication industry's supply chains.

Huawei Technologies was founded in 1987 by Ren Zhengfei, formerly a mid-level officer in the Chinese military. The company's early strategy was to copy existing technologies to produce phone switches for Asian markets. Over the years, the company grew rapidly, expanding its research and development program and bringing consumer products to international markets. By 2010, it was selling cell phones throughout the developing world and set its sights on the lucrative consumer cell phone markets in developed country markets.

Telecommunication companies in developed markets purchased Huawei phones to sell directly to their home country customers. These telecommunication companies were facing consumer, NGO, and government pressures for improved social and environmental performance. BT wanted suppliers like Huawei to go beyond compliance with local regulations, reduce their greenhouse gas emissions, and even share their knowledge about how to achieve these objectives.

For Huawei, the challenge of meeting developed market expectations was daunting because the terms of Huawei's social license to operate covered not only its own performance but its suppliers as well. Huawei had over 1,000 first-tier suppliers, most of which were smaller Chinese companies, who in turn had their own suppliers scattered throughout the country. While Chinese government regulations had become more strict over the years and were approaching the stringency of developed country regulatory standards, they were unevenly enforced. A violation or scandal within its supply chain could echo back to cause public relations and financial harm for Huawei.

Huawei's leadership, recognizing that improving social and environmental performance for itself and its suppliers would be key for its growth, established its Department of Corporate Social Responsibility and Global Supplier Management, which by 2010 had 240 staff working on supplier sustainability. The department created a supplier code of conduct and an auditing program aimed at ensuring its suppliers adhered to local laws and regulations and the conduct code's standards. Suppliers, however, were often not enthusiastic partners in helping Huawei achieve its goals, with many responding to audits evasively or by responding to the letter of the auditors' requests rather than spirit of Huawei's CSR code of conduct.

The challenges Huawei experienced in improving its supply chain CSR performance were quite common among manufacturing and production industries. Major telecommunication companies like AT&T, Deutsche Telekom, and Vodafone, like BT, purchased cell phones from producers like Huawei and passed them on to customers. Telecommunication companies in developed countries and their suppliers had long and complex supply chains that stretched broadly into the developing world. The attraction of lower costs from weaker environmental, labor, and social regulations was at least part of the reason supply chains had grown among developing countries in the first place. Supplier companies in the developing world were under less pressure for CSR performance. Public opinion and government regulations on environmental and social issues were more permissive. Relatively weak civil society organizations and international NGOs allowed developing country companies plenty of room for lax environmental and labor practices.

Meanwhile, telecommunication companies and cell phone producers were under mounting pressure to improve social, labor, and environmental practices in their supply chains. The challenge was not just avoiding scandal; stakeholders wanted assurances that companies were ensuring that suppliers' day-to-day operations were meeting expectations for social and environmental performance. For example, a company's climate strategy would simply not be credible with stakeholders if it did not address the greenhouse gas emissions of the products and services its purchased.

As Huawei discovered, improving suppliers' CSR conduct was particularly challenging for a single company working on its own. Managing supply chain CSR came with high costs – a company needed to develop a code of conduct for its suppliers and then conduct a monitoring program in many separate locations that were geographically distant and culturally diverse. Correcting suppliers' behavior was also challenging because a company might not have much leverage over its suppliers – if a company's code of conduct was too demanding, a supplier might simply switch to less demanding purchasers.

The CSR challenges in the cell phone supply chain were a collective action problem for the cell phone companies, cell phone producers and suppliers, and telecommunication companies. Each actor risked bearing a large share of the costs of the improvements while only receiving a fraction of the benefits. Responding to an audit and complying with a code of conduct's standards could put the supplier at a cost disadvantage if its competitors were able to dodge supply chain scrutiny. If a cell phone producer improved performance among one of its suppliers, the benefits of the improvement – lower reputational risk from scandal, improved standing with stakeholders – would accrue to others who purchased from the supplier as well. Meanwhile, the benefits of suppliers' CSR improvement would be shared broadly. Cell phone and telecommunications companies would receive reputational benefits from their stakeholders. The suppliers' communities and workers would experience better environmental and working conditions.

The industries' suppliers' cell phone companies would all benefit from more uniform standards, coordinating audit inspections, and sharing audit results. From the suppliers' perspective, a single supplier might face audit requests from many companies, and each audit carried costs. For cell phone and telecommunication companies, coordinating audit inspections and sharing results would lower costs, particularly if audits evaluated according to a uniform standard.

In 2010, three European telecommunications companies – Deutsche Telekom, France Télécom, and Telecom Italia – launched the JAC to create a standard auditing procedure for suppliers in the telecommunications industry. Other major companies joined over the next decade, including major players in international and global markets such as

AT&T, Verizon, MTN, MTS, Telstra, and Vodafone. JAC's goal was to improve CSR performance among telecommunication suppliers. JAC is a voluntary institution in that it promulgated a set of rules to govern the supply chain practices of participating telecommunication companies and their suppliers' CSR performance but lacked the formal legal authority of the state to compel participation. The JAC's rules included requirements for telecommunication companies' supplier codes of conduct and for how supplier audits were to be conducted. Telecommunication suppliers had incentives to cooperate with the JAC. They would retain access to lucrative markets and face potentially fewer audits with more uniform standards.

To incentivize telecommunications companies to participate, the JAC also provided benefits that could be allocated only to companies that formally participated in the program. For example, members would have more cost-effective monitoring. The JAC identified members' major first-tier suppliers and then divided auditing responsibility among its members. Suppliers turned out to be more responsive to JAC member audits – knowing that one audit was backed by many companies gave them more incentive to participate and meet the audit terms. The participating telecommunications companies would learn the outcome of other JAC members' audits while conducting fewer audits themselves. The JAC also offered members reputational benefits – members could use their JAC participation to reassure stakeholders that they were making serious efforts to improve suppliers' CSR performance.

Huawei started collaborating with the JAC in 2013, with a role similar to JAC's telecommunication company members. Huawei oversaw supplier audits and received the results of audits conducted by other JAC members. Through the JAC, Huawei could identify its highest-risk first-tier suppliers and ensure they received a JAC-supervised audit, thus reducing the risk of a supply chain CSR scandal.

While the JAC had some success, it was not a panacea for the supply chain challenges facing Huawei and the telecommunication companies. The size and depth of the industry's supply chains put many suppliers beyond the reach of even a well-organized auditing campaign. BT alone had over 17,400 suppliers. Suppliers deeper in the supply chain often had less motivation and expertise to meet JAC's higher CSR standards. Most of Huawei's suppliers were small and medium-sized enterprises located in areas of China where government regulations were at best unevenly enforced and the population and civic groups were not well organized to pressure local companies to improve environmental performance. To expand its capacity, JAC could look to expand its membership to include more telecommunication companies and companies in other industries, with the goal of sharing the burden of auditing deeper into the supply chain. It could also look to recruit like-minded NGOs. But expansion would come with costs – more participants means aligning more disparate views into a common strategy. A larger membership roster might lead to free-riding risks as participants may look to enjoy the benefits of membership with taking on the costs of maintaining the JAC's standards.

4.3 Conclusion

Like market strategy, nonmarket strategy focuses on the environment external to the company to identify threats and opportunities for sustainable environmental improvements. Government regulations, NGOs, activists, and citizens can all interact with a company in ways that have consequences for its environmental strategy, even if the consequences of stakeholder engagement can be difficult to measure directly in financial terms. NGOs can shape a company's relationship with customers through protests and endorsements. Competitors' environmental mishaps can damage the reputation of an entire industry. Companies also have opportunities to engage with institutions and change their rules and how they allocate environmental costs and benefits. Companies can lobby governments, influence their industry associations, and collaborate with other organizations, such as by creating a multisector partnerships.

Market and nonmarket environmental strategies can be mutually reinforcing, combining a low-cost strategy with a nonmarket strategy, as exemplified by Coca-Cola's water initiatives. As a beverage company, Coca-Cola is reliant on access to water, particularly in areas where access to clean water is expensive and cannot be taken for granted. Water efficiency and contributing to the health of local water systems have long been key components of Coca-Cola's environmental programs, and access to water resources may require the permission of local communities and stakeholders.

In 2004, Coca-Cola used 2.7 liters of water to make 1 liter of product; by 2016, it was using only 1.96 liters (Coca-Cola Company

2018). Facing mounting pressure from NGO and citizen protests, such as what occurred in Kerala, India, in 2007, Coca-Cola's CEO, Muhtar Kent, announced a company goal that by 2020 the company would return an equal amount of water to what it used in its finished beverages and production to local water systems. The company started a $20 million water conservation partnership with the World Wildlife Fund, a move that gained Coca-Cola expertise in water efficiency practices and, perhaps more importantly, enhanced credibility for its water initiatives (The Economic Times 2007). In 2017, Coca-Cola announced that it had achieved many of its water goals, well ahead of schedule, though at a cost of $2 billion (Schwartz 2015).

Coca-Cola's water initiatives complemented its nonmarket strategy. The initial goal was to lower costs through improved efficiency. Over time the programs focused on nonmarket domains that threatened access to key inputs. Eventually the programs added to Coca-Cola's market strategy by improving its standing with nonmarket stakeholders and Coca-Cola's brand. Coca-Cola's chief competitor, Pepsi, had to respond by expanding its own water efficiency and community water programs.

5 | *Environmental Strategy and Strategic Resources*

There is no one-size-fits-all environmental strategy. Different companies have different opportunities for environmental improvements, face different stakeholders, have different challenges for capturing value from their environmental improvements, and have different market and nonmarket strategies. The success of an environmental strategy also depends on the resources the company possesses, which this chapter investigates.

The resource-based view of competitive strategy identifies the source of a firm's sustained competitive advantage in the resources it holds and to which it has access, including its capabilities (Barney 1991; Teece 2007; Wernerfelt 1984). Companies need all sorts of resources to operate – material inputs to make products, production equipment, labor and skills to get jobs done, distribution networks, and so on. Strategic resources are the "assets, capabilities, organizational processes, firm attributes, information, knowledge, etc. controlled by a firm that enable the firm to conceive of and implement strategies that improve its efficiency and effectiveness" (Barney 1991: 101). A strategic resource is valuable, rare, difficult for others to imitate or otherwise acquire, and can be organized within the company to promote its competitive advantage. A resource is valuable when it helps the company improve its effectiveness or efficiency. A resource is scarce when it is not available to every company.

The resource-based view echoes market-focused theories in identifying why some resources might be difficult for competitors to imitate or acquire. The first company in a market where customers' switching costs are high can be seen as having a valuable resource – competitors will have difficulty duplicating the company's strategy to attract customers. A resource may be inimitable because legal copyrights and patent protections prevent competitors from imitating the company's strategy. A strategic resource can be something tangible, like a piece of machinery or geographic location. There are also intangible resources that do not exist in a physical form but help the company nonetheless. Examples of intangible resources include the company's culture, the capabilities and accumulated knowledge of its employees, and the relationships with its customers or other key stakeholders.

The resource-based view of the firm identifies additional reasons why a company's competitive advantage may be insulated from competitive mimicry. One reason is rooted in history: changing circumstances can make resources more or less valuable over time, and such historical change can bestow competitive advantage by raising competitors' cost of acquiring the newly valuable resources. Evolving technology can change the value of different types of resources, such as knowledge and skills. Knowledge and skills are costly to obtain, as any student facing a tuition bill quickly realizes. A company may find itself with a workforce whose skills have increased in value due to some change in circumstances, leaving its competitors paying extra costs to catch up. The value of a company's culture can change over time as well. Suppose a maverick entrepreneur founded a company years ago with a more informal and nonhierarchical organizational culture than the norm at the time. The entrepreneur may find her culture to be a competitive advantage in the labor market, especially if preferences shift over time and younger workers prefer her more informal working environment rather than that of her stodgy competitors.

Another reason a company's resources can be difficult to mimic is complexity – some organizational resources are too complex to be easily transferred or copied by other companies. This complexity is often embedded in tacit knowledge, particularly around subtle social interactions, routines, and organizational culture (Barney 1986). Knowledge about physical technologies like computers or production equipment can be difficult to learn but still transferable among companies – a company can hire personnel with the requisite expertise or train its employees. More difficult to imitate are the valuable practices that arise through a precise and delicate fit among people, organizational practices, and physical technologies.

Toyota's production practices during the 1980s provide an illustrative example of complex management practices that are difficult for other companies to imitate. By the 1980s, Toyota had achieved a competitive advantage through its lean manufacturing practices, what the company came to call the "Toyota Production System" (TPS). TPS was a production management system that combined just-in-time production with empowering employees to improve processes and quality, among other technical and managerial elements. The TPS was a source of competitive advantage for Toyota. It lowered production costs and produced more reliable cars with fewer defects. Other car companies unsuccessfully tried to emulate Toyota's practices, including GM. In 1991, Toyota and GM formed an alliance around the New United Motor Manufacturing, Inc. automobile manufacturing company in Fremont, CA. The joint venture helped Toyota to gain access to the American market and it gave GM access to Toyota's manufacturing practices and the opportunity to learn the complex processes it could only achieve through firsthand experience (Inkpen 2005; Shook 2010). Gary Cowger, GM's vice president for manufacturing and labor relations, later credited Toyota for hard-earned lessons in improving production practices. Cowger said, "the roots of our [GM's] improvement are in the Toyota Production System [TPS]. We learned from them [Toyota]. We've got to give credit where credit is due" (Inkpen 2005). The lengths GM went to learn from Toyota are a testament to the power of complexity as a barrier to rivals' attempts to mimic TPS.

This chapter examines how companies can use their competitive advantages to develop their environmental strategy. The chapter begins with a discussion of the types of resources that can contribute to environmental strategy. It then examines companies' organizational structures, including the roles of chief sustainability officers, and how organizational features can facilitate identifying and implementing programs to achieve environmental solutions. Building on a company's current capabilities and resources can help the company's chief sustainability officer and green teams develop a successful environmental strategy that achieves a triple bottom line win.

5.1 Resources for Environmental Strategy

The resource-based view takes into account the resources a company holds and offers insights into environmental strategy (Aragón-Correa & Sharma 2003; Sharma & Vredenburg 1998). Strategically using resources for environmental improvements may create opportunities to create and capture value. Environmental improvements can be competitively advantageous when they exploit a company's existing strategic resources (Amui et al. 2017). Why start from the ground up when you can build on your current strengths? As the management scholar Stuart Hart wrote, "it is likely that strategy and competitive advantage in the coming years will be rooted in capabilities that facilitate environmentally sustainable economic activity – a natural-resource-based view of the firm" (Hart 1995: 991).

The resource-based view also suggests criteria for choosing among opportunities for environmental improvements: opportunities that draw on a company's strategic resources are more likely to succeed. The specific resources that can be deployed for such environmental strategic advantage are likely to depend on complex factors, both internal and external to the company, as well as the company's environmental and broader strategic goals (Aragón-Correa & Sharma 2003; Hart 1995; Hart & Dowell 2011; Russo & Fouts 1997). It is, therefore, important for environmental strategy to identify which resources can be applied to environmental opportunities and produce sustainable value.

A company can leverage its resources for competitive advantage in market and nonmarket contexts. A company adept at product innovation may find new markets for its offerings. A strong company brand developed in the market arena may be a valuable resource in nonmarket arenas; the company's brand may make its promises to stakeholders more credible, allowing it to make more favorable informal agreements with stakeholders. The resource-based view focuses initial attention internally to identify which resources can generate sustained competitive advantage (Grant 1991, 1996). The resource-based view addresses the importance of achieving alignment among the external market and nonmarket opportunities and the internal resources it holds. Competitive strategies are achieved through alignment among market strategy, nonmarket strategy, and internal processes and resources (Grant 1991; Kaplan & Norton 2006). Alignment means that these different elements are structured in such a way that they synergize: the competitive strategy draws on and strengthens the resources, and the resources are informed by and reinforce the competitive strategy. Alignment can enhance a company's competitive advantage by making it more difficult for competitors to copy a company's source of success, thereby maintaining financial returns over a longer period.

The resource-based view also helps identify when a company is ill-suited for what otherwise appears to be a promising market opportunity. A company may identify a consumer segment with unmet demand, but this may not be a promising opportunity unless the company has the resources to sustain a competitive advantage. The evolution of the MP3 music player market shows the importance of a sustainable competitive advantage. The patent for an MP3 music player shows the importance of a sustainable competitive advantage. The patent was originally held by a British man named Kane Kramer, but in 1988 he was unable to raise the money needed to keep the patent from reaching the public domain. In the 1990s, a few small companies offered MP3 players, but they did not survive long once giant consumer electronics companies like Apple and Sony entered the market. Apple and Sony possessed the resources to sustain their advantage in the MP3 player market (Sorrel 2000). As this book has discussed, for a company to capture value from any environmental improvement, it must solve a common set of problems: identify the environmental improvements and costs, evaluate stakeholder demand, ensure a channel for value transfer, and ensure the exchange's credibility. Section 5.1.1 begins the examination of resources that can contribute to effectively achieving environmental improvements.

5.1.1 Assessing Environmental Impacts and Costs

As discussed in Chapter 3, an assessment of a company's environmental impacts and costs needs to be comprehensive – that is, to cover all environmental impacts and outcomes – and sensitive to changing circumstances. Such assessments can be challenging; they can take considerable time and effort and expertise in engineering, accounting, production and operations, supply chain management, and other areas. The term "life cycle assessment," often shortened to just "LCA," refers to the discipline of accounting for a product's entire "cradle to grave" environmental impact (Suh & Huppes 2005).

LCA starts by breaking down a product's life into phases:

- *Production* of materials refers to how the product's raw materials are collected, transformed, and transported to become the product's inputs. Recycled materials may have lower environmental impacts.
- *Manufacturing* is the process of combining raw materials into a product. An environmentally superior manufacturing process captures more pollutants before they are released into the atmosphere.

- *Packaging and distribution* are the raw materials and distribution channels for getting the product to consumers. A product can have an environmental advantage if it uses fewer packaging materials or requires fewer resources to distribute to consumers.
- *Use* is what consumers do with the product up to when they no longer own it.
- *Disposal* is how a product is managed at the end of its life. Whether a product is recycled or tossed into a landfill can have important environmental consequences.

A comprehensive LCA considers all relevant environmental impacts across all of a product's life cycle phases. LCA's comprehensive cradle-to-grave analysis provides a more precise picture of a product's total environmental impact. LCA also categorizes products by different types of environmental impact. There are many potential environmental impacts worthy of assessment – greenhouse gas emissions and contributions to climate change, exposing ecosystems to toxic chemicals, depleting local aquifers or ecologically important resources, and so on. Picking the right environmental impacts for a company's environmental strategy is no small matter. Adding more impacts to the analysis might seem better, but doing so can be expensive because many are quite difficult to measure. Sometimes an LCA gives a clear answer: one product may have better net environmental impacts than another across all impact categories. Other times, a comprehensive LCA clarifies trade-offs between products: one product may have better climate change consequences but puts a greater strain on scarce local water systems. While not every company will be in a position to evaluate its products with full LCA; the analytic skills for this type of analysis can help companies comprehensively identify and evaluate opportunities for environmental improvements.

5.1.2 Resources for Stakeholders Analysis Engagement

Stakeholder analysis measures the strength of stakeholder demand and the resources stakeholders can deploy to influence a company's environmental performance (Freeman 2010; Reed et al. 2009). The capabilities for stakeholder mapping are very similar, in some respects, to the capabilities necessary for understanding consumer markets, such as market research for identifying potential stakeholders and understanding their needs. However, environmental stakeholders are likely to be quite different, and are much broader than the company's customers, and therefore a stakeholder analysis is a more involved process than market research.

Companies can learn about stakeholders through market research techniques like surveys and focus groups. Some companies are more adept than others at identifying stakeholders and interpreting their needs (Barnett 2007; Crilly & Sloan 2014). This capability is transferrable to assessing environmental stakeholders, as companies are able to anticipate changing circumstances and trends as well. An environmental impact may be currently of little concern to stakeholders, perhaps because they are unaware of the problem or the impact is at relatively low levels. Understanding how these stakeholders will react when they learn of the problem or if the impact increases can help focus a company's environmental strategy. Stakeholder mapping is a helpful process for understanding not only a company's environmental stakeholders, but also the environmental harms and solutions. Engaging environmental stakeholders helps companies identify new environmental problems, adapt their environmental programs, and improve environmental performance (Dangelico et al. 2017; Dangelico & Pujari 2010; Henriques & Sadorsky 1999).

5.1.3 Channels, Resources, and Capabilities

An environmental strategy can reinforce a company's broader competitive strategy when both capture value through the same channels and draw on the same resources. A market-focused environmental strategy can reinforce a product differentiation competitive strategy by bringing new environmental products to market, as we discuss in Chapter 6. Likewise, an environmental strategy can reinforce a low-cost competitive strategy by improving operational efficiency (Porter & van der Linde 1995). Companies with resources for improving production and operations may have opportunities to capture cost savings through improved efficiency and reducing the risk and costs of accidental pollution releases and spills (Kleindorfer et al. 2005; Reinhardt 1999). For example, chemical companies with stronger capabilities for process innovation and implementation received greater cost savings when adopting advanced environmental management practices (Christmann 2000). Likewise, companies with more advanced quality-based management and inventory control systems, like ISO 9000 or

Total Quality Management, spend fewer resources to adopt advanced environmental management systems (Darnall & Edwards 2006). Such cost-saving capabilities may become more valuable as industries mature and the strategic focus shifts from adopting new technologies and expanding into new markets to harvesting efficiencies within current practices (Reinhardt 1999).

Walmart's sustainability efforts in the 2000s offer an example of how an environmental strategy can draw on supply chain management resources to identify and address environmental problems (Bowen et al. 2001; Spicer & Hyatt 2017). Supply chains are an important source of both environmental risk and opportunities for identifying areas of environmental improvements (Seuring & Müller 2008). The pressure for improving supply chain sustainability often comes from NGOs and activists (Roberts 2003), which can put the company's reputation at risk (Seuring & Müller 2008). For decades, Walmart used its supply chain expertise and considerable bargaining power with suppliers to drive down costs. In the 2000s, Walmart was facing pressure from NGOs to improve its environmental practices (Dauvergne & Lister 2012). Instead of offering new lines of environmentally differentiated products, which experience had shown were unlikely to be well received by its consumers, Walmart focused its sustainability initiatives on its supply chain. For example, Walmart told its fish suppliers that it would only purchase fish certified as sustainable by the MSC. But instead of paying higher prices for sustainable fish, Walmart used its supply chain skills and alliances with NGOs to compel suppliers to bear the costs of sustainability. Walmart did not advertise its MSC certification to consumers, but its sustainable fish policy helped shield the company from NGO publicity campaigns while also helping to ensure that Walmart would have a stable supply of fish in the future. Walmart's lessons apply more broadly. Companies that have effective supply chain management systems – that effectively share information across organizational subunits and have a well-trained supply chain workforce – are more likely to achieve cost savings through environmental supply chain initiatives (Bowen et al. 2001).

5.1.4 Credibility and Resources

Stakeholders who want environmental performance are rarely in a position to observe directly whether and how well a company is producing environmental value, as discussed in Chapter 3. Indeed, stakeholders are well aware that companies have incentives to exaggerate their environmental accomplishments and promise to produce an environmental improvement without actually following through with it. To overcome this problem, a company must be credible in its communications so that stakeholders believe its environmental commitments and improvements are genuine. Such credibility can come from a costly signal – a communication that will cost the sender (the company) significant value if it turns out to be untrue. Section 5.2 discusses how a company's culture and brand can compliment its strategy for communicating with stakeholders. Companies have incentives to keep their environmental communications consistent with the broader themes in their culture and brands.

Culture shapes how a company interacts with its stakeholders and how people within a company interact with each other. An effective company culture can enhance a company's ability to create and capture value. A culture can influence how employees will perform in the absence of direct orders or supervision. Effective cultures can lead to a more efficient workforce, better information sharing and cooperation among employees, and higher-quality products with fewer defects. A thriving company culture is often difficult for others to copy. But building culture is costly and can take time to produce. Cultures are often based on terms and concepts that are difficult to explain and convey to others or are rooted in the company's unique historical circumstances (Barney 1986). Chapter 7 discusses the role of environmental performance, employee relations, and company culture in more detail.

A brand is a mental image held by stakeholders about a company and its products. A brand conveys information that stakeholders would not otherwise be able to acquire – the quality of a product, how it was made, and how it will perform. Brands can convey emotional messages, such as how a consumer will feel when consuming a product, as exemplified in the 1980s when Coca-Cola used the slogan "Have a Coke and a Smile" to advertise its soft drinks. Like culture, a company's brand can be a strategic resource. A brand can help a company capture value. Customers may be more willing to purchase a branded product because they are more confident about the qualities they will receive in return for their money. Brands are costly to create; building a brand takes time and is built through advertising and other expensive communication campaigns. Brands are difficult

for competitors to mimic, and brand images, for example, are pro-
tected by copyright law. A company's CSR practices can influence
consumers' perceptions of its brand and product qualities, including
those not directly related to CSR (Shea & Hawn 2018). In the other
direction, the sustainability and CSR features of a product can change
how stakeholders view a company (Sen & Bhattacharya 2001; Siegel
& Vitaliano 2007). Likewise, a positive environmental brand image
can improve a company's standing with local communities and NGOs
(Bhattacharya et al. 2011). Chapter 6 discusses the importance of
brands for green product strategies.

A company's culture and brand can be valuable resources for
improving the credibility of its environmental communications with
stakeholders. Cultures and brands can be strategically valuable – they
help the company create and capture value in ways that are difficult
for competitors to mimic. If a company's environmental communications violate the terms of its culture or brand, stakeholders are likely
to lose faith in the broader cultural and brand messages and terms
they had previously believed. Without such beliefs, they may no longer
purchase from the company. For example, if a company with a reputation for high-quality products is found to be violating the terms of
its environmental pledges, consumers may come to doubt whether the
products are genuinely of high quality. The key to credibility appears
to be that stakeholders perceive the environmental action as intrinsi-
cally motivated by the organization's core values rather than extrin-
sically motivated by short-term financial gain (Bhattacharya et al.
2011). Conversely, environmental and social performance can boost
stakeholders' acceptance of a company's brand and culture.

5.2 Organizational Structure and Human Resources for Environmental Improvements

When a company adopts and manages an effective sustainability
initiative, its value is healthy for the planet's ecosystems as well as
the company's bottom line. Companies exist to identify and exploit
opportunities to create and capture value. Companies organize their
workforce so that employees work together to achieve these goals. If
some new innovation comes along that will improve the company's
position, it should adopt that innovation. We would expect the financial benefits to compel companies to adopt these programs quite easily,

just as we expect people to pick up twenty-dollar bills they find lying on the ground. Why is this not always the case? Even high-performing companies do not always make the changes they need to remain on top (Christensen 1997). Companies can make mistakes, and one reason they do so is that their executives and managers fail to adapt innovations that would benefit the company (Ocasio & Joseph 2018). It turns out that adopting innovations requires solving problems, and these problems turn out to be quite similar to the transaction cost problems discussed in Chapter 2, only now the problems exist within the company rather than between a company and its stakeholders. In this section we discuss why these challenges are particularly difficult for environmental improvements, starting with how companies aim to organize the workforce so that managers will make decisions that benefit the company as a whole.

In order for a company's managers to adopt profitable innovation, they must have the right authority, incentives, and information (Csaszar 2012; Garicano & Posner 2005). Authority means the manager is authorized to spend resources to adopt the innovation. The right incentive exists when the manager is rewarded for choosing to adopt an innovation that generates returns of greater value for the company than their costs (this also means that managers bear a cost for adopting unsuccessful innovations). The right information means managers have knowledge about the problem, the potential solution, and the costs and benefits from adopting the innovation (Gibbons & Henderson 2012; Gold et al. 2001; Leonard & Sensiper 1998).

Companies design managers' employment terms to encourage and enable them to identify and solve problems in ways that benefit the company as a whole. First, employment terms grant managers authority to make decisions and spend resources within a functional area, such as operations, supply chains, or marketing. Supply chain managers, for example, are responsible for procuring suitable inputs and making sure they are delivered on time and with the appropriate qualities and quantities. Marketing managers are responsible for buying advertisements to promote the company's products. A well-defined functional area has boundaries that contain the causes and effects of a common set of problems. Second, employment terms also specify managers' incentives: the salary and advancement opportunities the manager will receive in return for achieving goals and outcomes within their functional area. Operations managers might be rewarded for hitting production quotas and meeting quality targets. Supply chain managers might be rewarded for stabilizing input flows or finding lower-priced materials. Marketing managers might be rewarded for brand recognition. The rewards could include higher pay, promotion opportunities, or other forms of recognition. Finally, managers' employment terms also specify how they will acquire information about problems and solutions in their functional area. Managers can more efficiently acquire information about problems and solutions within their functional area by learning specialized knowledge, language, and culture specific to that area (Crilly & Sloan 2014). Such specialized expertise includes the capacity to better absorb information from external sources, such as stakeholders relevant to the area (Barnett 2007).

A benefit of specialization is equipping managers to make decisions within functional areas that produce the best outcomes for the company as a whole. But specialization comes with trade-offs. First, the more managers' incentives are tied to improvements within their functional area, the less managers have incentives to attend to problems and solutions outside their functional area. The downsides of such incentive structures are likely to be most salient for problems and solutions that have costs and benefits that span managers' functional expertise. If a manager's incentives are tied only to costs and benefits within her functional area, she is less likely to spend resources that produce value within another manager's functional domain. Second, the more managers develop a specialized expertise for managing information within their functional area, the less adept they become at exchanging information across functional areas. Third, the more managers have expertise specialized for solving problems within a functional area, the more difficult it is for them to share knowledge across functional areas (Gold et al. 2001; Leonard & Sensiper 1998). Managers' attention is a finite resource – managers cannot pay attention to everything. Attention paid to issues inside the functional area must come at the expense of attention outside the functional area (Joseph & Wilson 2018).

The trade-offs of specialization depend on circumstances. Specialization has larger downsides when business problems have costs and benefits that span organizational boundaries, and therefore solutions require collaboration and sharing information across organizational boundaries. In such circumstances, managers' incentives may be misaligned – an innovation may produce benefits within one manager's functional area while its costs accrue in another manager's area. Functional barriers within companies may also prevent information flowing into and within a company from reaching those in a position to use it to implement innovations – managers in one area may have the expertise to identify a problem occurring in another manager's area (King 1999). In such cases, a company needs to find ways to align incentives and information to ensure the adoption of valuable innovations.

5.2.1 Information and Incentive Problems for Environmental Improvements

For a company to implement an environmental innovation that provides value in return, its managers must have the information and incentives to implement the improvement. In some cases, the information, costs, and benefits for an environmental improvement all fall within the same area of a single manager. A supply chain manager, drawing on his subject area expertise, may identify inputs that lower costs and reduce pollution emissions among the company's suppliers. To implement improvements, the manager would pay the costs of time and effort to work with suppliers to adopt the new input. The manager would also realize important benefits from the improvement, such as lower input prices and a more stable supply chain due to the suppliers improving relations with their own local community stakeholders.

For scholars, what happens within companies to adopt environmental improvements has been difficult to study (Delmas & Toffel 2008) – the influence of external factors has been easier to measure and analyze relative to internal factors. One reason for this is that data on what goes on inside companies is harder to obtain, resulting in more case studies and smaller sample research. In an informative study, Andrew King showed that environmental departments could facilitate information flow within a company, thus helping to mitigate the trade-off between technical specialization and information flow within a company (King 1995). In environmental departments within companies that produced printed circuit boards, King found that managers in specialized environmental departments helped their company improve efficiency and environmental performance. The reason is that managers in the environmental departments had the incentive and capacity to acquire and disseminate information to operations managers about process improvements. The environmental managers' efforts may have been spurred by the need for the companies to respond to new water regulations, but nonetheless this is a powerful example of how environmental managers can solve information and incentive problems to implement environmental improvements (King 1995).

Companies looking to adopt environmental improvements are likely to experience more challenging information and incentive problems than they would when considering improvements in other areas. There are several reasons for this. First, environmental problems and solutions have causes and effects that are often distant from each other and are thus realized across different functional units within the company. Pollution generated deep within the supply chain may cause customers to choose to buy other products. The supply chain managers who oversee the purchasing of the pollution-generating inputs are likely to be far removed from the marketing managers who oversee customer relations and the company brand. Second, because the benefits of environmental improvements are collective goods, they are likely to be experienced by a broad range of diverse stakeholders (Tantalo & Priem 2016). Stakeholders who value pollution reductions could include customers who prefer green products, people living in communities that directly experience the pollution reduction, government regulators responsible for limiting pollution, and employees who prefer to work for an environmentally responsible company. The diversity of environmental stakeholders means that both the information about stakeholder demand and the benefits from satisfying stakeholder demand may be spread out across several functional areas within the company. The upshot is that, even when an environmental improvement could generate positive value for a company, the individual managers who would pay the costs of implementing it may not have the incentive or the information to do so.

To ensure that companies identify and implement favorable environmental improvements, companies need ways to align information and incentives with managers authorized to implement the solutions. The following discussion examines the organization of sustainability responsibilities within companies. First is an overview of the organization of sustainability in companies, focusing on the role of the chief sustainability officer (CSO).

5.2.2 Organizational Structure, Capabilities, and Sustainability within Companies

5.2.2.1 The Board of Directors and Senior Executive Management

The company's board of directors oversees the senior executives and its overall strategy and performance. Most boards have a person or committee responsible for CSR issues, including environmental performance, a sign that these issues are materially important for companies' financial success. In recent years, some boards have begun including CSR clauses in the employment contracts for senior executives, such as the CEO. Such clauses award executives with financial bonuses for achieving specified CSR criteria in a manner similar to compensation clauses that tie executives' salaries to companies' financial performance. There is evidence that such performance clauses can be effective at improving CSR and financial performance. Companies that adopt CSR compensation clauses end up with better financial valuations, lower pollution emissions, and more innovative environmental practices (Flammer et al. 2019). In general, senior executives are receptive to environmental improvement initiatives when they are framed with a business case justifying their value (Hafenbrädl & Waeger 2017). Below CEOs, facility managers are also likely to improve environmental performance when they receive financial compensation for doing so (Russo & Harrison 2005). Thus, there is evidence that board-level practices can incentivize managers to adopt environmental innovations.

5.2.2.2 CSOs and Sustainability Departments

Among executives, companies have a single senior executive whose responsibilities are most entirely or predominantly focused on the company's relationship with the environment (Greenbiz 2016). In some cases, this position is at the most senior level reporting to the CEO, and at other times it can be several layers lower in the organizational chart. The formal titles for this senior environmental position include "vice president for sustainability," "head of environment," "director of sustainability," and "chief sustainability officer" (see Table 5.1). For simplicity, in this book, we use CSO to refer to the most senior person in the company whose job entails full responsibility for the company's environmental affairs

Table 5.1 *Examples of senior environmental position titles*

Company	Senior environmental position title
Netflix	CSO
HP Inc.	Chief sustainability and social impact officer
Patagonia	Vice president of social and environmental sustainability
Levi Strauss	CSO

Source: (Wenzel 2020).

and issues (note that the acronym CSO can also stand for "chief science officer").

In practice, CSOs can oversee a wide range of functional responsibilities relating to environmental performance and sustainability. A CSO's responsibilities tend to reflect the evolution of the sustainability offices (Kanashiro & Rivera 2019). Often, the sustainability office's origin was within another functional unit, such as the operations office. Table 5.2 lists some potential CSO responsibility areas.

CSOs can have any combination of these responsibilities and others not listed Table 5.2. Some responsibilities are ongoing matters that require regular work. CSOs may oversee the company's annual sustainability report or engage in regular outreach with community stakeholders. Other responsibilities appear only from time to time as special projects. A CSO may work with facilities and operations managers on a special project to reduce a facility's impact on local water systems. As we will see in Chapter 9, members of Nike's sustainability office worked with the company's product design teams to improve the environmental performance of its apparel products and manufacturing practices. Environmental managers working under the CSO can be assigned to work on ongoing and special project responsibilities.

Importantly, CSO responsibilities are often in functional areas shared with other departments and managers. Facilities departments manage the building heating and cooling systems that play a big role in energy efficiency. Human resources departments recruit and train the company's workforce and run employee engagement programs. Environmental health and safety, which is primarily concerned with regulatory compliance, overlaps with workplace safety.

Table 5.2 *Potential areas of responsibility in a CSO's portfolio*

Responsibility areas	Examples
Strategy	Environmental strategy
	CSR strategy
Operations	Energy efficiency
	Recycling
	Environmental management systems (e.g., ISO 14001)
Product development and marketing	Designing sustainable products
	Promoting and marketing company sustainability practices and products
	Brand management
Human resources	Employee sustainability education
	Employee environmental engagement programs
	Recruitment and retention
Stakeholder relations	Community outreach for sustainability and environmental performance
	Partnerships and outreach to environmental groups
Environmental reporting	Compiling data for rating and certification agencies
	Annual sustainability report
Environmental health and safety	Regulatory compliance and reporting

Just because a company has a CSO and a sustainability office does not mean that the CSO has significant influence. The position of most CSOs is characterized by limited financial and staffing resources, shared business responsibilities, and only indirect roles in primary sources of revenue. CSOs tend to oversee sustainability offices with a relatively small staff of ten or fewer even in multi-billion-dollar companies and often fewer than five in large and medium-sized companies (Greenbiz 2016). Larger sustainability departments tend have staff with more specialized responsibilities and areas of expertise, such as energy efficiency or supply chain management. Sustainability department budgets also tend to be small, often less than $1 million in even the largest companies (Greenbiz 2016).

The upshot is that CSOs' institutional position within their companies is one of political weakness. A CSO with a senior title such as vice president is likely to find herself politically weak relative to vice presidents overseeing her company's major revenue centers. Mid-level environmental managers struggle to initiate environmental improvements beyond regulatory compliance without support from senior management (Cordano & Frieze 2000). Even in a company with lofty environmental ambitions, the vice president overseeing its core product is likely to have more sway in company priorities and policies than the vice president for sustainability.

CSOs and the managers working within environmental departments clearly have incentives to implement environmental improvements. After all, environmental problems are at the core of the CSO's functional area, and environmental improvements are part of their job description. The structure of the sustainability offices suggests that most CSOs lack the resources and internal political authority to influence the incentives for managers in other functional units to adopt environmental improvements.

When companies do not have a CSO, responsibility for environmental performance can be assigned another senior executive (such as vice president for production or operations) or distributed among multiple senior executives (production, strategy, marketing). The absence of a single senior environmental executive may dilute the focus on environmental issues. There is evidence that CSOs can influence environmental improvements, at least in some circumstances. Having a CSO leads to greater reductions in pollution emissions when companies face more stringent regulatory regimes (Kanashiro & Rivera 2019).

5.2.2.3 Green Teams

Developing "green teams" is an organizational practice that has become quite popular in recent years. A green team is a group of employees that work together to improve their company's sustainability practices (Dangelico 2015). Team members are generally volunteers from across the company's functional units. Informal green teams tend to develop their own goals and programs, usually focused on "low-hanging fruit" in areas where success does not require large investments, such as waste reduction, recycling, and behavioral approaches to energy reduction. More formal green teams can take on larger, more strategic sustainability initiatives. A potential benefit of green teams is in providing employees with an opportunity to contribute to causes that matter to them and increase the employees' workplace engagement (see Chapter 7).

Like CSOs, green teams can mitigate the downside of specialization within the organization by facilitating information flows within the organization and helping coordinate action across functional units. Meeting repeatedly to discuss shared concerns helps employees acquire additional areas of expertise and learn to share information more easily. However, quite often, green teams lack the resources that can incentivize other managers to adopt environmental improvements. Companies with stronger environmental performance and reputations are more likely to implement green teams, although it is unclear whether the teams cause the performance and reputation improvements or the improvements (or some other factor) cause the company to implement the green team (Dangelico 2015).

5.2.2.4 Company Culture

For most managers in most companies, contributing to an environmental improvement is an extra work assignment. The work is "extra" in that the manager takes on extra work outside her functional responsibilities without an explicit promise of additional reward or recognition (Wang et al. 2009). Companies often want employees to take on work assignments that are not precisely spelled out in their employment terms (Baker et al. 2002; Gibbons 2005; Gibbons & Henderson 2012; Rousseau 1995). The company may need employees put in extra work to meet a deadline that is important to the company. Employees may be willing to do the extra but may fear that they will not receive any compensation. They may also fear that doing the extra work may prompt the company to invent more emergency deadlines to squeeze more productivity from them. Sharing information about environmental problems and solutions often means a manager is talking to employees and stakeholders about topics that are unrelated to problems the company has formally assigned to them. Likewise, managers are taking on an extra work assignment when they contribute an environmental solution that produces benefits outside their formal area of responsibility.

A company's culture can provide employees with assurances that the company will recognize and reward these extra work assignments. Recall that we define organizational culture as a set of norms and values that are widely shared and firmly held throughout the organization (Gibbons & Henderson 2012; O'Reilly 1989; O'Reilly & Chatman 1996). A company may have a cultural norm that employees will receive some sort of compensation for taking on extra work assignments that lead to environmental improvements that benefit the company. Such a cooperative culture offers incentives to participate in environmental initiatives by suggesting that the extra work assignments will be rewarded. If the company does not provide such rewards, the manager and other employees will be reluctant to take on extra work assignments in the future. A collaborative culture – one that rewards information sharing and contributing to initiatives across functional areas – can thus solve the incentive and information problems for environmental improvements.

Research suggests that collaborative cultures help companies implement value-enhancing environmental improvements. Companies with employees who collaborate more effectively across functional units are more likely to improve their environmental performance and environmental reputation (Albino et al. 2012). More social contact among employees in a company means the company receives more efficiency gains from their environmental management systems (Delmas & Pekovic 2012). Such collaborative cultures translate into organizational practices that promote information sharing and collaborative interaction between the company and its external stakeholders, leading companies to be more innovative with their environmental practices and products. The capacity to assimilate divergent perspectives brought forth by a broad array of stakeholders enables a firm to consider outcomes that realize value returns over longer horizons. (Marcus & Anderson 2006).

5.2.2.5 Human Resource Capabilities for Sustainability
The discussion in this chapter suggests the types of employee capabilities that can facilitate the creation and implementation of an effective environmental strategy (Amrutha & Geetha 2020; Amui et al. 2017). One way to identify these capabilities is through the challenges of developing an environmental strategy as presented throughout this book. Companies may not adopt environmental improvements because they do not know what stakeholders want or even how to identify and talk to stakeholders to learn what they want. Companies may not know how to translate stakeholder demand into value-enhancing resources

Table 5.3 *Human resource capabilities for developing and implementing environmental strategy*

Environmental strategy elements	Example human resource capabilities
Identifying which dimensions of environmental performance improvements can create business value	Ecological or LCA analysis Stakeholder mapping and analysis Cost estimation Process and product innovation
Ensuring channel for value transfer	Supply chain management and logistics Product distribution Creating partnerships Stakeholder engagement
Ensuring credibility	Communication and marketing Measuring environmental performance (LCA, data analysis, and reporting)
Capturing value from environmental improvements	Market and nonmarket strategy Strategic capabilities

that can improve their competitive position. Companies may not know how to reassure stakeholders that the environmental improvements are genuine.

Table 5.3 lists the environmental strategy challenges and examples of relevant capabilities. A theme than unifies these capabilities is that they lower the costs for creating and implementing the Coasian exchanges that underlie environmental strategy.

As we discussed earlier in this chapter, the transaction costs that undermine win–win exchanges between companies and their stakeholders are similar to the internal transaction costs that obstruct managers from adopting value-enhancing environmental improvements. Managers may not have the information to identify opportunities and solutions outside their functional area. Managers may also not have the incentive to take on the costs of environmental improvements when the benefits fall outside their functional area. Thus, many of these capabilities listed in Table 5.3 are also relevant for environmental managers as they work to implement environmental improvements and programs. Stakeholder analysis skills, for example, are also applicable for identifying the needs and resources of other managers and employees within the company whose support is important for implementing the program. Likewise, skills for creating synergistic partnerships, such as identifying the resources partners can contribute and the values they can receive, are applicable to creating an internal coalition of supportive managers.

Even while lacking internal political clout to change incentives with the organization, environmental managers with the necessary capabilities can still be influential within companies. The key to their effectiveness is how they use their capabilities to lower internal transaction costs. As CSOs and their environmental managers work in different areas, they learn the language and cultural norms of those areas. CSOs can thus be internal information conduits, helping expertise flow across organizational areas and thus mitigating the downsides of organizational specialization (Fu et al. 2020; Kanashiro & Rivera 2019). Effective communication can help environmental managers encourage employees to participate in the company's environmental programs. Employees are more likely to participate when the environmental programs are clear and well communicated. Employees are also more likely to participate when senior managers support communication and information sharing among employees and when they recognize and reward subordinates' contributions (Ramus 2001; Ramus & Steger 2000).

Environmental managers can use their capabilities to shape other managers' incentives to adopt environmental improvements. Expertise in cross-functional dialogue can help redefine environmental improvements so that other managers see them as solutions to problems within their own functional area. For example, suppose a company improves environmental practices among suppliers deep within its supply chain. The environmental improvements may help improve relations with nonmarket stakeholders in remote communities. An adept CSO may help translate the environmental improvements as solutions to problems confronting marketing managers who are looking to increase sales. The supply chain environmental improvements may be an opportunity to attract new customers by offering an environmentally differentiated product. Beth Adcock Shiroishi, vice president of sustainability and philanthropy AT&T, made the case for cross-functional communication skills in sustainability: "I think of myself and my team as chameleons. Being able to think and communicate in the same fashion as a business unit we're working with is, for me, the most important skill set needed to be successful" (Vox Global 2012: 7).

5.3 Conclusion

Chapters 3 and 4 discussed the external circumstances that shape environmental strategy. This chapter has focused on the internal resources that companies can draw upon when creating and implementing an environmental strategy. Identifying a company's existing strategic resources can help sharpen an environmental strategy and determine what environmental improvement will be successful. An effective environmental strategy reinforces competitive strategy and draws on the company's existing strategic resource and capabilities. A company's capabilities for interacting with stakeholders and communicating credibly about its CSR activities are particularly important resources for environmental strategy.

Even if an environmental strategy identifies opportunities for environmental improvements, there is no guarantee that a company will adopt them. Managers within the company must be authorized to make the improvements, have the right information to identify the problem and evaluate potential solutions, and have incentives to take on the costs of implementing the improvements. The board and top executives can assign authority and incentives for overseeing environmental improvements. CSOs and mid-level environmental managers can facilitate the adoption of environmental improvements through information provision, even if they lack their own significant political authority and incentives to compel other managers' cooperation. A company culture that encourages collaboration and rewards employees taking on extra work assignments can also facilitate the adoption of environmental improvements.

6 | Green Products and Services

In 1983, Samuel Kaymen and Gary Hirshberg were running a school for organic farming in rural New Hampshire. Kaymen and Hirshberg were committed environmentalists. Kaymen had originally founded the school to teach sustainable farming practices and during the 1970s and 1980s, and was active in regional organic food certification initiatives. Hirshberg grew as up an east coast skier and outdoorsman, and studied environmental science in college, but started his career on a more traditional corporate path (Koehn et al. 2012). During a 1982 visit to Disney's Epcot exhibits, he had an epiphany in response to a Kraft Foods exhibit extolling the promising future of industrial food production. The exhibit struck Hirshberg as "cartoonish chemistry gone mad." Thinking about the Kraft exhibit, Hirshberg realized that "to become effective rather than eccentric, I had to somehow create a truly sustainable business that actually made money – and the more the better" (Hirshberg 2008: 6).

Not surprisingly, Kaymen and Hirshberg's school needed money; debts were mounting, and the school could not pay its rent. Kaymen had learned some yogurt-making tips while visiting an Orthodox Jewish community in Brooklyn, New York. After some at-home experimentation, he refined an old family recipe to make a great-tasting yogurt. To keep their school afloat, they decided to sell yogurt made from the milk produced by their farm's cows. In keeping with the school's mission, they made it without pesticides and fertilizers. Kaymen and Hirshberg were as pragmatic as they were committed to the environment. They created their business, Stonyfield Farm. Their original mission has not changed much over the years: they aimed to create value for their shareholders, employees, and the environment by making high-quality organic products.

With a tiny advertising budget, but convinced that the world would love their special yogurt, Kaymen and Hirshberg set out to attract consumers. They got a fortunate break – five nearby Stop & Shop grocery stores gave Stonyfield shelf space for its yogurt along with a twelve-week window to pass out in-store samples. Kaymen and Hirshberg talked to customers, trying to get every shopper and store manager who would talk to them to sample Stonyfield's yogurt. People liked the yogurt's taste and smooth texture. Within a year, Stop & Shop was selling Stonyfield yogurt in stores across New England. Their yogurt sold well, and over the next decade, Kaymen and Hirshberg had transformed the organic farming school into a full-fledged yogurt company.[1]

Through the 1980s and 1990s, Hirshberg was constantly looking for low-cost ways to market Stonyfield's yogurt. After hearing that a Boston radio host claimed on air that, instead of eating yogurt, he would "rather eat camel manure," Hirshberg spotted an opportunity. He and his wife hopped in their car, stopped off at a nearby animal farm, drove to Boston, and talked their way into the studio. On air, the host sniffed a spoonful of camel manure, then tasted Stonyfield yogurt, and said: "Ok, I admit it. The yogurt does taste better" (Hirshberg 2008: 90). The on-air mentions continued over the next few months and boosted Stonyfield's sales.

As Stonyfield's sales grew, it started selling frozen yogurt, soft-serve ice cream, and even holiday-season eggnog. Kaymen and Hirshberg sold Stonyfield's herd of cows to one of its milk suppliers, expanded its yogurt production, and in 1989 opened its own production facility. By 1990, Stonyfield products were in supermarkets throughout the northeast and natural food stores across the country, and in 1992, Stonyfield had its first profitable year. Stonyfield's growth continued through the 1990s, with new flavorings and products, such as its "YoBaby" yogurt for infants. In the 2000s, it added ice cream and Greek-style yogurt under the brand name "Oikos."

Stonyfield's early yogurts were made from natural ingredients and family farm milk and used fruit-based sweeteners. In the 1990s, Stonyfield took a stance against milk from cows fed growth hormones and began to pursue organic certifications for all of their products. Over the next decades, Stonyfield's sustainability efforts went well beyond its products. Kaymen and Hirshberg installed solar panels at

---

[1] Several Harvard Business School case studies have told Stonyfield's story (Bhide & Thurber 1995; Koehn et al. 2012), as did Hirshberg himself in a book reflecting on lessons he learned about business sustainability (Hirshberg 2008).

their facilities, purchased offsets for the company's greenhouse gas emissions, and later installed an anaerobic digester to transform yogurt waste into methane gas for energy production. Stonyfield changed its product packaging over the years as more sustainable options became available.

In 2000, Group Danone, eager to expand in natural food markets, purchased Stonyfield in a deal that valued the New Hampshire company at $125 million. The sale rewarded investors – many of whom were friends, family, and employees – who had stuck with the company through thick and thin. Hirshberg stayed on with management control of the company as CEO and board chair. Stonyfield now had access to Danone's mass production and marketing expertise (Kaymen ended up working in the organic wine industry). Hirshberg's influence would later help Danone with its CSR programs and its goal to expand organic sales in Europe. In 2018, Danone sold Stonyfield for $875 million to Lactalis, the privately held French dairy company. While organic foods have become ubiquitous, as we will see in this chapter, the Stonyfield story provides a useful illustration of the strategic challenges facing companies launching green products.

The goal in this chapter to identify the challenges to solve and the conditions that make green products successful. Some green product challenges are essentially the same as those for conventional products, such as whether the company can bring a product to market that meets significant consumer demand; the product's impact on the company's operations, other products, and brand; and the product's effects on the relations with the company's suppliers and other collaborators. These challenges, along with strategic considerations for overcoming them, are described well in other places (Kotler & Keller 2015), so we won't cover them in this reading. Instead, our focus is on the additional challenges presented by green products.

6.1 Strategy for Green Products and Services

These days, environmentally committed consumers in the United States can quite easily find a more sustainable option for just about any product or service they want to buy. Green consumers can choose sustainable food, cleaning supplies, toiletries (e.g., toothbrush and toothpaste), and household furniture. Almost every vacation destination in the world offers an eco-tourism option. Even personal services, like dry cleaning and massage therapy, offer environmentally friendly options. For simplicity, this book uses the term "green products" to refer to anything consumers can purchase that has a sustainability feature, including services.

The supply of green products parallels trends in public opinion surveys in which people express progressive environmental attitudes and beliefs. Gallup surveys show a strong majority of people in the USA are concerned about the degradation of the environment and support more government action to improve environmental conditions (Gallup Inc. 2020). Consumers often state that they are willing to buy green products, even when they cost more (Casadesus-Masanell et al. 2009; White et al. 2019), and companies compete in a "market for virtue" to supply products with the environmental and other CSR features that consumers want (Vogel 2007). According to a 2019 study, over two-thirds of US consumers said they consider sustainability when making a purchase and are willing to pay more for sustainable products (CGS 2019). One estimate puts the size of the "green economy" in the United States at $1.3 trillion, or 7 percent of gross domestic product, and it continues to grow (Georgeson & Maslin 2019).

Though there seems to be a sustainable option for just about every type of product and service, and there is no shortage of people who say they are willing to pay extra for sustainable products, this does not mean that every business will find it profitable to offer sustainable versions of its products. Surveys often overstate how much consumers are actually willing to spend when purchasing green products in real-world circumstances (Delmas & Colgan 2018). Behind all the options available in today's market lies a graveyard of green products that never found their market niche. Before its colossal 2010 oil spill in the Gulf of Mexico, the giant oil company BP had been looking to transform itself into a company known for producing more clean energy. The company centered its marketing efforts around a "BP: Beyond Petroleum" campaign (Barrage et al. 2020). BP's 2010 oil spill disaster in the Gulf of Mexico left the company's environmental reputation in tatters.

An environmental strategy can help companies identify which products have the potential for market success and what they must do to make them successful. First, the strategy identifies why consumers may be less willing to buy green products. An important reason why the green economy is smaller than public opinion surveys would suggest lies within the unique features of ethical purchasing. The environmental benefits of a green product are enjoyed broadly by the full range of environmental stakeholders, even when the stakeholders do not pay any of the costs. Meanwhile, when choosing products at the store or browsing online, the potential green consumers think about how they will feel about purchasing the product and how it will benefit them. An environmental strategy also helps companies identify which consumers are willing to pay extra for a green product and why they are willing to do so. A green product needs to offer consumers private benefits – some value the consumer can experience only by purchasing the product (Delmas & Colgan 2018). Some benefits stem directly from how the product functions. Other benefits stem from more psychological and social rewards. Understanding these benefits and the consumer segments who value them can help companies successfully design and market green products. Finally, an environmental strategy helps guide the marketing strategy for green products. Consumers are rarely in a position to fully evaluate the potential benefits of a product's environmental features. They usually are not able to directly see the product's environmental benefits. Green product marketing needs to assure consumers that the product will deliver its promised benefits.

Throughout the chapter, we examine how Stonyfield addresses the challenges of creating and marketing a green product. In this brief summary, Stonyfield Farm's yogurt story looks similar to other companies' experiences. The two entrepreneurs developed a tastier yogurt recipe and included sustainability in their company's mission. They navigated financial perils (and other harrowing episodes, including Hirshberg heroically saving their facility from fire by hooking a blazing dumpster to a tractor and pulling it to safety), expanded production, and built a successful mass-market food company. But this short story obscures the strategic choices Hirshberg and Kaymen confronted as they pursued the financial and sustainability goals at the core of Stonyfield's mission. With great yogurt as a start, they also identified environmental problems and paths for improvement, reworking paths that were not immediately achievable. They identified customer segments and honed messages that conveyed the benefits customers would receive in return for Stonyfield's higher prices. Success meant that by purchasing a container of Stonyfield yogurt, a customer was showing their confidence that the company was truly delivering high quality and presumably also that they valued its environmental sustainability.

6.2 Identifying Green Products' Environmental Benefits and Costs

Successful companies are constantly on the lookout for a competitive advantage. They look for ways to lower their production costs and differentiate their products in ways that increase customers' willingness to pay. In the right circumstances, a company can achieve a competitive advantage by improving the environmental performance of its products. The strategy for achieving a successful green product begins with identifying the environmental improvements a company can achieve in its products, perhaps even at a lower cost than its competitors.

Every product offers consumers a bundle of benefits through its features and attributes. Core product features are the generic attributes of products that apply to all products in a category and offer consumers direct value from ownership. All consumer toothbrushes have a handle and bristles and offer owners value through the opportunity to scrub their teeth. Augmented product features are unique attributes that distinguish the product's value from others in its category. For toothbrushes, product augmentations include features such as a curved, ergonomic handle or stiffer bristles, which some consumers are willing to pay more for, while others are not. Augmented features are what differentiate products within a product type.

A green product is differentiated from similar products through an augmented sustainability feature. There are many ways to differentiate a green product because products can have environmental impacts across their life cycles, as noted in our LCA discussion in Chapter 3. Organic food is differentiated in the production phase because it is grown with fewer pesticides. Household appliances can reduce their environmental impact by being more energy efficient. Recycling can make paper and packaging more environmentally sustainable.

This definition of a green product is perhaps different to what some people would want to use. An ardent environmentalist might object that a green product with *some* sustainability benefits may not make *enough* of an environmental contribution to be considered a green product. The environmentalist might question whether any product can be "sustainable" because all consumption has negative environmental consequences. For any product marketed as environmentally friendly, it is easy to develop alternative products that would be better for the environment. A stay-at-home vacation in Cleveland would cause less environmental harm than an eco-tourism trip to Costa Rica. For brushing your teeth, simple baking soda may be better for the environment than even the most sustainably produced toothpaste. Committed environmentalists often use these types of comparisons as grounds for accusing companies of greenwashing – when a company or group promotes green-based environmental initiatives or images but actually functions in a way that is detrimental to the environment or that is counter to the goal of the projected ideas (Delmas & Burbano 2011), as discussed in Chapter 3. Later in this chapter, we return to the issue of credibility and stakeholder reactions to sustainability claims.

These alternative definitions of green products, and the criticisms they imply, are based on comparing the sustainability profiles of products with fundamentally different core features. A Clevelander considering a vacation is unlikely to see a staycation in her home city as offering the same core features as a tropical winter getaway. However, our Clevelander may be willing to consider, and perhaps even pay more for, a vacation that takes her to a more sustainable Costa Rican eco-tourism option rather than a traditional Costa Rican tourist destination. Costa Rica, after all, is a well-known eco-tourism destination and is able to capture a price premium from environmentally conscious tourists (Rivera 2002). While perhaps not a definition that satisfies the most committed environmentalists, we define green products from the potential consumer's perspective: what are the other product options against which consumers compare the green product? Most often, the relevant comparison is an identical, or very similar, product that does not offer the green product's augmented sustainability feature.

When Kaymen and Hirshberg started out making yogurt, it was easy to identify the initial environmental improvements Stonyfield yogurt would provide. The co-founders were both committed to making healthier and more environmentally sustainable food. They wanted to sell all-natural yogurt made out of milk from local farms and produced through low-environmental-impact practices – something that was quite rare in consumer markets at that time. As Stonyfield grew, they looked for further environmental impacts to address. In 1994, Stonyfield commissioned a rigorous third-party environmental audit of its operations, and as Stonyfield grew, the auditor studied the company's environmental impacts throughout its operations and supply chain through detailed energy audits and environmental analyses. Stonyfield's management team expected that yogurt production, with all the heating and cooling it required, was the company's biggest source of greenhouse gas emissions. A general lesson from these studies was that Stonyfield's material inputs, such as milk and packaging materials, had bigger environmental impacts than producing the yogurt or the disposal of yogurt containers. In fact, the audits revealed that Stonyfield's biggest environmental impact was from cows producing methane while making the milk Stonyfield purchased.

6.3 Demand for Green Products

Selling any product is challenging – why would a consumer pay for the product being offered? A successful product strategy answers this question by positioning the product to provide value to customers that exceeds the purchase price. Consumers can receive different types of value from the products they purchase. How well a product performs a particular task or meets a specific consumer need is always an important consideration. Will this hammer help effectively pound nails? Consumers also have other reasons for choosing a product to purchase beyond how it functions. Buying a product can fulfill emotional needs, helping consumers feel warmth and satisfaction for living closer to their moral values. Purchasing a brand of breakfast cereal may conjure fond childhood memories of happy morning meals. Treating oneself to a fine chocolate candy may induce warm feelings of luxurious self-indulgence. Buying a product may also reinforce consumers' sense of identity. Eating at an ethnic restaurant can reinforce a diner's sense of family heritage. Consumers can also receive value through the message it conveys to others. The North Face markets its outdoor attire with the motto "Never Stop Exploring." This phrase can describe features of The North Face's clothes: they are rugged and designed for extreme conditions. The message also aims to reflect the mindset of the person wearing the clothes – someone who enjoys outdoor adventure.

For a company considering launching a green product, the important task is to define the market segment for that product: who are the potential consumers for the product, and why are they willing to pay for a green product versus a traditional product? An environmental strategy for a green product focuses on stakeholder mapping to identifying customers, thus resembling the market segmentation and analysis companies use to develop their marketing and competitive strategies. Market segmentation identifies consumers with common needs and hence willingness to pay for the products the company offers. There are several different approaches for grouping consumers into market segments, such as geographic location, demographic profiles, personality profiles and values, and behavioral characteristics and activities (Gupta 2014).

Green products face an additional challenge. The differentiating feature of a green product is the benefit it provides for the environment. However, the person making the purchase receives only a small part, if any, of the product's environmental benefit. It is no mystery why consumers express strong desires for seeing environmental conditions improved but a weaker willingness to pay extra for products that provide such environmental benefits – they bear the higher costs of the environmental improvement but do not receive much, if any, of its benefits.

6.3.1 Co-benefits and Green Products

Successful green products offer customers additional value, something beyond improved environmental conditions, to offset the products' higher prices. Such additional value comes from one or more co-benefits that are bundled with the environmental benefit (Delmas & Colgan 2018). A co-benefit offers private value to just the purchaser, but this value is inseparable from the product's environmental feature.[2] Customers evaluate green products' co-benefits in the same way they value other products – how does the consumer benefit from this purchase? Green product co-benefits include how the product will function, the emotions consumers experience when purchasing and using the product, and even how the product influences how consumers perceive themselves and are perceived by the people around them.

6.3.1.1 Functional and Quality Co-benefits
A functional or quality co-benefit adds value through the utility the purchaser directly receives from purchasing and consuming the product. Buyers derive many different types of utility from products, depending on the nature of the product and what they want from their purchase. A green product's environmental feature may enhance any

---

[2] Goods that jointly offer public and private benefits are also called "impure public goods" (Kotchen 2006).

of these benefits while also providing environmental benefits. Here are some examples of common co-benefits that green products offer.

Performance or functionality. Some green features improve how a product performs. In the 1990s, Walmart noticed strong consumer demand for a line of yoga pants. Walmart had decided not to advertise the fact that the pants were made from organic cotton. Instead, consumers appreciated the pants' softer feel and comfort that came from the organic cotton (Spicer & Hyatt 2017).

Health. A product that is healthier for the planet may also be healthier for the people who purchase it. People see organic produce as healthier to eat because it is grown without chemical pesticides and people see organic produce as healthier for the environment because these same pesticides do not end up damaging ecosystems (Padel & Foster 2005).

Efficiency. Products that consume fewer resources when used put lighter demands on the planet and on owners' wallets. Efficient washing machines use less water, energy, and detergent, making them cheaper for their owners to operate, even as features put fewer resource demands on the planet.

Durability. Products that last longer benefit the environment because they avoid the environmental damage caused when their replacements are produced. For example, compact fluorescent light (CFL) bulbs last longer than older incandescent bulbs. Owners benefit from the newer bulbs because they do not need to buy LED bulbs as often and perhaps they spend less time climbing creaky ladders to replace burnouts.

6.3.1.2 Emotional Co-benefits

For some consumers, the willingness to pay for a green product stems from the emotions they feel when they make the purchase or use the product. Positive emotions may arise because their purchase aligns with their core moral beliefs. People are more likely to pay extra to support environmental and social causes when they believe in the moral values underlying the cause (Antonetti & Maklan 2014). Such emotional responses suggest the higher price consumers pay for a green product is akin to making a charitable donation; in return for financially supporting a cause a consumer believes in, they feel emotional satisfaction, feelings that are sometimes called the "warm glow" (Andreoni 1990), as discussed in Chapter 3.

Empathy, understanding, and sharing others' experiences are other potential sources of emotional co-benefits derived from purchasing a green product. Empathy can motivate a consumer to buy a green product because the consumer feels better when they can imagine the people, wildlife, or ecosystems that are healthier as a result of their purchase. Humans can feel empathy toward animals, especially toward charismatic, aesthetically appealing, happy-looking animals such as dolphins. In 1998, a marine biologist named Sam LaBuddle shared a video of Panamanian fishers killing dolphins brought on board their ship as by-catch during tuna fishing, to the horror of environmentalists and even regular tuna consumers (Wright 2000). As tuna sales dropped, the tuna industry quickly responded, adopting "dolphin-safe" fishing practices and an accompanying product certification, which helped restore sales (Teisl et al. 2000). Knowing that they now support dolphin-saving fishing practices, consumers may receive an emotional co-benefit from their tuna purchase.

Finally, for some consumers, the emotional returns from buying a green product stem from reinforcing their sense of self-identity. Such motives mean consumers evaluate not just what values are inherent in the product, but the values of the company that produced them. Nike's sneakers are known for their performance, comfort, and styling. An avid runner might buy a pair of Nike running shoes purely for functionality: comfort, fit, and durability. But for some consumers, wearing Nike shoes can also be an expression of identity. Think about images from Nike's "Just Do It" advertising campaign. Many of the print ads have common themes: pictures of a lone morning runner on a long dirt road, often bundled against the cold or rain. While images convey some information about how Nike running shoes function – they are sturdy on dirt roads – they also convey a range of other potential emotional values. Running in Nike sneakers reinforces a runner's self-image: "rain or shine, I run hard every day. I 'just do it.' These running shoes reflect who I am." For some consumers, Nike's "Just Do It" campaign emotionally rewards purchases by reinforcing a positive self-image, thus increasing a consumer's willingness to pay. Similarly, a TV advertisement for Dawn dish soap, aired during the aftermath of the Deepwater Horizon oil spill, played up the emotional co-benefits a consumer would receive from the soap. Although Dawn's dish soap was not the "greenest" on the market, the advertisement showed wildlife experts using Dawn dish soap to clean birds covered from Deepwater

Horizon's spilled oil. The advertisement reinforced Dawn's "tough on grease, yet gentle" marketing message (Kaufman 2010).

6.3.1.3 Social Co-benefits

People often use their purchases to make a statement about themselves (Sexton & Sexton 2014). Luxury brands may signal the owner's social status. Other products signal the person's willingness to engage in pro-social activities. National Public Radio (NPR) often gives gifts in return for large donations. Many of these gifts prominently display the NPR logo on items that the owner uses in public settings, such as umbrellas and tote bags. Importantly, NPR is careful to ensure that these items only go to donors. Walking around in public with an NPR tote bag or umbrella sends a clear message: "I'm a nice person. I donated to NPR." When tote bags, coffee mugs, and umbrellas prominently display NPR logos, they are signaling to the world that their owners are the kind of nice people that become NPR members.

Green products can likewise be a vehicle through which consumers make social statements about themselves. People are more likely to buy a green product when they are shopping in public places and are primed to think about their social positions (Griskevicius et al. 2010). The Prius, Toyota Motor's hybrid car that first entered US markets in 2000, exemplifies the potential of social signaling to motivate environmental purchasing. With its then unique hybrid battery power system, the Prius offered several points of differentiation to appeal to different market segments: lower fuel costs from high gas mileage, reduced smog and greenhouse gas emissions, a better driving experience, and a distinctive look. But what seems to have been most attractive to many owners was the social signal that came from driving a Prius. In a 2007 survey, 57 percent of Prius owners reported that a top reason for purchasing their car was "it makes a statement about me"; 37 percent cited fuel economy; only 25 percent cited lower emissions (Maynard 2007). Products that are immediately distinctive, like the Prius with its idiosyncratic shape, are more apt to provide social co-benefits, whereas products that are easily copied by nonsustainable producers are not.

So far in this section, we have focused on social co-benefits that signal a consumer's environmental behavior to others. Consumers can also be influenced by how they perceive other people are behaving. Reminding people that many other people are doing a pro-environmental behavior makes them more likely to do it themselves. Hotel guests were more likely to recycle their towels after being told other hotel guests had already done so (Goldstein et al. 2008).

A consumer's decision to purchase a particular green product can be motivated by one or more of these co-benefits. Many of the Prius owners who wanted to make a statement about themselves also appreciated the car's better fuel efficiency and lower pollution emissions. Unlike functional co-benefits, where the product's function provides a clearer view of the private value consumers receive, emotional co-benefits can be much less tangible.

6.3.2 Complexities with Green Products and Their Co-benefits

The co-benefits of a green product can depend on who is buying the product and their motives for buying it (Bhattacharya et al. 2011; Delmas & Colgan 2018; Zdravkovic et al. 2010). Warm glow emotional co-benefits are generally stronger motivations to buy a green product among consumers with stronger environmental attitudes. But such warm glow motives are not uniform across all products, even for a particular environmentalist consumer. For example, committed environmentalists are more likely to pay a price premium for green products when they are purchasing luxury goods than when they are buying basic necessities (Strahilevitz & Myers 1998). A possible explanation for these changing motives is that doing an "extra, morally good act," such as paying more for a green product, provides the moral license to indulge in other behaviors, like eating tasty chocolates and drinking fine wine (Merritt et al. 2010).

Just as environmentalists can receive a warm glow from their green purchases, people can be less willing to buy green products if doing so conflicts with their values and political beliefs. For people opposed to environmental regulations, purchasing a green product can induce a "cold shadow" that makes them less willing to buy the product than if it offered no environmental benefit at all. In other words, people avoid making purchases that are misaligned with their values, even when those values are in opposition to environmental regulations. Take, for example, purchasing energy-efficient light bulbs. Even people who oppose environmental regulations are still willing to buy energy-efficient light bulbs, and even pay extra for them, when the product marketing emphasizes that the bulbs will save them money (Gromet et al. 2013). But when those same bulbs, with the same energy-saving benefits, are labeled as good for the environment, these same people are less willing to make the purchase.

Like emotional co-benefits, a "halo effect" occurs when the presence of an environmental feature in a product can change how people view the quality of other product features. For example, in blind taste tests, people reported that granola bars tasted better and were more nutritious when first told that the producing company engaged in charitable CSR practices (Peloza et al. 2015). These people were eating the same granola bars in the same conditions – the only thing that changed was that some were told about the company's CSR practices. Other, similar studies have found that consumers believed food tasted better when it was presented to them with a label indicating the food was environmentally friendly. Foods that people might see as an indulgence to consume, such as chocolate (Lotz et al. 2013), coffee (Sörqvist et al. 2015), and wine (Wiedmann et al. 2014), may be particularly prone to these halo effects.

The halo effect can be a double-edged sword, sometimes boosting consumers' perceptions of product quality and other times lowering perceptions of product quality. Consumers have stereotypes about sustainable products: consumers tend to believe that green products have more "caring and gentleness" qualities and less "power and strength" qualities (Luchs et al. 2010). An environmental product feature can increase willingness to pay, like when purchasing baby shampoo. People are willing to pay more for sustainable baby shampoo than for regular shampoo, reflecting the fact that their stereotype may cause them to associate "sustainability" with "caring and gentleness." An environmental feature can conversely decrease willingness to pay when consumers want a product that is strong and powerful. When purchasing dish soap, many people want a product that is strong and powerful because they need a tough product to take care of the grease. Some people are less willing to purchase sustainable dish soap as compared to classic dish soap. Along similar lines, other studies have shown that when told that a cleaning product is "environmentally friendly," people apply it in greater quantities, perhaps because they doubt these products are powerful enough to clean at a normal dose (Lin & Chang 2012).

Table 6.1 *Green products and co-benefits*

Product	Environmental benefit	Potential co-benefits
Residential rooftop solar	Renewable energy	Cost savings on utility bills Social prestige from neighbors Warm glow from doing good against climate change
Upcycled clothing	Lower resource usage Less demand on landfills	Warm glow Possible social co-benefits if upcycled qualities can be communicated
Electric cars	Climate change Air pollution	Cost savings, especially with high gasoline costs Social prestige Warm glow Identity if technologically advanced

Table 6.1 presents examples of green products, their environmental benefits, and the potential co-benefits for markets segments. The examples illustrate a few considerations for green product strategy. First, co-benefits are not necessarily fixed across all consumers in all circumstances. The financial savings from rooftop solar depends on local conditions like the amount of cloud cover. Rooftop solar's social benefits depends on how much neighbors' reactions and its warm glow benefits depend on the owners' environmental values. Second, the same consumer can receive multiple co-benefits from the same product. Take, for example, someone who is a technology enthusiast and who lives in an area with high gasoline prices and with many people who share her technological and environmental inclinations. Purchasing one of the first Tesla automobiles would provide this consumer with several co-benefits at the same time through cost savings, social prestige, and warm glow feelings. These examples suggest the importance of matching a green product's environmental benefits to the desires and circumstances of specific market segments.

6.3.3 Stonyfield's Yogurt and Its Benefits to Consumers

As committed as they were to sustainability, Hirshberg and Kaymen always believed that the most important attribute of their yogurt was its taste. Stonyfield's yogurt was more expensive than most of what was on the market. Customers needed direct experience to appreciate how well it tasted. For Hirshberg, the lessons from their taste test marketing approach were clear – "we clearly proved that great taste was our key customer hook" (Hirshberg 2008: 89). Stonyfield's marketing strategy continued to employ tasting for years, such as offering free trials to public transit commuters and activists at environmental protests and demonstrations.

In addition to its taste, Stonyfield's yogurt also offered consumers the benefit of purchasing a sustainable product. Stonyfield's marketing materials emphasized that the yogurt's sustainability features also offered consumers health co-benefits. Even before the USDA launched its organic yogurt certification, Stonyfield's advertising suggested that its yogurt, made from sustainably produced ingredients, had benefits for human health, something Hirshberg often discussed face to face at Stop & Shop stores when he was offering free tasting opportunities. Hirshberg wrote about those interactions, stating: "Many yogurt lovers see healthy eating as a cause. When they discovered that Stonyfield was genuinely pure as well as delicious, they couldn't wait to tell their like-minded friends" (Hirshberg 2008: 89). For Hirshberg, it was also important for Stonyfield's customers to feel an emotional bond with the company. He wrote, "we expanded our customer base largely by making an emotional connection with those who sample our product" (Hirshberg 2008: 93). Such connections could be established in supermarket aisles as customers tasted Stonyfield's yogurts, and Hirshberg could connect with them in face-to-face conversations.

Over time, Stonyfield found that some consumers were also responding to messages that combined its products' health and sustainability benefits with the broader values held by customers. Purchasing from Stonyfield promised a warm glow benefit. Baby boomers, in particular, "wanted to have their purchases count for something more than just a purchase. They liked the idea that their grocery dollars could go to causes that they cared about" (Koehn et al. 2012). A 2001 Stonyfield magazine advertisement featured the famous documentary filmmaker Ken Burns saying:

I'm committed to:
History, our greatest teacher
Jazz as an original art form
America's great baseball culture
Dairy Farmers who don't use growth hormones
Strawberry Fruit Blends Yogurt
Companies that do what's right.

Stonyfield's logo and a picture of a container of its yogurt appear at the bottom of the ad, alongside the words: "I like Stonyfield because it's an environmentally responsible company that avoids synthetic hormones, and artificial thickeners, sweeteners and preservatives in its yogurt. ... Stonyfield is good for the planet, great for your body, and a treat for your taste buds." The Ken Burns ad showed Stonyfield's value bundling in its yogurt: taste, health, and the warm glow that comes from purchasing a product aligned with the customer's moral values.

After the success of his "yogurt tastes better than camel dung" radio performance, Hirshberg found more guerrilla opportunities to market Stonyfield's yogurt through eye-catching promotions that combined social cause with a dash of good humor. In Chicago, a Stonyfield exhibit featured a giant fiberglass cow that every ten minutes "pooped" out fresh organic soil for kids to pack into planting pots made from recycled Stonyfield yogurt containers. The kids took the pots home to watch the seeds grow into plants. The giant cow, the kids, and Stonyfield yogurt were featured in media stories. Stonyfield eventually used more traditional marketing campaigns. In the later 2000s, Stonyfield produced humorous television commercials featuring Hirshberg and a farmer trying to plant and grow a vial of chemical dye in soil. According to Hirshberg, "[t]he idea is to reach about a million people with an amusing experience that, instead of just showing Stonyfield in a thirty-second television spot, creates an emotional connection to us" (Hirshberg 2008: 120). Hirshberg's marketing efforts helped establish Stonyfield's brand as a company that not only delivered environmental value and good yogurt but also appealed to customers' emotions and sense of identity.

6.4 Channels for Selling Green Products

Companies these days can usually sell green products through market channels, often alongside traditional products, as discussed in Chapter 3. Consumers can find green product offerings in supermarkets, specialty stores, and online retailers – virtually everywhere they shop. These outlets make selling green products relatively easy: consumers know where to find green products and how to compare offerings among competing products, and companies' know how to get their products to where consumers can find and buy them. Transactions in these channels are therefore relatively easy to execute, with money as the basis for the exchange. Of course, selling green products does come with some transaction costs. As we have seen, finding market segments willing to pay for environmental products requires matching the products' co-benefits to the needs of consumers already interested in the product for its core and other augmented features.

As Stonyfield expanded its sales nationally during the 1990s, it found the most success in natural food and specialty stores. At the time, few supermarket consumers valued sustainable or even all-natural products, and it was hard to induce customers to pay more for just the promise of better-tasting yogurt. Supermarkets wanted to see traditional advertising and large sales volumes to justify a product's shelf space. Such marketing was unfamiliar to Stonyfield and anathema to Hirshberg's low-cost guerrilla-marketing mindset. Eventually, organic foods became mainstream, and Stonyfield's yogurts were on supermarket shelves throughout the country.

6.5 Green Lemons and the Credibility Challenge

The environmental benefits of green products are often very difficult for consumers to observe directly. Consumers know that sustainable products are usually more expensive to produce and that companies' pursuit of profits leads them to cut costs where they can. When stripped of packaging and marketing materials, organic food looks pretty much the same as nonorganic food (older readers may recall times long ago when organic produce was very often less visually appealing than nonorganic produce). The credibility problem often stems from the fact that green products' environmental benefits are often beyond the consumer's direct experience. Our morning coffee looks and tastes the same regardless of whether its production damaged the Amazon rainforest, which few coffee drinkers will ever even see first hand. Absent credible information about the product's sustainability features, most green products offer environmental benefits that a consumer cannot easily and directly evaluate prior to purchase or even after consumption.

Without the reassurance of the green product's credentials, consumers may suspect the product is "greenwashed." People are reluctant to pay extra for a product feature when they are unable to judge its quality. Again, we see the "green lemons" problem introduced in Chapter 3: in a lemons market, sellers know more about the quality of a good than do buyers. Fearing they will receive a low-quality good when they paid the price for a higher-quality one, consumers refuse to pay anything but rock-bottom prices, and sellers end up not producing the higher-quality goods. If consumers were fully informed, those who want higher quality would pay higher prices, fully confident they were getting what they paid for. Informing hesitant consumers about product quality is not an uncommon challenge that companies face – particularly when they are bringing new products to the market.

6.5.1 Certifications

An environmental certification is a recognition that a company (or its products) has met a set of performance standards or rules. In return for complying with these rules, a company can use the certification in its marketing efforts to help reassure consumers about its environmental qualities (Potoski & Prakash 2009; Prakash & Potoski 2006). Certifications include standards that define the products' environmental attributes; for example, certified organic food is produced without pesticides. Certifications can also have rules that address whether the products actually achieve the standards of environmental performance. Other certifications require companies to disclose information about their product. The difficulty of overcoming the green lemons problem helps explain why there are so many voluntary certification programs for environmental products and company practices. When successful, a voluntary environmental program solves the information gap between companies and green consumers by providing a credibility signal about a company's environmental performance.

Product certifications are no panacea for solving the credibility challenge. The certification's rules can influence how well it signals that its members have achieved superior environmental performance (Potoski & Prakash 2013). Some have more stringent standards stipulating that companies achieve better environmental performance to become members. Others require less environmental improvements. Some certifications require members to receive third-party audits to verify that they are complying with the program's standards, while other certifications allow members to self-declare their adherence to the standards. The ISO 14001 certification requires companies to implement stringent environmental management practices and procedures and have them verified by external audit. Responsible Care requires similar environmental management practices and procedures, but does not require an external audit. Research suggests that companies participating in ISO 14001 improved their environmental performance while companies participating in Responsible Care did not (King & Lenox 2000).

Even a well-designed certification may not function well in certain context. The certification's sponsor may lack credibility, leaving stakeholders to doubt the program's efficacy (Darnall et al. 2010, 2017). For a certification to provide credible assurance, the company's targeted consumers or stakeholders must recognize the certification and understand that it signals the environmental product features they desire. While organic food and Energy Star certification are both fairly simple and well understood by consumers, in other cases, consumers can find certifications quite confusing; for example, when there are several sustainability certifications, such as in the wood and paper industry. In such cases, the company may need to take extra steps to communicate about its own environmental performance or the meaning of the certifications it has achieved, lest consumers end up unsure about the company's environmental performance.

6.5.2 Co-benefits and Credibility

Marketing strategies for green products need to focus on the product attributes that matter most to consumers. The attributes could the environmental benefits or they could be something else. A durable product may be good for the environment, but its marketing may need to focus on its lower lifetime cost and overall convenience if these are the values that motivate consumers' purchase. Sometimes, advertising misses the mark by focusing on values that are not important to consumers. "Green marketing myopia" occurs when companies emphasize a green product's environmental benefits at the expense of its co-benefits that consumers actually want (Ottman et al. 2006). For example, in 1994, Philips introduced energy-efficient CFL bulbs to the US market. The bulbs were called "EarthLight" to emphasize their environmental benefits, but the bulbs also used less energy and lasted longer than traditional incandescent bulbs. For years, EarthLight sales were modest, perhaps because the bulb's awkward design made them ill-suited for some uses, or perhaps because their emphasis on environmental benefits failed to spark consumers' interest in costs and convenience. Philips redesigned its CFL bulb and relaunched it in 2000 under the name "Marathon" to emphasize its consumer appeal as a long-lasting light bulb. The Marathon saw healthy sales growth over the next several years (Ottman et al. 2006).

Additional credibility challenges can arise when a green product's co-benefit is not tightly linked to other, more easily verified product features. In such circumstances, increasing consumers' confidence about the product's environmental benefit may not improve their confidence in the co-benefit. A consumer considering a product for its social signaling co-benefit may not need reassurance that the product provides an environmental benefit. Instead, the consumer may need reassurance that others will hold the consumer in higher esteem when they see them with the product, perhaps because they already believe in the product's green features.

Consumers may also need assurance to experience emotional and identity co-benefits. Consumers' experience of emotional and identity co-benefits depends not just on whether they believe the company has actually produced an environmental good but on their perceptions of why the company has produced it. Consumers rate a company and its products more negatively (or remain neutral) if they perceive that the company had only financial motives for producing CSR or environmental improvements. But if they perceive that the company has altruistic motives, along with profit motives, for producing CSR and environmental improvements, they perceive the company and its products more favorably (Bhattacharya et al. 2011; Chernev & Blair 2015; Ellen et al. 2006; Vlachos et al. 2009).

6.5.3 Branding

As discussed in Chapter 3, a company's brand helps consumers make inferences about product qualities they are unable to evaluate prior to purchase, such as the reliability of a car or how great a bag of cheese snacks will taste, while also influencing how customers relate to the company, such as their feelings and sense of connection (Holt 2003). Strong brands can also convey the "story" of the company – how it came into being and the cultural values and aspirations it pursues.

For green products, a brand helps companies solve credibility problems in several ways. Consumers are more likely to believe companies' marketing messages if the company already has a well-established brand image that reinforces the company's environmental claims. A strong brand reputation for product quality and trustworthiness helps reassure consumers that a company's environmentally differentiated products do not sacrifice product quality and are, in fact, better for the environment (Bhattacharya et al. 2011). Tom's Shoes established itself as a socially conscious company, with its one-for-one business model of donating a product (shoes, glasses, etc.) to a person in need for every product purchased. With this reputation established, consumers are likely to believe the company's claims about vegan and sustainably produced shoes. A company brand can also inform how consumers interpret the motives behind a company's environmental actions, such as whether a company's sustainability practices are authentic, altruistic extensions of its values and culture, or mere ploys for extra profits (Bhattacharya et al. 2011; Ellen et al. 2006).

Early on, Kaymen and Hirshberg did not have easy ways to convince customers that their yogurt provided the environmental and health benefits promised in Stonyfield's marketing campaigns. They could tell consumers how their yogurt was made – often in the face-to-face conversations during sample handouts. But back in 1983, it took a complicated conversation to explain how Stonyfield's practices – pesticide-free milk production, all-natural ingredients, and so on – were better for the environment. Stonyfield could label its food as "natural," but so could other companies that produced food with less sustainable practices than Stonyfield, all to the confusion of customers. As Hirshberg described the problem, "[b]eing 'natural' is a good thing, but despite all the talk about natural food these days, we still lack tough standards defining exactly what the term means for consumers" (Hirshberg 2008: 116). USDA organic certification did not exist when Kaymen and Hirshberg founded Stonyfield.

During the 1980s and 1990s, environmental groups and some state governments started creating certification standards for organic foods. The organic standards were different and sometimes even competed with each other. As a result, consumers were often confused. For Stonyfield, differing standards meant that competitors could claim an organic certification despite using less sustainable practices. Hirshberg welcomed the USDA's efforts to create a national organic certification standard. He reflected, "[t]he organic food business is the only industry I know that actively seeks increased government regulation. It's our way of remedying public confusion about the meaning of organic. ... The upshot [of government-defined organic standards] is that the word 'organic' is more credible than ever" (Hirshberg 2008: 93). He added, "[t]he reason we want our government to validate and defend a strong set of organic standards is that we would like everyone – consumers, farmers, and processors – to know exactly what it means to be organic" (Hirshberg 2008: 93).

Assuring consumers about its yogurt's taste and environmental benefits was not enough. Stonyfield also needed a strategy to assure consumers that its yogurt aligned with their personal values. For these consumers, purchasing Stonyfield yogurt promised the positive emotions of fulfilling their own moral values and even their self-identity. But to deliver on such values, consumers need reassurance not just about what Stonyfield did but also about why it did it. Stonyfield's social and environmental practices needed to be authentic. Hirshberg recognized that his customers needed to believe in what his company stood for. For him, the sale of a cup of yogurt was not just a financial exchange but a "handshake" agreement over values well beyond financial payment. As Hirshberg wrote, "once a connection is formed and the figurative handshake exchanged, we use every customer interaction to strengthen the pact we've made. That means providing high-quality yogurt, doing all we can to protect the environment and promote sustainable farming methods, and living up to our mission to prove that socially and environmentally responsible business can still be profitable" (Hirshberg 2008: 93).

6.6 Conclusion

Stonyfield's journey shows the challenges in growing a company offering environmental products. Hirshberg and Stonyfield's environmental managers prioritized Stonyfield's environmental impacts with a practical eye. They understood that they could not remove cows from the equation, so they went ahead making other environmental improvements to areas that would allow their business to continue. Sometimes, they found opportunities to make substantive environmental improvements, even in nonobvious areas. For example, in the 2000s, Stonyfield stopped producing recyclable yogurt containers and switched to containers made from plant-based plastics that had fewer greenhouse gas emissions even when thrown into landfills. But Stonyfield did not implement all the environmental improvements its impact assessments identified. Stonyfield recognized that some improvements were too costly and would not generate enough financial value in return. For example, while 32-ounce yogurt containers were significantly better for the environment than single-serving containers, Stonyfield's consumers highly valued the smaller containers' convenience. According to Hirshberg, "[n]ot every environmentally good idea is a sound business idea as well" (Hirshberg 2008: 141).

Stonyfield's yogurt offered customers yogurt they enjoyed eating and provided emotional and identify co-benefits that were tightly coupled with the company's sustainability mission and its quirky company culture. Sustainability was part of the ethos of striving to do the right thing, which would benefit consumers who held sustainability as an important ethical value and who saw environmentalism as part of their personal identity. In the early 1990s, access to markets to sell products was a challenge for organic foods, and Hirshberg needed to be resourceful to get Stonyfield's yogurt onto supermarket shelves. For Hirshberg, consumers could believe in Stonyfield's commitment to social and environmental causes because, from its inception, Stonyfield went the extra mile to pursue the social and environmental goals its founders believed in: "Maintaining our side of the bargain means we don't just meet customer expectations; we exceed them" (Hirshberg 2008: 93).

Stonyfield's environmental and marketing strategies were mutually reinforcing. Sustainability was part of Stonyfield's founding vision when it grew out of the organic farming school Kaymen had founded.

While Hirshberg and Kaymen may not have pursued every social and sustainability lead, they did more than most companies. They supported family-owned farmers and organic milk production, often by paying higher prices. They installed solar energy at their New Hampshire facility. Instead of festooning container tops with yet another Stonyfield logo, it used the space to promote other social and environmental causes. With each of these initiatives, and there are more than can be listed here, Stonyfield built a company and culture that would show the authenticity of its social and environmental practices.

7 | *Employee Engagement*

Diana Glassman had always wanted her career to leverage private sector skills and resources to find creative win–win opportunities that improved financial, human, and environmental well-being. She earned master's degrees from Harvard's Business School and its Kennedy School of Government, and she hoped to leverage both parts of her education in her future job. She spent the early part of her career in consulting and had helped start an environmentally focused investing program at Credit Suisse. In July 2011, Glassman started a new role as head of the environment for TD Bank's US operations. In this job, the challenge for Glassman was to expand the business value of TD Bank's environmental programs and initiatives. How could the bank reduce its environmental impact in ways that contributed to its business goals?

When Glassman arrived in 2011, TD Bank had grown to become one of the United States' ten largest banks, with over $7 billion in revenue (Van Hasselt 2011). More than 28,000 employees staffed its 1,300 retail banking locations (called "stores" in the bank's terminology), most clustered in metropolitan areas along the eastern seaboard from Florida to New England. TD Bank jostled with national and regional chains for retail banking business in an industry where growth and profits were generally low, which would seem to limit the potential for the bank's environmental programs.

A first place to look for potential environmental improvements in the banking industry is targeting investing and lending programs. Sustainable investing and lending was a small but growing business throughout the banking industry in 2011. While TD Bank did have a sustainable investment and lending businesses, they were not under Glassman's purview. Her assignment was to the TD Bank's retail banking operations, and this was where she chose to focus her efforts.

The environmental impact of TD Bank's retail banking operations may appear slight when compared to industrial activities like heavy manufacturing or transportation. Yet TD Bank had long been committed to sustainability. In 2010, TD Bank became one of the largest banks in the USA to declare itself "carbon neutral," an achievement it reached through energy efficiency improvements and purchasing renewable energy credits and carbon offsets. When Glassman came on board, TD Bank had environmental programs to reduce greenhouse gas emissions and paper use, achieve LEED certification for its buildings, and promote forest conservation through employee tree-planting days and partnerships with TNC. It encouraged customers to switch to paperless bank statements by touting the convenience and environmental benefits of internet banking (which was relatively new in 2011 and became standard practice in the industry over the next few years).

Looking over TD Bank's financial reports, Glassman realized TD Bank's environmental initiatives did not have a large financial impact on the company's expenses and cash flow. Some programs, like paper reduction, reduced mailed mailings, and limiting business travel, reduced costs, but they were all just tiny portions of TD Bank's expenses. Like most service companies, labor costs were a significant driver of TD Bank's expenses. If TD Bank's environmental programs could have even a small impact on labor costs, the financial returns would be substantial.

In retail banking, most of the competitive focus was on acquiring new customers: people tended to change banks infrequently, suggesting customer switching costs were high. Each new customer or new service provided to an existing customer added revenue with low marginal costs; meanwhile, the bank's fixed costs – mostly operating and staffing 1,300 store locations – were relatively high. Other than the store's location, retail banking's core features – customer deposit accounts, personal checking, and so on – were essentially identical across banks. TD Bank's checking and savings accounts paid the same interest rates and offered the same features as its competitors. Even in this competitive environment, Glassman spotted an opportunity for TD Bank to increase its appeal to important consumer segments that mattered to TD Bank in 2011. TD Bank's internal market research showed that younger people – the segment that tends to open new bank accounts – wanted their bank to be environmentally friendly. Moreover, TD Bank operated many stores in cities and neighborhoods with large Hispanic populations. TD Bank had commissioned public opinion surveys that showed that environmental issues were particularly salient among Hispanics, suggesting additional opportunities for revenue growth in key markets.

Stepping back from the financial statements, Glassman understood that increasing employee engagement among the 16,000 employees working at TD Bank's stores could significantly lower labor costs. Keeping sales associates, traditionally known as bank tellers, in their jobs through improved morale would substantially lower the cost of employee turnover. Sales associates were the frontline employees who interacted most directly with potential customers. If sales associates believed in TD Bank as a sustainability leader, they might recruit new customers more effectively. Fortuitously, many of these new customers were of the same age group as TD Bank's sales associates – younger people with strong environmental values were the ones likely to open a new account with TD Bank.

Glassman was hired at TD Bank in 2011 with a mandate to engage employees through sustainability. Glassman and her small staff at TD Environment – Brad Peirce, TD Environment's program manager, and Sarah Healey, TD Environment's program associate – set out to build and grow programs to boost employee engagement throughout the bank's workforce. Within a year of Glassman's arrival, the team started a new program – TD Green Leaders – that created regional teams to be internal champions of TD Bank's environmental programs and objectives. The teams would tell employees about opportunities to add sustainability activities to their regular jobs and how this would be valuable to the employees and their careers. Each team was made up of volunteers – senior executives in each region, up-and-coming mid-level employees, and an "ambassador" from each store. To reach the rest of TD Bank's workforce, Glassman and her team created "the Green Pledge" – six specific commitments for action that all employees could take to help TD Bank reach its paper reduction and greenhouse gas emission goals. The Glassman team added new programs for employees to reduce business travel by using video meetings, and encouraged employees to reduce, reuse, and recycle office supplies, and to conserve energy by turning off unused appliances. Glassman had set up programs though which TD Bank employees would have the opportunity to participate in environmental activities that reflected their values, offered the potential for learning and demonstrating workplace skills, and provided a fun, social environment to engage with like-minded peers.

TD Environment offered several resources to support the Green Leaders. Green Leaders could reach fellow employees through TD Bank's Green Network, an online program that uses the company's internal social media platform and internal website. TD Environment also supplied a playbook and suggested narratives for Green Leaders' own weekly email communications, including information regarding TD Bank's corporate sustainability goals and practices, "Green Tips" for saving energy and paper, and customer conversation starter ideas. TD Environment encouraged Green Leaders to customize the messages to make them relevant to their local audience. Green Leaders had access to nominal financial incentives ($5 gift cards, $25 prize drawings), along with TD Bank's established channels for employee performance recognition to reward employees for strong environmental performance.

TD Environment's goals were ambitious and aimed to create value by lowering costs and raising revenues. TD Bank's costs would be lower, mostly through increased employee engagement, with additional, though smaller savings through lower business travel, paper use, and other expenses. On the revenue side, engaged employees and an energized workforce would help increase customer acquisition, particularly among younger people and Hispanics. Glassman successfully leveraged her cross-disciplinary knowledge to create a program that aimed for a triple bottom line win for TD Bank – improved working conditions for the employees, environmental improvements, and a financial benefit for the company.

In this chapter, we examine environmental strategy through its potential to engage a company's employees. Section 7.1 looks at companies' general environmental performance and programs and how employees respond to them. Environmental performance can influence employees' choices about where to work and their engagement once on the job. Under the right circumstances, a company's environmental performance can help attract higher-caliber employees, increase their productivity, and improve retention. We focus on the strategic choices companies make to identify environmental improvements and present them to employees in ways that are more likely to increase employees' work engagement. Section 7.2 examines employee environmental engagement (EEE) programs. The section investigates how a company can identify the environmental improvements for these programs and the employees who would participate in them. It also considers the

EEE program's value proposition – how these programs can benefit volunteers and other employees and how a company can capture a portion of the value the program creates. The section concludes with a discussion of how companies can establish credibility for their programs. The discussion throughout examines Diana Glassman's experience at TD Bank.

7.1 Employee Engagement and Companies' Environmental Performance

Take a look at one of the many of the "great places to work" lists, and you'll find some of the most financially successful companies in their industry. There is compelling evidence that companies on such lists end up with higher profits than their industry peers (Edmans 2011). One explanation for the link between engaged employees and higher profits is that, as Diana Glassman in the TD Bank example suspected, engagement increases productivity and lowers employment costs. Engaged employees feel a psychological commitment to their company and their work roles within it, leading them to be more productive and keeping them from leaving for greener pastures elsewhere. Having an engaged workforce also helps attract talent: potential recruits may be more likely to join companies where their co-workers will be more engaged at work.

Few people choose a job "just for the money." Beyond a paycheck, most people also want a job that offers nonfinancial value such as opportunities for learning, growth, career advancement, a pleasant social environment, enjoyable work assignments, and a specific geographic location (Christian et al. 2011; Kristof 1996). Many employees report in surveys that a company's environmental and social responsibility practices are a source of the value they receive from a job (Bauman & Skitka 2012). Fifty-eight percent of US employees consider a company's social and environmental performance when deciding where to work (Cone Communications 2016). Of course, different people place more or less emphasis on pay, employee benefits, and their employer's record on environmental and social issues, as with the example of younger workers being more excited about environmental initiatives at TD Bank.

Many companies have programs in which employees can volunteer to take on extra work assignments to participate in producing environmental goods and improvements (Harter et al. 2002). We refer to these as EEE programs. The idea behind these programs is that employees' engagement increases when their work activities contribute to the moral values they hold dear, and the benefits of increased engagement are greater than the costs of the programs that get employees more engaged. By providing employees with work that aligns with their values, companies enjoy a more engaged and productive workforce, on top of the environmental value the employees produce. The combination of sustainability and employee engagement offers a compelling appeal that yields a win across the triple bottom line: companies have a more engaged and committed workforce, employees enjoy the satisfaction of achieving their own social and environmental values, and the world's ecosystems become healthier (Mirvis 2012).

7.1.1 Environmental Improvements for Employee Engagement

Companies choose who participates in the process to decide which environmental improvements to address. The participants bring their perspective, expertise, and values to the process and, therefore, may be more likely to identify environmental improvements they understand and care about. Identifying opportunities often requires coordinating diverse expertise because environmental problems and improvements need to be understood across multiple dimensions. Their ecological impact, financial costs and benefits, effects on the companies' processes and stakeholders, and fit with social, legal, and economic circumstances all need to be considered.

In a top-down process, senior management selects problems for the companies' environmental strategy to address. An advantage of this approach is that senior managers may be better positioned to identify an environmental problem that facilitates strategic alignment between the company's environmental strategy and its broader strategic objectives and resources. The problem may exploit a company's competitive advantage, such as a core competence. Or, the problem may be salient with key external stakeholders, such as an influential environmental NGO.

In a bottom-up process, employees identify environmental problems, with senior management setting the infrastructure through which target environmental problems are chosen (Ramus 2001). An advantage of this approach is that employee involvement may increase employees' sense of ownership from working to improve it. Likewise, a bottom-up approach may produce more creative, out-of-the-box choices. On the other hand, employee-chosen problems may be less strategically aligned and less likely to produce financial returns for the company. Finally, a hybrid approach, in which senior management and employees negotiate the project to work on, can balance the advantages and disadvantages of top-down and bottom-up approaches. For example, in 2015, BASF, the large chemical company, asked employees to submit proposals for employee volunteering projects in one of BASF's core areas of food, smart energy, or urban living. Employees formed teams, submitting 500 project ideas. From these, BASF selected 150 to implement (Polman & Bhattacharya 2016).

7.1.2 Stakeholder Demand and Employee Engagement

Employees are often environmental stakeholders – they care about their employer's environmental performance and respond to it in ways that affect the company's financial performance. For example, a 2019 survey of office workers, most of whom do not have direct job responsibility for environmental matters or experience their employer's environmental impacts, showed the importance of a company's sustainability practices to its employees. In the survey, 61 percent of office workers agreed that "sustainability is no longer a nice [thing] to have for companies, it's a need to have," and 40 percent reported they would look to change jobs if their employer did not implement sustainable business practices (Hewlett-Packard 2019). Employees value a company's environmental improvements because of the co-benefits they receive from them. As with green products, we can break down the potential functional, emotional, and social co-benefits employees may receive from their employers' environmental performance.

Functional co-benefits. Functional co-benefits of a company's environmental practice come from the utility stakeholders receive from the company's environmental improvement. Some employees may experience environmental risks at work, such as potential exposure to pollutants through spills and accidents, and can directly benefit from a company's improvement of these environmental risks. More often, however, employees are not able to directly experience the environmental benefits their company produces.

Emotional co-benefits. A company's environmental and other CSR practices can influence employee engagement. People feel stronger emotional attachment and identification when they share moral values with their organization (Bauman & Skitka 2012; Rupp et al. 2018). Engaged employees feel a stronger and more positive emotional commitment to their work and employer. When an employee believes her employer has strong CSR practices, including environmental and sustainability programs, she is likely to experience more positive engagement about her work and her affiliation with the company (Gond et al. 2017; Rupp & Mallory 2015).

Social co-benefits. Some jobs provide a level of social prestige to their holders. A company's CSR programs, including its environmental programs, can provide social prestige co-benefits for employees. When employees believe that external stakeholders recognize and appreciate a company's environmental improvements, they feel greater pride in their work roles (Jones 2010; Jones et al. 2014). And being surrounded by happier, more engaged employees makes a job more pleasant.

For most employees, the primary co-benefit of their employer's environmental performance is the emotional satisfaction, warm glow, and a sense of purpose that comes from working for a company whose behavior aligns with their moral values (Bansal 2003). Different groups may have more or less for a company's social and environmental performance and their accompanying co-benefits. Companies that operate in regions with environmentally conscious cultures or have younger or more educated workers are especially likely to benefit from environmental programs that target employee engagement.

7.1.3 Channels for Capturing Value

Employee engagement is a component of the informal labor contract between employees and their employer (Baker et al. 2002; Gibbons 2005; Gibbons & Henderson 2012; Rousseau 1995). Engaged employees put in extra work, stay longer at their jobs, and are generally more productive, beyond what is required by the formal written contract terms. Employees are more likely to remain engaged when their efforts is rewarded and supported by the company. Recall that we defined organizational culture in Chapter 4 as a set of norms and values that are widely shared and strongly held throughout the organization (Gibbons & Henderson 2012; O'Reilly 1989;

O'Reilly & Chatman 1996). Culture can thus function as a form of social constraint and incentive in labor contracts' informal areas. The constraints and incentives influence both the company and its employees. When company culture is strong and effective, the company can be more confident that employees comply with its cultural norms, even when employee behavior is unsupervised or otherwise difficult to observe. Likewise, employees can be more confident that their engaged behavior will be recognized and rewarded by the company.

This type of informal labor contract, backed by a company culture that promotes cooperation between employer and employees, is a channel through which a company can capture value from employees in return for improving its environmental performance. Formal employment contracts do not promise employees that their employer will produce environmental goods beyond the requirements of laws and regulations. Nor do formal employment contracts require employees to feel pride in and emotional engagement with their work. Instead, the company chooses to produce the environmental improvement hoping that employees will see the improvement and realize their own co-benefits from it. In response, the employees will be more engaged with their work and identify more closely with their employer. Employee engagement can yield financial returns by lowering labor costs and increasing productivity (Attridge 2009; Shuck & Wollard 2010).

Labor costs. A company's labor costs are the amount of money it spends on items such as employee salaries, health insurance, taxes, and recruiting and onboarding new employees. Lowering labor costs improves a company's bottom line because the company has lower production costs for the goods and services it sells. Receiving co-benefits from a company's environmental and other CSR practices could translate into employees' willingness to accept lower wages for employment. Surveys report that 55 percent of US employees would choose to work for a socially responsible company, even if the salary was less (Cone Communications 2016). Of course, survey responses may not be accurate because people may be responding based on what they hope they would do or what they think the survey interviewer wants them to say, rather than what they would actually do.

Fortunately, we have some strong research evidence suggesting that employees may choose lower wages in return for working for a socially responsible company. Vanessa Burbano conducted a series of studies in online labor platforms where prospective employees submitted bids for work assignments to be performed online while working for a company (Burbano 2016). Half the prospective employees were randomly provided information about the company's CSR practices, and the other half were not. In all other ways, the prospective employees were evaluating the same jobs, from the same companies, and in the same conditions. Employees who saw the company's CSR practices were willing to work for significantly lower wages than those who did not. Other research corroborates Burbano's finding that some employees accept lower wages to work for a company with stronger CSR practices (Ariely et al. 2008; Gond et al. 2017; Grant et al. 2011; Rupp & Mallory 2015).

Workforce productivity. The productivity of a company's workforce is the number of products and services it produces per employee over a period of time. Increasing productivity without raising wages contributes to the bottom line because the company can sell more goods and services without raising costs. Again, we can turn to Burbano's field experiments for evidence on how a company's CSR practices can increase productivity. In another study, online gig workers at two labor platforms were given the opportunity to perform extra work without pay. Half the employees were randomly given information about their employer's charitable giving practices, and the other half were not. Again, the employees were otherwise performing the same job, for the same companies, in the same conditions. The employees who learned that their employer donated to charity were more likely to volunteer to take on extra work assignments (Burbano 2019).

Burbano's experimental findings echo research from a nonexperimental setting, which shows that CSR increases employee engagement and that more engaged employees are more productive employees (Beaudoin et al. 2019). When working for companies with strong CSR programs, managers are more likely to choose options that benefit the company as a whole, even at the expense of their own self-interest (Beaudoin et al. 2019). Engaged employees work harder at their job (Flammer & Luo 2017), are less likely to be absent from work or quit their job (Carnahan et al. 2017), and are more effective company ambassadors by projecting a more positive image to customers, clients, and other external stakeholders (Edinger-Schons et al. 2019). Engaged employees participate more in voluntary workplace activities, adhere more closely to company policies, and perform desired work behaviors (Grant 2012; Ramus & Killmer 2007; Rodell 2013).

When employees believe in their employer's CSR performance, they are more creative in their work roles (Glavas & Piderit 2009; Hur et al. 2018). Companies' environmental programs can lower labor costs by attracting and engaging employees who are more productive, stay longer in their jobs, and even accept lower wages.

7.1.4 Credibility and Employees

To achieve credibility with employees and to ensure that motivations for environmental improvement are clearly communicated, a company must overcome several challenges. First, employees must believe that the company has actually produced the environmental improvements it claims to have produced. This part of the challenge is similar to the credibility challenge companies face more generally – stakeholders suspect companies' profit motives lead them to overstate their environmental improvements, particularly when the stakeholders are not able to observe the improvements directly. If employees believe the company is generally motivated by short-term profits, they will believe its environmental improvements are motivated in the same way (Donia et al. 2017). For employees to experience emotional co-benefits from the company's environmental performance, they need to believe that the company's actions were caused by the its moral values or some other deeply held facet of organizational culture (Donia & Sirsly 2016; McShane & Cunningham 2012). Likewise, the employees need to believe that the company's moral values are aligned with their own moral values and identity (Bansal 2003). Employees who care about the environment put in more effort at work when they believe their employer authentically shares their values (Donia et al. 2017; Scheidler et al. 2019). When these elements are in place, a company's environmental improvements can increase employee engagement, leading to more productive and loyal employees.

Companies can improve credibility with their employees by choosing environmental and CSR priorities that align with the company's culture (McShane & Cunningham 2012; Scheidler et al. 2019). Including employee input while developing an environmental strategy can increase authenticity because it may more fully reflect participants' values. Companies can also improve credibility by carefully choosing the messenger. Employees are more likely to believe CSR messages conveyed through their workplace peers than through traditional company communication channels (Potoski & Callery 2018). Employees are more likely to see environmental improvements as authentic when they trust the company and its leadership (Farooq et al. 2014).

Part of the role of a company's culture is to help employees anticipate how the company will perform in the future. A company with stronger environmental performance may treat its employees well in the future (Walker 2010). Some elements of a positive and trustworthy organizational culture must be developed slowly over time as employees and other stakeholders observe a company's behavior and make inferences about its motives and values. Over time, they learn culturally acceptable behaviors and what to expect of their employer and each other, and begin to adapt their own behaviors. Employees update their beliefs about culture as they observe the company's actions and make further judgments about why those behaviors occurred. Once harmed, a positive culture can be difficult to reestablish. Companies can leverage cultures to help internally reinforce the credibility of their environmental strategy motives and objectives in the eyes of their employees.

7.2 EEE Programs

Companies often combine their employee engagement programs with their environmental strategy (Siemens Industry Inc. & McGraw-Hill Construction 2009). EEE programs offer employees opportunities to participate in company-sponsored activities with the goal of increasing employees' engagement. Of course, an EEE program has the additional dimension of producing environmental benefits, which can be an opportunity for the company to create value for other internal and external stakeholders. Some programs look to reshape regular work tasks, routines, and the work environment. Other programs provide special events that break employees out of their normal roles and routines to provide opportunities for bonding and enrichment.

An effective EEE program improves a company's environmental performance while increasing employee engagement in ways that generate value for the company. The key to efficacy is to create EEE programs that are credible to both internal and external stakeholders and create channels for the company to capture value from the program's environmental improvements. Under the right circumstances, an EEE program is an opportunity for a company to create and capture value. To find these opportunities, we first focus on the value the programs can generate for the company's employees and stakeholders and then identify channels through which some of this value can be channeled back to the company. We then address how companies can improve the credibility of their programs. EEE programs come in many different shapes and sizes. These challenges should be addressed in light of the outcome goals for the environment and for the employees.

7.2.1 Environmental Problems for Engagement Programs

While companies have many options for improving their environmental performance, not all environmental improvements are suitable for EEE programs. To gather employee participants, EEE programs must align with the employees' willingness and ability to participate in workplace environmental activities, which restricts the types of environmental impacts the EEE program can look to address. Environmental impacts distant from the employee experience and work activities are ill-suited for EEE programs; for example, a project centered around planting trees might not be the best choice for a New York City-based law firm.

Diana Glassman looked for ways to engage TD Bank's employees through environmental programs. TD Bank's environmental priorities were largely in place upon Glassman's arrival. TD Bank had been working on its greenhouse gas policies for some time before achieving its carbon neutral goal in 2010, and its other environmental programs were up and running as well. Glassman and her team, however, saw opportunities for bottom-up input from TD Bank's employees, so they helped Green Leaders tailor their activities to fit the employees in their region. Over time, they used the Green Network to allow TD Bank employees to suggest new directions for TD Bank's environmental program. As Brad Peirce, TD Environment's program manager, explained, "[w]e started them on paper and energy so that they could coalesce as a group and prove – to themselves and the bank – they could demonstrate business results" (Clancy 2013). As the programs matured, Pierce continued, TD Environment could ask employees "to expand, innovate, and help lead the program by layering on additional environmental issues that are important to them, their families, and their communities" (Clancy 2013).

Employee engagement programs come with costs. There are the administrative costs of setting up and managing the program, and making sure that it is running properly. Then there are the costs of the time, effort, and resources employees spend while participating in the program. Employees may be "volunteering" to participate in the EEE program, but their work comes at the expense of time spent on their regular work assignments. Employee time spent planting trees or cleaning trash from a neighborhood park is time spent away from doing the normal job they were hired to do.

While developing TD Bank's Green Leaders program, Glassman kept an eye on keeping costs low. Much of the program was built on top of what was already in place, such as the bank's internal communications systems and existing environmental programs, so that Green Leaders did not require a significant financial investment. The highest cost of the programs was in the time employees devoted to it. While TD Environment's team of three employees may seem small in comparison to the bank's 28,000-person workforce, its programs drew significant volunteer time from across the workforce.

7.2.2 Employee Demand and Environmental Engagement Programs

Participating in an EEE program requires employees to do more than their job descriptions require – taking an extra step out of their work routines to engage in new and unfamiliar work activities. Some employees may value the EEE program work in itself, in the same way that some people simply enjoy gardening. However, for most employees, the extra work requires some extra incentives (Grant 2012; Rodell et al. 2016). Very rarely do employees receive additional financial compensation for participating in an engagement program. For a source of nonfinancial incentives for employees to participate in the EEE program, we once again turn to co-benefits.

An EEE program co-benefit is the value an employee receives from participation that he would not receive if he did not participate. Many employees would like sustainability to be part of their workplace duties. According to a 2016 survey, 71 percent of US employees reported that it is important that their employer provide them with hands-on activities to promote environmental sustainability (Cone Communications 2016).

Functional co-benefits. Some employees may experience direct value from participating in the EEE program. The functional co-benefits from EEE program participation come less from the environmental goods themselves but from the employees' involvement in producing them. Important functional co-benefits from EEE program participation can stem from the opportunity for employees to learn new skills and knowledge to advance their careers. According to the Cone Communications survey, 53 percent of US employees would prefer volunteer activities that are a balance between skills they use every day and skills that are not related to their job (Cone Communications 2016). An EEE program can thus provide the benefits of a stretch assignment, a work task or project that is beyond the employee's current capabilities and requires the employee to expand and increase their abilities in order to be successful. An accountant assigned to work on a company environmental newsletter may learn skills for writing, editing, and graphic design. The accountant might also build project management skills by leading the team. Employees are more likely to volunteer for a CSR program when they can develop relevant career skills (Jones 2016; Caligiuri et al. 2013).

Emotional co-benefits. The goal of employee engagement programs is to increase employees' commitment to their jobs and their employer and to improve their workplace motivation. Contributing through work to an environmental cause that an employee values may elicit a "warm glow" emotional response, akin to making a financial contribution to a charitable cause or purchasing a green product. Such warm glow emotions arise when employees feel their work life is aligned with the moral values that are core to their identity. Employees volunteering for an EEE program may also feel more pride in working for the company (Jones 2010). For some employees, workplace volunteering can enhance their emotional responses to the company's environmental and other CSR contributions, leading to stronger employee engagement (Attridge 2009; Shuck & Wollard 2010).

An EEE program can offer a welcome and exciting change from work routines (Attridge 2009; Shuck & Wollard 2010). Many, if not most jobs, have routine patterns and tasks, the regular day-to-day elements of the job. Over time, an employee settles into the position and develops skills to handle these everyday tasks. The job becomes easier, and the routine can become boring. An EEE program can offer novelty, excitement, and a chance to get out of the office. Participants may have the opportunity to use different skills, enjoy a social context with different people, and experience the challenge of tackling new problems. Such positive excitement can translate into employees feeling happier at work and more committed to their job (Rodell et al. 2016).

Social co-benefits. Volunteering to participate in an EEE program may provide social signaling value by allowing an employee the opportunity to show commitment to environmental causes and that the employee is a trustworthy and cooperative person. After all, the employee is volunteering for a good cause. Volunteering may have an additional signaling value that is unique to the workplace: the opportunity for an employee performing in new roles to be seen by senior managers (Peloza & Hassay 2006). Such visibility may help an employee earn additional responsibilities and perhaps even promotion to more senior positions (Rodell 2013; Rodell et al. 2016).

At TD Bank, Diana Glassman's efforts targeted two stakeholder groups that were strategically important to TD Bank: new customers and employees. The TD Environment team estimated that about 10 percent of TD Bank's employees were passionately committed to the environment. As Sarah Healey, TD Environment's program associate, described the recruitment strategy, "[t]hese employees are most passionate about our green efforts. In some sense, they were 'lone wolves' waiting for the arrival of our program to give them a sense of belonging, a voice, and an urgency to lead ... We want to celebrate what they do, build on their passion, and provide them with additional benefits for going above and beyond" (Clancy 2013). These employees would be most motivated to volunteer for an environmental program and would be the target recruits for TD Environment's programs.

Beyond emotional awards, TD Bank's programs offered participants potential social and career advancement rewards. The Green Leaders program was a high-profile initiative that offered volunteers visibility within the company. Green Leader volunteers were invited by senior managers to join their teams and had the opportunity to hone and display their management and leadership skills. TD Environment's online systems for the program allowed senior managers to identify which Green Leaders were the most successful in engaging employees, such as getting the full range of TD Bank's employees to take the Green Pledge. When an employee achieved an environmental accomplishment, he or she received a nice thank-you email from TD Environment, which was also visibly copied to the employee's superior.

When employees choose to volunteer at work, they are often seeking co-benefits. When Cone Communications asked what would lead US employees to participate in a workplace volunteering program, their responses were "professional growth" (87 percent), "making a meaningful difference" (85 percent), "financial incentives" (e.g., bonuses or gift cards) (85 percent), "personal recognition" (79 percent), "a meaningful personal experience" (76 percent), and "perks" (e.g., better parking spaces, "casual Fridays") (74 percent) (Cone Communications 2016). Employees often want to participate in EEE programs for many of the same reasons they want to work for companies that have strong environmental and CSR programs. They may feel warm glow emotions from work that is aligned with their own moral values. They may feel pride in working for a company whose environmental performance creates public admiration and receive social co-benefits from this. But to experience these benefits, an employee just needs to show up for work each day. A desire to work for a socially responsible company may not be sufficient inducement for enthusiastic volunteering in an EEE program. Likewise, employees, even younger people, may overstate how much they would be willing to volunteer in an EEE program.

Table 7.1 provides examples of different types of employee engagement programs. As with the green product examples discussed in Table 6.1, the co-benefits from these programs are likely to vary across circumstances. Some employees may greatly value participating in a workplace recycling initiative, others may see it as an extra work burden, and others may not care at all. Employees can receive direct benefits from neighborhood cleanup programs if they live where the program occurs. The table does not list the benefits to the company from more engaged employees, such as higher productivity and better retention. Instead, it shows other co-benefits that may accrue to the company from the program's environmental improvements.

7.2.3 The Value of EEE Programs

An effective EEE program increases employee engagement among participants and the broader workforce, thus lowering labor costs and increasing productivity through a more committed workforce. Just as some employees are attracted to work for companies with stronger environmental and CSR programs, there are also job seekers who

Table 7.1 *Co-benefits from EEE programs*

Employee engagement program	Environmental benefit	Potential co-benefits
Workplace recycling	Reduce waste stream	Employees: warm glow from work that reflects moral values Company: lower disposal costs
Neighborhood clean up days	Litter reduction	Employees: cleaner neighborhood, warm glow, identity Company: social license to operate
Replace travel with video conferencing	Greenhouse gas savings from reduced travel	For employees: time savings from reduced travel, warm glow For company: cost savings

prefer to work for companies that offer opportunities for workplace volunteering (Jones 2010; Jones et al. 2016). Once on the job, volunteering programs can motivate employees. When employees volunteer for an EEE program, companies receive the benefits of the increased engagement among the volunteers: more workplace productivity, better retention, and more workplace cooperation (Rodell et al. 2016). Employees who volunteer are more productive in their jobs and are less likely to voluntarily leave the company (Bode et al. 2015; Rodell et al. 2016). Companies also benefit when volunteering enhances employees' skills (Jones 2016; Jones et al. 2016). These positive effects of workplace volunteering can be stronger among employees who believe in the cause for which they are volunteering (Gatignon-Turnau & Mignonac 2015), and, perhaps more importantly, among employees who are not fully fulfilled by their regular work assignments (Rodell 2013).

After two years, Glassman and her TD Environment team stepped back to assess how well their programs were working. For TD Bank, a primary channel for capturing value was to increase employee engagement, with the aim of lowering labor costs by reducing turnover. TD

Bank tracked employee engagement through internal surveys. Their data showed that the disengaged employees were more likely to end up leaving their jobs, and the EEE programs were showing results with rank-and-file employees – they became more engaged with their work and were taking extra steps to advance TD Bank's goals. Employees reported more awareness and pride in TD Bank's environmental programs and more commitment to working at TD Bank after Glassman rolled out her engagement programs. According to Glassman, "[w]hen we showed these results to our CEO, it was the pride and commitment levels that really struck a chord, because we are a service culture and those are believed to be indicators of retention and customer satisfaction, that in turn support TD Bank's core business goals of revenue and profit" (Clancy 2013).

The cost of recruiting and training a new sales associate was high; it cost TD Bank the equivalent of several months salary to properly train them, and a new hire often stayed on the job for less than a year. TD Bank's human resources department saw the potential of TD Bank's sustainability programs to help recruit and retain employees. As Diana Glassman later recounted, "[i]n fact, it was Human Resources starting with recruiting who came to us as soon as we created the TD Environment department in summer 2011" (Clancy 2013). TD Bank's human resource managers saw Glassman's engagement programs as a solution to problems within their functional area – recruiting and retaining employees – and were therefore willing to contribute to making the programs effective.

The Green Leaders were actively communicating with employees in their areas and encouraging participation in TD Bank's environmental programs. About 12,500 employees took TD Bank's Green Pledge. Senior management staff supported TD Environment's programs and actively participated in them as well. TD Bank's surveys showed that employees were more comfortable talking about the bank's environmental programs with customers, and there was anecdotal evidence that customers noticed what was happening too. Store managers reported stories of sales associates having customer conversations about the bank's environmental programs, reinforcing TD Bank's employee surveys. As TD Environment's Green Leader program grew, it started to show spillover benefits in other areas of the company. One senior executive noted that TD Bank's environmental reputation was helping in negotiations with local communities. "There are a growing number of communities and businesses that will only do business with people who share values of environmental leadership," he said. "By coming into the discussions [with communities where TD Bank wants to expand] from day one with a green business agenda, we get a lot more support early on" (Clancy 2013).

7.2.4 Credibility and EEE Programs

The credibility challenges for EEE programs are similar to the credibility challenges companies face when their employees evaluate more general environmental performance. An EEE program needs to be designed and implemented with an eye toward ensuring its credibility and legitimacy with targeted employees and company stakeholders. The company needs to show EEE program participants that the environmental improvements are real, that the company's motives for producing them are genuine, and that the EEE program and its activities are part of the company's informal labor contract and its culture. With EEE programs, it is relatively easy for companies to show participants that the environmental improvements are real because the participants have firsthand experience in producing them. In fact, employees become more engaged with their work when they engage with assignments that have more clear and visible social and environmental impacts (Chandler & Kapelner 2013; Grant 2008a, 2008b, 2012).

Employees participating in an EEE program want the program to be an authentic representation of the company's core values and culture rather than an insincere short-term profit grab (Gatignon-Turnau & Mignonac 2015). There is some evidence that the mere act of participating in a workplace volunteer program reduces employee cynicism toward their employer (Rodell 2013; Sheel & Vohra 2016). Endorsements from trusted senior managers can ensure employees that volunteering is important to the program, particularly when senior managers themselves volunteer to participate (Ramus & Steger 2000). When managers engage in workplace environmental behaviors, their subordinates are more likely to follow (Kim et al. 2017; Robertson & Barling 2013).

Companies can make volunteer recognition part of the informal labor contract and company culture by committing to rewarding employee volunteers. Take, for example, how law firms use junior associates in pro bono legal cases (Burbano et al. 2018). A pro bono case is when a law firm provides legal services to a client who cannot afford them or to other worthy causes. Law firms typically assign junior associates to these cases as stretch assignments – the junior associate has roles and responsibilities beyond what they would normally perform and, while their performance is monitored and reviewed, have less direct input from more senior colleagues. The law firm benefits from these arrangements because the junior associates learn skills they will need for working on more lucrative assignments, and the firm gets information on how well the associates perform when working independently. A similar informal commitment to recognizing EEE program participation could reassure employees considering whether to volunteer.

Should credibility efforts fail, employees may suspect that volunteering opportunities are merely ploys to burnish the company's image and increase profits (Rodell et al. 2016). While some employees may be motivated purely by the environmental cause, most employees who take on the extra work assignments need assurance that their efforts will be rewarded (and, of course, not punished). Employees who volunteer in order to learn new skills and show their abilities to managers need some confidence that their efforts will pay off in their employee evaluations or through opportunities for higher wages and career advancement (Rodell et al. 2016; Rodell & Lynch 2016).

Diana Glassman and her team addressed these credibility challenges in several ways. First, most of the communication employees received about the bank's environmental programs was coming from their peers who had volunteered to participate in TD Environment's engagement programs. Second, to show that TD Bank's EEE programs were part of the bank's culture, Glassman recruited senior executives to be involved in the programs, both as supervisors and as participants. She created the TD Green Council, a team of senior executives who would supervise and champion TD Environment's programs, and helped the council's chair recruit volunteers from across the company. Members of the TD Green Council included the CEO's chief of staff, chief marketing officer, the deputy chief financial officer, and the chief information officer. Glassman also made sure that senior executives were engaging in the same volunteer efforts that she was asking of rank-and-file employees. Glassman tracked how many senior executives took the "Green Pledge" and monitored their progress toward meeting its goals, which was then reported back to TD Bank's rank-and-file employees.

Finally, Glassman and her team made sure her program produced results that would be credible to internal and external audiences. She and her team, with a small dose of outside help, designed and implemented ways to measure key components of the engagement programs. They used TD Bank's in-house employee surveys to monitor participation in the programs and evaluate their impact on employee engagement, and used internal data sources to track other outcomes, such as paper purchasing and business travel. Their broad measurement approach allowed them to craft messages explaining the program's performance in language tailored to diverse audiences. For example, rigorous measures and analyses that connected data to financial measurement were particularly important in discussing the programs' value with skeptical senior executives. Glassman and her team made a significant effort to create EEE programs that were credible and widely accepted by TD Bank's executives, managers, and other employees.

7.3 Conclusion

The popularity of EEE programs is not evidence that they are always producing value. Some social science research shows that similar employee-focused programs do not always work. Field experiment research, with rigorously randomized treatment and control groups, shows that workplace wellness programs may not improve employees' health and productivity (Jones et al. 2019). A further pitfall of EEE programs is the risk of employee and external stakeholder scorn should the programs turn out to be yet another form of corporate greenwashing. Companies need to design environmental improvements and EEE programs to yield more engaged employees, resulting in employee behavior that helps the company's bottom line by accepting lower wages, avoiding quitting, working harder, and directing work effort toward the organizations' values and norms. Companies can do this by offering engagement opportunities the provide functional, emotional, and identity co-benefits and by ensuring the program's credibility with employees.

TD Bank's successful employee environmental engagement programs highlight the key challenges companies must address to create and implement a successful EEE program. Diana Glassman and her team sought input from across the company to target environmental improvements that would appeal to the bank's internal and external stakeholders. They structured the program to provide co-benefits for the participants and value to the bank through improvement in employee engagement. Finally, Glassman and her team ensured the programs' credibility by translating their benefits into the various languages and terms of their stakeholders so they could better understand the programs' value.

8 | Environmental Groups

Chapter 1 opened this book with a story about the 65,000 emails Timberland CEO Jeff Swartz received from angry Greenpeace supporters. The emails accused Timberland of "supporting slave labor, destroying Amazon rain forests, and exacerbating global warming" (Swartz 2010: 39). Timberland had become the target of an activist campaign organized by one of the world's strongest and most aggressive environmental groups. This chapter revisits Swartz's efforts to develop an environmental strategy to respond to Greenpeace's activist campaign.

Swartz later wrote about his experience in a short article published in the *Harvard Business Review*:

My first response to the emails was to be pretty angry myself. Of all the environmental problems Timberland has been actively committed to addressing, deforestation tops the list. We've planted a million trees in China; we host community regreening events in cities all over the world. Our logo is a tree, for crying out loud. How much more ridiculous could this campaign be? (Swartz 2010: 40)

Swartz was angered by Greenpeace's accusations against his company. Timberland had been founded in 1952 by his grandfather and later run by his father and uncle. Swartz joined Timberland in 1986. Swartz strongly believed in social justice and related causes. He originally pursued a career in medicine, and he brought his passion for helping people and the planet to his work at Timberland. As CEO, Swartz had overseen a remarkable period of growth – between 1992 and 2005, the company's stock price increased by 300 percent (Schechter 2012) while it also became a leader in corporate social and environmental responsibility. The company paid employees for up to thirty-two hours they spent volunteering each year. The company supported charitable causes; they helped City Year, a fledgling education nonprofit, to grow into a multicity enterprise. Swartz believed he had already proved Timberland's social credentials; why would Greenpeace target his company?

Swartz knew about Greenpeace and its approach to environmental activism. As an organization, Greenpeace began in the 1960s and 1970s with environmental activists who sought to deter US atomic weapons testing by sailing their vessels close to ocean testing sites.[1] By the mid-1970s, Greenpeace branches were operating worldwide, continuing the tradition of aggressive and confrontational environmental activism. Greenpeace was a formidable environmental group, with strong support among environmentalists. In early 2000, Greenpeace's mission statement read: "Greenpeace is an independent, campaigning organization that uses non-violent, creative confrontation to expose global environmental problems, and force solutions for a green and peaceful future" (Eden 2004: 595).[2]

In 2009, Greenpeace published the results of an extensive investigation into international supply chains that sourced material from the Amazon region. The lengthy report detailed how the Brazilian cattle industry was producing leather and beef from livestock raised on apparently illegally cleared rainforest land (Greenpeace International 2009). The report called out large consumer products companies, including Audi, Adidas, Kraft, Walmart, and Timberland, that had purchased products from supply chain intermediaries who had obtained the Amazon-sourced cattle products. The controversy was picked up in media outlets around the world and clearly found a following among Greenpeace supporters.

As he composed himself, Swartz could see the scope of the problem that Greenpeace's campaign had brought to light. Despite Timberland's many social and environmental programs, including planting trees in China and supporting social and environmental causes, the company was vulnerable. If 65,000 people were willing to send an email, many more were likely to be sympathetic to the cause, including many of Timberland's customers. Swartz had worked for years to make

---

[1] For a history of Greenpeace, see Eden (2004).
[2] Over the years, Greenpeace's mission statement has shifted toward a less confrontational stance. Today it reads: "Greenpeace is a global, independent campaigning organization that uses peaceful protest and creative communication to expose global environmental problems and promote solutions that are essential to a green and peaceful future."

Timberland an example of how commerce, justice, and the environment could coexist and even thrive together in a financially successful company. Now, the reputation of his company was under threat, and Swartz needed to take action. Would the cost and headache of cleaning up its supply chain pay off with Timberland's customers and stakeholders? Would surrendering to Greenpeace's "guerrilla tactics" make Timberland a bull's-eye target for future activist campaigns? Swartz needed an environmental strategy to weigh the trade-offs in these difficult circumstances.

This chapter applies the environmental strategy framework to the nonmarket arena. It examines how companies can make the right choices about their environmental improvements and their interactions with environmental groups. We start by taking a closer look at the business model of environmental groups, what kinds of goods and value they produce, and how they garner recourses to support their efforts. The chapter then examines the choices that companies make when interacting with nonmarket stakeholders through activist campaigns, using Greenpeace's campaign against Timberland as an illustrative example. The chapter then examines cooperative partnerships between companies and environmental groups.

8.1 Environmental Groups and Sustainability

As discussed in Chapter 3, a company's nonmarket stakeholders are those who do not conduct business but have preferences about how the company performs. Nonmarket stakeholders, including activist organizations and governments, can have important impacts on companies. Environmental groups like Greenpeace can launch protests and boycotts. Governments create and enforce environmental regulations and decide what types of environmental impacts are permissible and where they can occur. Environmental groups can organize a demonstration to protest a company's environmental harms or lobby their government for intervention. A company's relations with nonmarket stakeholders can yield important financial consequences. For example, being the target of an activist campaign can damage a company's stock price (Bartley & Child 2011; King & Soule 2007). Companies can also benefit from interactions with nonmarket stakeholders. If a company and a community of activists can come together to resolve a potentially contentious environmental issue, they may be able to reach a compromise that benefits the local environment and the company's stock price (Dorobantu & Odziemkowska 2017).

Understanding nonmarket stakeholders from their own strategic perspective can shed light on how a company can constructively interact with them. This chapter focuses on environmental groups because they are often the important stakeholders facing a company and can influence the success of an environmental strategy, for better or for worse. Environmental groups are nonprofit organizations whose "business model" is based on capturing rewards from stakeholders in return for contributing to the production of environmental public goods. For these groups, as for companies, the challenges groups face are (1) distinguishing themselves in a competitive landscape with other environmental groups, (2) capturing value to support their activities, and (3) communicating to stakeholders about the value they provide. Just as a company's competitive strategy aims for consistency between the market segments it targets, and the quality and price of its products, an environmental group seeks consistency between its targeted stakeholders and the causes and tactics it pursues (den Hond & de Bakker 2007; Heyes & Martin 2015; Taylor & Van dyke 2004). Confrontational tactics include protests and boycotts that pressure companies to improve their environmental performance, with the goal of renegotiating the terms of a company's social license to operate (Aguinis & Glavas 2012; Gunningham et al. 2004) and are more often chosen by more "radical" groups (den Hond & de Bakker 2007; Eesley et al. 2016). With nonconfrontational tactics, such as cooperative partnerships, both the business and the environmental group contribute resources to a project that produces an environmental good (Seitanidi & Crane 2009; Van Tulder et al. 2016).

8.2 Environmental Groups and Their Strategy

An environmental group is a formally organized association that seeks to improve environmental conditions. Environmental groups combine stakeholders' preferences into a more focused voice. In the Timberland example, Greenpeace saw that many people cared to protect the Amazon rainforest. Greenpeace identified the root of the problem, identified the move visible companies that could be linked creating it, and came up with a strategic plan to leverage support from its supporters' voices to improve supply chain practices. Greenpeace provided a structure to channel its members' voices into a cohesive message, which gave them more influence with Timberland than they would have otherwise had.

While all environmental groups seek to improve environmental conditions, they can be quite different in many ways. Some environmental groups seek a large number of followers and members. Others have a smaller cadre of highly committed members.[3] Environmental groups can pursue different types of environmental causes, with some focused narrowly on one or two issues and others pursuing a broader portfolio. Environmental causes can be local, national, or global. Environmental groups also differ in their tactics for achieving environmental improvements (Taylor & Van dyke 2004). Some NGOs, such as Greenpeace, focus more on organizing activist campaigns and protests. Others focus on lobbying politicians and governments to produce better environmental legislation. Sometimes NGOs produce environmental goods themselves, such as when TNC purchases wildlife habitat for conservation and preservation.

Every environmental group needs financial resources. Larger NGOs need financial resources to pay their employees. Even small, all-volunteer NGOs have expenses – rent and office supplies, mailings and fundraising, and other sundries. The need for financial resources means the NGO must operate with some sort of business model – the strategy through which it receives resources from stakeholders in return for producing environmental goods.[4] Environmental groups operate in a competitive environment (Minkoff 1997). Groups compete for publication attention (King et al. 2007) and donations (Grant & Potoski 2015). There is a limited pool of stakeholders from which environmental groups can receive support. Even groups united by a common cause and common foes directly compete with each other for resources from the same stakeholders (McCarthy & Zald 1977; Rose-Ackerman 1996).

Environmental groups need to produce environmental goods in ways that not only generate value from gratified stakeholders but do so better than other environmental groups do. An environmental

---

[3] For more on nonprofit management and strategy, see (Bryson 2018).

[4] Of course, no environmental group has a business model in the strictest sense, since as nonprofits they are legally prohibited from returning residual "profits" to shareholders.

group can have a competitive advantage by having a unique approach to creating and capturing greater value from stakeholders. An environmental group may be able to lower its costs by using expert volunteers while its competitors rely on paid professional labor. Or, a group may have a superior ability to produce environmental goods, stemming perhaps from its staff's scientific expertise, lobbying skill, or grassroots-organizing ability. Competitive advantage may also stem from increasing stakeholders' willingness to contribute. Environmental groups with more persuasive communications expertise can garner more stakeholder support, even if they are otherwise less effective.

Compared to for-profit companies and even some other nonprofits, environmental groups face two additional challenges that further complicate their ability to create and sustain themselves in a competitive context. First, environmental groups face the challenge of capturing value from the environmental improvements they create. For a company, capturing value is relatively easy; the company sells products that consumers want and receives financial payment in return. Of course, this is complicated by competition from other companies, suppliers, and consumers, who all want the value for themselves. Environmental groups also have the challenge of capturing value from environmental goods without the facilitation of markets. As we discussed in Chapter 2, people can enjoy the benefits of environmental improvements even if they did not pay to produce them.

The second important challenge for environmental groups is establishing credibility for producing the values their stakeholders want. Just as consumers are unwilling to pay premium prices for goods whose quality is not clear, stakeholders can be unwilling to support environmental groups that cannot credibly convey their environmental contributions. An environmental group's stakeholders, including those who would support the group financially and otherwise, are rarely able to evaluate directly the quality of the environmental goods the group produces. Even when stakeholders can directly evaluate the quality of environmental outcomes, they may be unable to determine who deserves credit for making them happen. This is especially likely because environmental improvement is often the result of collaborative efforts among coalitions of business, governments, and NGO groups; in other words, they are coproduced (Ostrom 1996). For example, consider how many people and groups can claim to play an important role in passing a new environmental law: legislators, the president, political parties, and of course many environmental groups. An environmental group that claims to have been influential in getting the bill passed would see its claims competing with the claims of politicians, political parties, and other groups that also had a hand in passing the legislation. It is hard for environmental groups to show stakeholders that they deserve value for making environmental improvements because there are so many other parties involved, many of whom also want to claim to have been instrumental in making the environmental improvement happen.

A business strategy is essential for an environmental group, in the same way that a business strategy is crucial for a for-profit business. Developing strategies for partnering with companies and organizing an activist campaign can help ensure that the group's efforts are effective. Understanding an environmental group's competitive advantage can help them leverage their best assets to move forward with their activities.

8.3 Environmental Groups and Activist Campaigns

Boycotts and activist protest tactics aim to coerce firms to produce environmental goods against their will. An activist campaign is usually organized and led by an environmental group that identifies the environmental problem, company, or industry to target, and the tactics for the campaign, and then calls upon like-minded activists and groups to join the campaign. The leading organization must also capture value from the campaign to sustain its own operations. A campaign of activists, organized with common demands and messaging, can exert more pressure than the same activists working alone. The organization of a campaign is a form of collective good for the participants and, as we saw in Chapter 3, a collective good can yield greater value than the sum of the individual contributions. This leadership comes with costs – advertising the cause and recruiting allies, organizing the campaign, and negotiating with the targeted company all require time and resources.[5]

Boycotts and protests aim to pressure the company through lost revenue from lost sales, damage to the reputation of its brand, and

---

[5] Several recent papers review environmental groups, including their relationships with activists (Eesley et al. 2016; Heyes & King 2020; Lyon 2020).

disruptions to its operations. In the summer of 1990, Earth First! organized "Redwood Summer," a month-long protest against logging practices in the Pacific Northwest, aiming to disrupt what it claimed to be the destruction of old-growth forests. According to a story in the *Los Angeles Times*, "with equal measures of guerrilla theater and guerrilla war, Redwood Summer saw as few as one, and as many as 1,500 activists dress as owls and sing protest songs, chain themselves to heavy equipment and block logging roads, suspend themselves by wires above state highways and stand between angry tree fallers and ancient redwoods" (Stein 1990). Along with attracting public attention, the protestors sought to disrupt logging operations by blocking access to roads and chaining themselves to trees. The outcome of these protests remains unclear, with even some environmentalists questioning their efficacy (Gabriel 1990).

Activist protests can also look to block a company's access to resources. In 2021, activists launched a campaign against Hindustan Zinc in Gujarat, India over its plans to open a zinc-smelting plant in the community (Bavadam 2021). The protestors charged that the plant would pollute local waterways with heavy metals and its water usage would overburden the local reservoir. The protests escalated to violent conflict with police. As of March 2022, it is not certain that Hindustan Zinc will open its smelting plant in Gujarat, despite the support of the local government.

8.3.1 Targeting for an Activist Campaign

An activist campaign aims to compel the targeted company to pay the costs of the improvement while directing the value created by the improvement to the environmental group and its stakeholders. An environmental group considering a campaign against a company may have little concern for how much an environmental improvement costs the company. The group instead focuses on the costs incurred in creating the campaign. A company can assess its environmental impacts to identify what environmental groups might target. Some companies have environmental impacts that are not well known or understood by stakeholders and thus not currently the subject of their concern. Perhaps the impacts occur deep within the supply chain so that the company's connection to the problem is obscured by layer upon layer of transactions. When stakeholders are not actively asking for improvements, a company might be tempted to neglect to look for them. But a company should not ignore environmental impacts just because stakeholders appear unconcerned about them. Unanticipated problems, such as leather sourced deep in a supply chain, can precipitate an activist campaign. Formerly acceptable environmental practices may no longer be acceptable, and stakeholders may learn that a company is not conforming to the social license's standards of conduct (Dorobantu et al. 2017a).

An activist campaign targets both an environmental problem and the company that produces it, and both can have features that make them more or less attractive campaign targets. What makes environmental problems more attractive? An attractive environmental problem has a large pool of potential activists who can be motivated to become participants – stakeholders who care enough to become mobilized in the campaign, have the resources to participate, and are likely to respond to the campaign's call to action. An environmental problem can also be a more attractive campaign target when it elicits an emotional reaction among potential activists. For instance, regardless of the ecological consequences, people become more engaged in causes to protect "charismatic megafauna" – large animals such as panda bears that people find more physically attractive – compared to species that they find distasteful, such as slugs and spiders (Ando & Langpap 2018). Such attractive causes also attract media attention to help advertise the campaign. Finally, environmental groups look to target environmental problems where they have a reputation and standing with their members.

Environmental groups are similarly strategic in choosing companies to target for campaigns (Bartley & Child 2014; Eesley & Lenox 2006; McDonnell et al. 2015; McDonnell & King 2013). Companies with a more visible public presence, such as consumer products companies, can be more attractive candidates. Such companies are better known among potential stakeholders and may have more to lose from the negative publicity of a campaign. Companies are also more attractive targets when their customers and stakeholders overlap with the environmental group's supporters. Groups organizing campaigns in the apparel industry were likely to target companies that did business with colleges and universities, like Nike, because the companies' consumers were also a prime source of campaign activists (Bartley & Child 2014). Companies with more resources to resist the campaign, such as those with higher profits and larger capital reserves, are less attractive targets (Baron & Diermeier 2007; Lenox & Eesley 2009).

The targeting calculus is not always simple. Companies with weaker reputations for CSR performance would seem to be ideal targets for campaigns since their malfeasance would be better fuel for activists' ire (Baron & Diermeier 2007; Rehbein et al. 2004). However, a strong record for environmental and CSR performance is not always a perfect shield (King & McDonnell 2015; McDonnell et al. 2015). A potential explanation is this: what motivates campaign activists can be not just a company doing something wrong but doing so hypocritically – the company is discovered to be doing something wrong despite its claims that it is doing better. Stakeholders' responses to the campaign may be tied to their perceptions of how the company was already performing. Stakeholders react more strongly to negative behavior by a company with a more positive reputation than the same negative behavior by a company with a negative reputation (King & Carberry 2018; Wagner et al. 2009).

In choosing an issue for its Amazon campaign, Greenpeace targeted an environmental problem deep within Timberland's supply chain. In fact, Timberland simply did not know if any of its leather was tainted, and neither did its leather suppliers. Nonetheless, Amazon deforestation was an issue that mattered to Greenpeace's stakeholders, and after the problem was brought to light, the group pressured Timberland to make a change. Timberland's experience with Greenpeace shows that even companies with a proven track record of environmental and CSR achievements can become the target of an activist campaign. Timberland was a ripe target because it would motivate Greenpeace's stakeholders to take action. Timberland was a large consumer products company with a brand and reputation for sustainability that was well recognized among Greenpeace's stakeholders, many of whom may even have been Timberland customers

8.3.2 Nonmarket Stakeholders and Demand for Environmental Improvements

Activist campaigns are efforts by organizers, usually an environmental group, to mobilize people to engage in action to influence a company's environmental activist. Participants may be members or an environmental NGO or other people whom the NGO motivates to activism. Activist campaigns can help environmental groups achieve their strategic objectives by creating synergies between the organizers and the campaign activists. Organizers provide collective goods that help the participants be effective, such as information about the target's transgressions and the need for a campaign, coordination among stakeholders and other activists, publicity for the campaign, and negotiations with the target. Participants provide clout that gives the campaign its compelling force, such as by engaging in protests and campaigns, writing letters, and boycotting products. Achieving these synergies comes from strategically selecting an environmental problem at a targeted company and at the same time ensuring that the cause offers co-benefits that appeal to potential participants.

8.3.2.1 Activist Campaigns and Co-benefits

Activist campaigns need participants to perform the activities: march, boycott, demonstrate, sign petitions, and the like. These are costly ways for people to express their demands for environmental improvements (Innes 2006). What then mobilizes people to participate in an activist campaign? Participation in an activist campaign can provide activists with co-benefits, a value that they would not receive without participating in the campaign. Again, we can classify the co-benefits according to the functional, emotional, and social value they provide.

Functional co-benefits. People who support a campaign's cause and are evaluating whether to participate in an activist campaign are likely to consider the prospects for success (Klandermans 2007). After all, they will share the value of the company's environmental improvements through direct benefits and perhaps co-benefits as well. Moreover, people can have preferences not just for environmental outcomes, but how those outcomes are achieved (Aldashev & Verdier 2010), such as by forcing companies to "clean up their own mess." But, functional co-benefits are likely to be less important for motivating activists, as we discussed earlier with the challenges of motivating people for collective action (Knoke 1988).

Emotional and identity co-benefits. People may be motivated to participate in a campaign because doing so aligns with their self-identity (Polletta & Jasper 2001). Participating in a group's campaigns can reinforce their sense of identity toward a group (Andrews et al. 2010; Han 2016). Emotional and identity co-benefits require some important conditions to motivate campaign activism. First, stakeholders must see themselves as members of the collective. This could mean identifying with the environmental group organizing the campaign, such as believing, "I am a member of 350.org." It could also mean identifying with the campaign's cause, such as believing, "I am an environmentalist who fights for the health of the planet." Collective identities often lie latent, out of regular consciousness, and become salient when activated by an external stimulus. We may not think of ourselves as alumni of our alma mater until our school's fundraising letter arrives and reminds us of our golden college days. Second, the stakeholders must believe that participating in the campaign aligns with their collective identity. A 350.org member who participates in a climate march may have in their identity the sense that "to be a member of 350.org means being willing to attend protest marches and rallies." When a collective identity is salient, people receive positive emotional responses from acting in accordance with it (Akerlof & Kranton 2005; Polletta & Jasper 2001). We feel good because writing our check to the annual giving campaign aligns with our identity as alumni and our belief that we should reciprocate for the gift our school gave us when we were students.

Social co-benefits. Some people join groups and campaigns for the social connections they provide (Knoke 1988). Many people become campaign activists because they were recruited by a friend or acquaintance (Diani 2007). Friends and acquaintances can be effective recruiters. They are credible about the organizers and cause. They often share identities and attributes with potential activists and signal the type of people who are active in the campaign. People value spending time with people like themselves, particularly when they are engaging in activities that express their shared identity (Diani 2007). Some activist campaigns provide similar social opportunities, such as protest marches and demonstrations. Other campaigns, such as consumer boycotts and letter-writing campaigns, are largely performed in social isolation. Social media platforms, like Facebook, now allow activists to participate in a campaign individually, such as by signing a petition, and they can also broadcast their action to friends and family.

Greenpeace's Timberland campaign provided activists with a low-cost way to take action. They could be activists at their computer desks, copying and pasting text into an email message – an easy way to earn a warm glow. Many activists probably also appreciated the campaign's confrontational tactics as a way to live in accordance with their identities as environmental warriors.

8.3.3 Channels: The Value Consequences of Activist Campaigns

Activist campaigns are a form of negotiation between the company and the activists. Campaign leaders present the targeted company with a demand, reward, and threat (Baron & Diermeier 2007). The campaign's demand is the environmental improvement the activists want the company to make. The reward is what activists offer the company in return for meeting the demand. Rewards could be simply ending the protest or boycott, or the rewards could be the additional value provided to the company, such as positive publicity or an endorsement of the company's improved environmental practices. The threat is the action that the activists will take to harm the company, should it not comply with the demand. Threats include continuing, escalating, or expanding the protest, disrupting the company's operations, and creating negative publicity.

The threats often carry significant weight. Being the target of an activist campaign can hurt companies financially. Activist campaigns can raise costs for the targeted company, such as by requiring the company to switch to more expensive inputs (Franks et al. 2014; Henisz et al. 2014). Boycotts and campaigns can reduce the targeted company's sales (Bartley & Child 2011) and may cause additional revenue loss by damaging the company's reputation and brand more generally (King & McDonnell 2015; McDonnell & King 2013). Revenue reductions from activist campaigns can also occur through nonmarket channels. Activists' campaigns may close off opportunities to expand into new markets, suggesting that they can jeopardize a company's social license to operate. Walmart withdrew proposals to open new stores in areas where it saw that community protests were likely (King & McDonnell 2015; McDonnell & King 2013). Being the target of an activist campaign can hurt a company in political and policy arenas, too. Targeted companies have been less likely to be invited to testify before US congressional committees and even received fewer federal procurement grants (McDonnell & Werner 2016). Such financial consequences are noteworthy for investors – being the target of an activist campaign can reduce a company's stock price (Bartley & Child 2011; King & Soule 2007; Koku et al. 1997; Vasi & King 2012).

An obvious way for companies to respond to the threat of an activist campaign is to avoid becoming a target in the first place.

Beyond identifying vulnerable areas and improving their environmental performance, companies can take additional proactive steps to position themselves to respond more effectively should they become a campaign target. A strong reputation can help insulate a company from an activist campaign (Rehbein et al. 2004), in part because stronger reputations render environmental groups' criticisms less credible with potential activists (Baron & Diermeier 2007). Companies that produce more CSR and environmental goods and avoid causing social harms experience smaller financial losses from product recalls and other negative events (Minor & Morgan 2011; Shiu & Yang 2017). As we have seen, a positive CSR and environmental reputation can sometimes make companies more attractive to activist campaigns (McDonnell et al. 2015) by making the company more vulnerable to accusations of hypocrisy, should stakeholders find out the company is not living up to their expectations (Effron et al. 2018).

Once a company becomes a target of an activist campaign, additional factors can increase or decrease its negotiating leverage relative to the campaign's organizers. The campaign may raise costs and reduce revenues for the targeted company to such an extent that the sensible response is to acquiesce to the campaign's demands. If the costs of acquiescence are too high, the company can deploy its own resources and tactics to mitigate the campaign's costs and perhaps improve its bargaining position. Time is an important resource for targeted companies. In most cases, time is on the company's side. Activists' anger, fueled by learning of the target's environmental malfeasance and perhaps its hypocrisy, can dissipate over time. Media attention can fade as the focus shifts to the new stories. Campaign organizers may need to spend additional resources to attract and mobilize activists and keep the pressure on targeted companies. A company can also look to weaken the activist campaign with its own publicity campaign. Companies with a stronger reputation can help mitigate the downsides of being an activists' campaign target by publicizing their own social performance targets of a campaign (McDonnell & King 2013). The company's publicity can defend the merits of the company's actions or cast doubt on the campaign and sponsor's credibility (Chiroleu-Assouline & Lyon 2020). Companies also have resources for negotiating a resolution to the campaign. A company can help an environmental group with its need to satisfy stakeholders' demands for environmental improvements, even without acceding to all the campaign's demands. A company can also help with the environmental group's need for credibility. A company might single out a group or group of activists for praise, extolling their assistance in helping to solve the environmental problem.

Swartz understood the strategic choices Greenpeace had made that lead to the 65,000 angry emails. Greenpeace's Amazon email campaign was motivated in part by the quest to sustain itself, which meant choosing the aggressive campaign tactics that its supporters wanted. Swartz later wrote: "There's no question the organization cares about saving rainforests, but it also cares about recruiting new members and collecting membership fees. Making headlines by attacking companies helps it do that ... phone calls and press conferences aren't as sexy as an attack campaign and wouldn't have riled up Greenpeace's member base, which is part of what drives its revenue" (Swartz 2010: 42). Greenpeace did not have a reputation for working cooperatively with companies. In 2014, US sustainability executives ranked Greenpeace's credibility as the seventh worst among thirty major environmental groups, according to a Greenbiz survey (Davies 2014: 43).

Greenpeace picked Timberland as a target for its Amazon campaign and chose a noisy activist protest – "guerrilla tactics" in Swartz's words – for achieving its goals. Swartz clearly felt the sting of Greenpeace's Amazon campaign. The protests and negative publicity harmed the company's brand and threatened its sales. When deciding how to respond to Greenpeace's campaign, Swartz saw a couple of options. He could simply wait out the controversy, pointing out that Timberland's contribution to the problem was minuscule at most and touting Timberland's numerous environmental good works. Nike and Adidas were also Greenpeace targets and surely would take some of the heat. Or, Timberland could simply change its supply chain – it would not be hard to replace the 7 percent of its leather supply that Timberland sourced from Brazil – and tell its customers it was on the right side of the issue. Weighed against its history of social and environmental activism, Timberland's customers and stakeholders would be satisfied if Timberland's leather supply caused no harm to the Amazon.

Swartz would have preferred that Greenpeace started with a cooperative partnership approach from the start. He later wrote:

If Greenpeace wanted to start a dialogue with the footwear industry about how our supply chain might be hurting rain forests, I strongly feel that someone there should have picked up the phone. The organization could have convened the industry's CEOs to talk about these issues and craft a solution – and then held a press conference where it took credit for getting us to address the problem. There isn't one executive in our industry who wouldn't have wanted to be at that press conference. (Swartz 2010: 43)

Timberland may have responded to a cooperative invitation from Greenpeace, and their partnership may have helped improved conditions in the Amazon just as effectively (and perhaps more so). But companies may choose to ignore such invitations, particularly if media attention is scarce. Greenpeace's Amazon campaign certainly attracted Timberland's attention enough for it to take action. In choosing its activist tactics, Greenpeace had little concern about the costs Timberland would face to clean up the supply chain, though it did know that a damaged reputation would be a cost to Timberland. Swartz certainly recognized Greenpeace's calculus. He wrote: "So [Greenpeace] came at us instead [with an activist campaign], leading us to waste a ton of energy fighting a goopy mess rather than making meaningful progress" (Swartz 2010: 42).

8.3.4 Holdup Problems, Credibility, and Activist Campaigns

When an activist campaign does not fizzle out, or the activists otherwise give up, its resolution often ends up as an agreement that the company has met or will meet some portion of the campaign's demands, such as when the company makes specific pledges about how it will meet the campaign's goals. Sometimes there is even a formal written agreement between the company and the environmental group. Consumer boycotts often end with agreements and endorsements from the environmental groups, as we saw with the resolution to Greenpeace's campaign against Timberland and its McDonald's campaign that ended with a tree-hugging Ronald McDonald. Similarly, the Naturewatch Foundation organized a boycott of Natura, the parent company of The Body Shop and other cosmetic companies, to compel the company to stop selling products that had been tested on animals. The campaign ended successfully in 2017 when Natura announced its companies would no longer sell any animal-tested products, and Naturewatch invited The Body Shop and other companies to become endorsed as a "cruelty-free company" (The Naturewatch Foundation 2017).

The credibility challenge for the company is to show the organizers and activists that it will follow up on its terms in the agreement. This may not be as much of a challenge if activists can see the company's actions first hand or the company can otherwise credibly commit to making the environmental improvements. The cost of losing credibility or hurting brand reputation may be enough to hold the company and the environmental group to their promise. Backing out of a deal made in good faith can create doubt about trustworthiness in other areas.

The credibility challenge is often quite difficult – each side may have an incentive to renege on the agreement. The company may revert to its same old environmental practices: the ones that inspired the campaign in the first place. If the environmental group can no longer mobilize a campaign, perhaps because the passage of time has diminished activists' concerns, the company may not face any sanctions for backing out of the deal. The company can have similar fears that the environmental group will back out of the deal and find some reason to renew protests. Some agreements require the company to invest resources to make an environmental improvement, such as buying new equipment for its production processes. These investments are "asset specific" to the extent that they lose value if the company deploys them for other uses (Williamson 1985). Once the company has made asset-specific investments to improve its environmental performance, environmental groups may have an incentive to reignite their campaign and demand yet further environmental improvements. Without the assurance that the company and the environmental group will remain faithful to the deal, neither side may want to reach an agreement in the first place. It can be hard to reach a deal if the negotiators lack confidence that the other side will keep to its promises.

Eventually, Swartz reached out to Greenpeace and engaged in discussions about solutions that would appease Greenpeace and its activists. After a month of work, Timberland developed policies to ensure that its leather supply would not come from rainforest-cleared land. Timberland then worked with Greenpeace to ensure that other apparel companies would adopt similar practices as well, aiming to improve conditions in the Amazon and help ensure that Timberland was not the only one paying for the supply chain reforms.

Greenpeace responded to Timberland's Amazon supply chain improvement with a press release praising Timberland's leadership and the company's promise to protect the rainforest. The press release stated: "Timberland has raised the bar for environmentally and socially responsible leather sourcing policies in the Amazon" (Greenpeace 2010). The public endorsement was certainly valuable – it helped Timberland improve its standing with stakeholders and customers – even if the value would be difficult for Timberland to precisely detail in increased sales or lower costs. Swartz returned the favor, stating, "Greenpeace has done an outstanding job gathering data, creating a complete and compelling case for the issue, and mobilizing its tens of thousands of supporters. Their effort has driven change into the system. We applaud their activism" (Swartz 2010: 43). Swartz's statement showed Greenpeace's supporters that their activism, and Greenpeace's leadership, together contributed to a successful and credible environmental improvement.

8.4 Partnerships between Companies and Environmental Groups

A green partnership is a formal or informal collaboration between a business and an environmental group launched with an objective to improve environmental outcomes jointly (Brewer et al. 2013). Partnerships between companies and environmental groups have become quite common. It is not surprising when a company with a strong sustainability reputation teams up with a prominent environmental group to advance an environmental cause. Unilever is a consumer products company with a strong environmental reputation. Unilever uses palm oil in many of its food products. As part of its ambitious environmental agenda, Unilever has partnered with the World Wildlife Fund to certify the sustainability of 60,000 hectares of Malaysian forests from which it receives palm oil (Unilever 2020). Sustainability can also sometimes make seemingly strange bedfellows. Dow Chemical, a company whose reputation among environmentalists is less than heroic, teamed up with TNC to build and protect wetlands for its wastewater treatment facility in Freeport, Texas (Max 2014). Most media stories report partnerships that appear to be successes – a company and its partners cooperated to improve environmental conditions in important ways. But partnerships, of course, can fail to deliver their promise and even end up in bitter conflict, with both sides wishing they stayed home from the beginning.

8.4.1 Environmental Problems for Partnerships

Like activist campaigns, partnerships involve an environmental cause, the environmental improvement to be achieved, and a partner environmental group that engages the company to produce it. Environmental groups engaging in partnerships target environmental problems with specific features. First, the problem is one that can be solved through a partnership, usually between a single company and a single group. This means the environmental problem is typically narrower, with a harm the company has a direct hand in producing. Second, the problem is one that can be solved in a manner the environmental group's supporters will find credible. This requires that there be a clear way to show that the partnership provided environmental improvement. As we have seen, some environmental groups specialize in pragmatic solutions to environmental problems, which they often look to achieve through partnerships with companies. The Environmental Defense Fund, for example, has a long-running partnership with McDonald's. For these groups, specialization helps create a reputation that feeds further pragmatic partnerships. Donors and supporters come to trust that the group's partnerships deliver results. Groups that engage in partnerships tend to attract supporters with a pragmatic mindset: those who focus more on the group's results rather than the means it uses to produce them. Businesses trust that the group will be a cooperative partner who promotes the win–win spirit of the partnership.

The environmental goods produced through green partnerships can run the gamut of environmental improvements. A partnership may aim to improve the company's products, such as by reducing the impact of product packaging or improving its recyclability. The partnership may clean up the company's supply chain, perhaps by improving suppliers' environmental performance or helping the company switch to lower-impact inputs. The partnership can focus on the problem – production processes that are environmentally benign in one location may turn out to be problematic in another location where the company is opening a new facility. For example, water-intensive processes may cause greater environmental harm in arid regions than in rainier locales.

When assessing the costs of environmental improvements, a company naturally tends to focus on the costs it would pay to make the improvement itself or how much it would have to pay for the resources and expertise to help produce the improvement. Partnerships with environmental groups provide opportunities to lower these costs. For now, it is worth noting that a company's assessment of its environmental impacts and costs for improvements should consider the cost of acquiring inputs under diverse scenarios, particularly its potential environmental group partners.

8.4.2 Demand and Partnerships: Environmental Groups and Their Stakeholders

Environmental groups participate in partnerships with businesses to fulfill their objectives – producing environmental goods while capturing value to sustain themselves. In a partnership, an environmental group can receive value from the partnering business, perhaps from supporters who make financial donations. Thus, similar to analyzing stakeholder demand for activist campaigns, analyzing stakeholder demand for partnerships requires looking at both the environmental groups and their supporters.

The environmental group must choose a combination of company and environmental problems that will motivate its stakeholders. Environmental improvements with broad and diffuse benefits can have a large number of weakly motivated stakeholders. Conversely, when a partnership produces environmental benefits that are large but narrowly focused, the key stakeholder group can be small but highly motivated. In general, it is easier for an environmental group to receive value from a smaller, highly motivated group than from a broader but less motivated stakeholder group. When a partnership produces an environmental improvement with broad but shallower benefits to stakeholders, it may be more challenging to capture value from stakeholders.

On the company side, more visible companies allow environmental groups to leverage public opinion to pressure a company into the partnership. But broad visibility may not always be necessary. In some cases, a company faces an environmental problem that motivates a small but highly influential group of stakeholders. The stakeholder group may hold significant leverage over the company, blocking its expansion into new markets or disrupting its operations. Perhaps the company's operations threaten local water systems, giving rise to stiff community resistance. A company in such circumstances may welcome an environmental group partnership that can help resolve its stakeholder conflict and solve the environmental problem.

8.4.3 *Partnerships and Channels for Capturing Value*

A partnership is more likely to produce benefits for participants when it is grounded on a clear understanding of what resources each side can contribute, how these resources can be combined to produce an environmental good, and how the environment and the participants can all benefit from the partnership. Each partner contributes resources to the joint endeavor. These can be tangible resources, like money, goods, and services, or intangible resources like expertise on how to produce the environmental outcome or credibility that the project's environmental improvements are genuine. Sometimes resource contributions are financial, particularly from companies, but quite often nonfinancial contributions are more important (Dahan et al. 2010).

Partnerships between environmental groups and businesses can take different forms. Simple partnerships are arm's-length relationships where resources are exchanged in a direct quid pro quo. Such transactions may spell out each side's contributions and responsibilities, sometimes with contractual precision. Here are some examples of the forms that these collaborations can take:

- *Philanthropic support.* A company donates money or material resources to an environmental group. Donations to the nonprofit can either come through an employee giving program or directly through the corporate philanthropy division.
- *Board service.* Company leadership serves on the board of the environmental group. The board member can contribute to strategic planning and fundraising efforts. Board members are often expected or required to make significant charitable contributions.
- *Employee volunteer programs.* Company employees are encouraged or subsidized to volunteer for the environmental group and its programs.
- *Endorsements.* Nonprofits can endorse a company's environmental practices.

Other partnerships are more intensive relationships in which the business and nonprofit work more closely and contribute more sources of different types. Intensive partnerships involve more activities, from identifying environmental problems to implementing solutions. Here are some examples of higher-intensity partnerships:

- *Consulting engagements.* A nonprofit or company may choose to engage the other because of the superb expertise in one area the other has to offer (and perhaps the associated credibility and exposure that may come along with it). For example, for a mining company with operations that conflict with a rare species, a specialized wildlife conservation nonprofit may be the only source of expertise regarding how the company can manage its impact on the species. Similarly, it may be natural for an environmental group working on renewable energy development to engage with cutting-edge renewable energy startups on a consultancy basis to seek guidance on certain technologies.
- *Green certification schemes.* A company may work with an environmental group to develop a certification for environmental practices. A certification scheme may be a stepping stone toward developing a voluntary or regulatory standard for greening an entire industry.

Partnerships can start off narrowly focused and then expand to cover more environmental issues. In 1990, McDonald's and the Environmental Defense Fund worked together to eliminate McDonald's reliance on polystyrene food containers (Environmental Defense Fund 2010; Livesey 1999). Since then, the two organizations have engaged in partnership after partnership. In 2018, for example, the Environmental Defense Fund announced a program that helped McDonald's reduce its food waste by 30 percent (Environmental Defense Fund 2018).

Unlocking the win–win potential of successful partnerships requires identifying synergies that allow each partner to capture more value than they could by working independently. The synergies from an environmental partnership come from the resources each side contributes and how they are combined to produce the environmental good. Synergies may lower the costs of producing the environmental improvement or increase its quality (Austin & Seitanidi 2012a, 2012b). Potential sources of synergies include:

- *Resources resulting from organizational slack.* Organizations often have some resources kept in reserve to be activated when unforeseen events threaten operations (Bourgeois 1981). Businesses and environmental groups may, at least temporarily, contribute such slack to the partnership. Such contributions can lower costs when the organizations have different types of slack resources to contribute.
- *Resources with high fixed costs.* Partners may have cost advantages in contributing resources based on their fixed-cost investments. Costs can be lower when one or both participants contribute resources from sources that have high fixed costs but low marginal costs when deployed to the partnership. A new piece of machinery can be a large initial expense but lowers the cost of additional production units. This means that the owner of the machinery can contribute its products to a partnership at a lower cost.
- *Complementary resources.* Some resources are more productive when used in combination with another resource. For example, resources can be complementary if they lead to economies of scale in production. Such complementary resources lower costs and improve productivity. An employee of an environmental group may have expertise that, when applied to the company's machinery and production processes, makes them more efficient and less polluting.
- *Nonrivalrous resource and network effects.* For some resources, consumption does not diminish quality once they are produced (Ostrom 1990). For example, a stakeholder "consumes" an environmental group's reputation when she uses it to infer the credibility of the group's claims. The reputation remains available for other stakeholders to consume (Prakash & Potoski 2007). In some cases, there may be network effects in which one person's consumption of a good actually increases its value to others. For example, social media platforms like LinkedIn and Facebook are valuable because so many other people use them.

8.4.3.1 Partnerships' Contributions and Benefits

Companies often partner with environmental groups as part of their environmental strategy. In a partnership, synergies arise from the combination of resources each side contributes and the value each side receives in return. A company can contribute financial resources by directly paying the group for its partnership participation. The environmental group often contributes nonfinancial value. A 2011 partnership between Dow Chemical and TNC in Freeport, Texas provides an example. Dow Chemical supported the partnership financially, including payments to TNC, along with some substantial environmental problems TNC could help improve. Dow Chemical, after all, was not known for its sustainability achievements. For its part, TNC contributed technical expertise and advice on how the company could reduce its environmental impacts in financially beneficial ways. In addition to its advice on wetlands protection, TNC also advised Dow Chemical on how to reduce local ozone pollution levels so that they no longer exceeded regulatory limits. Instead of installing a smokestack scrubber at its Freeport facility, Dow Chemical could instead reduce smog by planting a thousand trees (Max 2014). In Section 8.4.3.2, we first look at common resources that partnership participants can contribute. We then look at the different types of benefits partnerships can produce.

8.4.3.2 Contributions

The environmental problem and credit. The company provides an important "resource" to the partnership by providing an environmental problem that the partnership will solve. From the perspective of an environmental group, the environmental problem is a resource because it needs solvable environmental problems to garner resources from stakeholders. If the problem is solved through a partnership with the business, the group can credibly claim an important role in solving the problem. It can tell its stakeholders, "look, the company had this environmental problem until we partnered with them to fix it. Therefore, we really are the ones who deserve all the credit."

Claiming credit for having produced an environmental solution can sometimes be nonrivalrous. Both the environmental group and the company can each claim to its own stakeholders that it has produced the environmental good. One side's claim may not interfere with the other's claim if their stakeholder groups do not overlap. Such credit claiming may help explain why activist campaigns are often resolved with a collaborative partnership between the targeted company and the organizing environmental group – each can look to claim credit with its own stakeholders for solving the environmental problem.

Technical expertise. Specialized knowledge particular to the environmental group or the business can lower the cost of producing the

environmental improvement, thus contributing to the value the partnership creates. As they conduct their operations over time, an organization can develop specialized knowledge and skills (Lam 2000).
Such knowledge can be valuable when applied in domains outside the
organization but can be difficult to convey to others who might want
to use it for themselves.

Environmental groups can have strategic capabilities, often with
highly technical expertise, in the environmental areas of their focus.
Environmental groups may have special expertise in mitigating the
damage from pollution, restoring species' habitat, and managing
water systems. Perhaps less obviously, environmental groups can also
have technical expertise in areas such as communications and public
relations. They may know how to identify key environmental stakeholders and their needs. These skills can focus on specific environmental problems, like science communication around climate change
or working with community groups. Greenpeace has a stronger presence among more left-leaning environmental activists, while Ducks
Unlimited works with hunters.

Companies can similarly have substantial expertise to contribute to
partnerships. A company will certainly know their own production
processes and inputs and how customers use their products. A company's employees may have highly technical science and engineering
expertise that can be deployed to address an environmental problem.
Businesses can also offer basic management expertise, like project and
financial management, operations, and legal issues.

Reputation. An environmental group can contribute its reputation to the partnership by endorsing the environmental benefit the
partnership achieves. As nonprofits, environmental groups have an
obvious source of credibility and legitimacy – people believe in nonprofits' commitment to the public causes because they are legally
prohibited from distributing residual profits to private shareholders. The company's stakeholders are more likely to believe the partnership's environmental improvements are genuine when a credible
environmental group endorses them. The credibility boost of such
endorsements may be particularly effective when the company's
reputation is weaker and the environmental group's reputation is
stronger (Irmak et al. 2015). An environmental group's endorsement
can provide credibility at a lower cost than a company could achieve
on its own.

8.4.3.3 Benefits

Just as the resources contributed to an environmental partnership can include financial and nonfinancial benefits, the value a company receives from the partnership can take various forms. A partnership may lower a company's operating costs. In 2008, the Environmental Defense Fund helped Poland Springs reduce its fuel costs (and greenhouse gas emissions) by implementing a company program that monitored drivers and created incentives for them to reduce engine-idling time. The program saved $20,000 in fuel savings for Poland Springs while eliminating seventy-seven tons of greenhouse gas emissions (Environmental Defense Fund 2014). However, such savings are often not enough to cover the company's costs for producing the environmental improvement, even with contributions from the partnering environmental group. The company must look to other sources of value to offset the costs.

A successful partnership may yield an environmental improvement that the company can present to stakeholders, thus creating an opportunity for the company to capture value in return. Consumers may react positively to an environmental partnership (Irmak et al. 2015), boosting the company's brand and perhaps its sales. Such brand benefits can be more salient when the company sells consumer products, the partnership is highly publicized, and the environmental issue has a broad stakeholder base. Even with these ideal circumstances, though, capturing stakeholder value can be challenging. Very rarely are there market channels to facilitate the value transfer. The stakeholders who receive the environmental benefit may not purchase products from the company or sell goods and services to the company.

Companies can also look to capture value from stakeholders through nonmarket channels. Stakeholders may hold sufficient political clout to revoke a company's social license to operate. For example, a partnership with the World Wildlife Fund helped Coca-Cola to reestablish its social license to operate in India, as we saw in Chapter 3. With a precisely crafted environmental improvement, a partnership can provide a low-cost path to improving the company's relations with small but influential stakeholder groups. A smaller group of local stakeholders can bring their cause to broader attention. Finally, a partnership with an environmental group can insulate the company from being a target of future environmental activism (Odziemkowska & McDonnell 2019).

8.4.4 Credibility and Partnerships

Partnerships are at risk of holdup problems. Each partner has its own goals, and each may contribute resources to the partnership that are at risk if the other side does not uphold the deal. In the early 1990s, Greenpeace and a small German appliance company named Foron formed an alliance to develop new refrigerator models that did not use ozone-depleting chemicals such as Freon (Stafford et al. 2000). Greenpeace helped Foron with the technology and the promise of a financial return from 70,000 customers who said they would buy the new refrigerators (Morgan 2018). Foron started selling refrigerators that were more environmentally friendly in 1993. They were an environmental and financial success. However, the partnership had a tension – Greenpeace's goal was to protect the ozone layer, which meant distributing the refrigeration technology to other appliance companies, while Foron had a competitive advantage in exclusively selling refrigerators that consumers wanted. Greenpeace quickly moved to share the Freon-free technology with other appliance manufacturers.

The Greenpeace partnership did not rescue Foron. Its market advantage disappeared as larger manufacturers copied its recipe for success, and it soon went out of business (King 2007). For Greenpeace, the outcome was less clear. Greenpeace enjoyed short-run success in advancing the ozone technology as it soon became widely used in the industry. Greenpeace could tout this accomplishment to its stakeholders (Morgan 2018). But this episode may also have hurt Greenpeace's reputation as a cooperative partner for businesses, making them less likely to work with Greenpeace in the future.

A solution to the holdup problem is for companies and environmental groups to codify their agreement in a legally binding contract. If either side backs out of their contribution, the other side can ask the court to enforce the agreement. A community benefit agreement (CBA) is a legally binding contract in which a company promises to produce some social good, and the community groups provide some value in return, such as accepting and promoting the company's social license to operate. Some Canadian mining companies, for example, have entered into CBA contracts with indigenous groups living near their mines (Dorobantu & Odziemkowska 2017; Odziemkowska & Dorobantu 2020). In the CBA, the groups consented to the mines' operation or expansion, and the companies agreed to provide value to the groups, such as by paying for local infrastructure, ice-skating rinks, hiring, and so on (Dorobantu & Odziemkowska 2017). These agreements codify these agreements codify costs borne by the company, in return, the company benefits from avoiding the disruption that community protests can cause. Likewise, the community benefits from knowing that the contract requires the company to produce its promised benefits. Beyond mining, CBAs are used in areas where companies make large asset-specific investments, such as real estate (Cain 2014) and onshore wind energy (Cowell et al. 2011).

Successful partnerships can build trust and help participants establish reputations for being cooperative partners. Success signals to other prospective partners that the company or environmental group will not take advantage of holdup opportunities. Such reputations can help constrain partnership participants from exploiting the holdup problem for their own advantage and at their partner's expense (King 2007). Environmental groups may be reluctant to partner with companies that have reputations for acting in bad faith and may even target them for activist campaigns. And, as we saw with Greenpeace and Foron, environmental groups exploiting the holdup problem may lose their credibility as cooperative partners. A company and an environmental group may choose to engage in a lower-intensity partnership with the hope that it grows into a higher-intensity partnership. For example, to test the waters for a collaboration, a company might consider inviting an environmental group to host an Earth Day event to begin building relations and plant seeds for further collaborations.

8.5 Conclusion

Activist campaigns and partnerships with environmental groups are important nonmarket components of an environmental strategy. Activist campaigns pose risks for companies. Campaigns can impose significant costs by harming a company's reputation, reducing sales, and disrupting operations and supply chains. The company does not choose the environmental problem under attack, the groups that organize the campaign, or the terrain on which the campaign will be addressed. While understanding that environmental harms and risks can shed light on what might attract the attention of campaign organizers and thus allow the company to take preventive measures, in the end, there is no sure-fire way to ensure the campaigns do not happen.

Once targeted for a campaign, taking stock of a company's resources can help prepare a strategy to respond to the campaign's demands.

A company considering an environmental partnership needs to identify the types of environmental and private values to produce through the partnership. An effective partnership targets a problem whose improvement benefits both parties, has a clear and specific agreement about what each partner will contribute, and understands how the partnership will create synergies and benefit both parties. An effective partnership is based on both sides having confidence that the other will make their promised contributions. Like any investment decision, a partnership needs to be designed and executed strategically, with an eye toward the company's strengths and weaknesses and its market and nonmarket context. What types of values will the partnership produce, and how can the company capture part of those values? Not every company would see noticeable improvements in its brand image or standing among stakeholders by doing good environmental activities, though there may be other benefits, such as improved efficiency.

Jeff Swartz's 2009 experience with Timberland reinforces a lesson about nonmarket stakeholders: a company may not be able to choose its nonmarket stakeholders, and it cannot always define the precise nature of its interactions with them. Swartz did not want the Greenpeace campaign, but Greenpeace saw the protest as an opportunity. Nonetheless, Swartz was able to develop a response that identified the environmental problem at the core of the controversy and met the demands of the important stakeholders: Greenpeace and its members. In the end, with Greenpeace's help, Swartz sought to set use the improvements in its supply chain as an opportunity to pressure Timberland's competitors to improve their practices as well, thereby helping not only Timberland's bottom line but also important Amazonian ecosystems.

9 | Conclusion

Bill Bowerman and Phil Knight started making running shoes for elite athletes in the 1960s, and together they founded the athletic apparel company that would become what we know today as Nike. From the beginning, the founders sought to create innovative shoes to meet athletes' needs, epitomized most famously in the early 1970s when Bowerman used his wife's waffle iron to develop running shoe soles with better traction. Nike's business model combined innovative design, low-cost, independent manufacturing, and sports star–driven consumer marketing to bring athletic apparel to elite athlete and consumer markets. For example, in 1978, Nike introduced air-cushioned soles in a limited-edition running shoe, called the Tailwind, and sent 250 of them to a few local retailers ahead of the Hawai'ian marathon. Nike went on to introduce air-cushioned soles in many of its other shoes, notably the iconic Air Max running shoes and Air Jordan basketball shoes (Nike 2019).

Over the following decades, Nike expanded product offerings to include other apparel items as it grew into a multi-billion-dollar shoe and apparel behemoth. The Nike "swoosh" symbol was recognized around the world. Nike's global brand and changing public expectations put the company under a higher level of scrutiny for its CSR practices. In the 1990s, Nike came under criticism from labor activists for unfair labor practices at some international suppliers and producers' factories. A series of high-profile protests and boycotts targeting Nike risked alienating customers and threatened Nike's important alliances with US universities and their athletic programs. Speaking to the National Press Club, Nike CEO Phil Knight acknowledged the threat: "the Nike product has become synonymous with slave wages, forced overtime, and arbitrary abuse" (quoted in Henderson et al. 2009). Nike hired its first vice president for corporate responsibility in 1998. In 2001, Nike established a board-level Corporate Responsibility Committee to oversee its labor, environmental, and community affairs activities and soon after published its first corporate responsibility report.

In the early 2000s, Nike expanded the focus of its social responsibility programs to include environmental sustainability and environmental issues. Instead of reacting to activists' protests as it had with labor issues, Nike's environmental specialists started collaborative processes with other units within the company, including its product design team. Their aim was to identify and solve environmental problems before they blossomed into public relations troubles.[1] Hannah Jones, Nike's vice president of sustainable business and innovation, saw how Nike's labor lessons could inform its strategy for environmental issues. As she later told Harvard Business School case researchers: "I realized that you can either solve a worker's rights issue by monitoring every single factory 24 hours a day for whether they're wearing personal protective equipment, or you can innovate a new glue that removes all the toxics so you don't have to have the personal protective equipment" (Paine et al. 2013: 7).

Jones and Nike's senior executives realized the company needed strategies to manage CSR risks in its supply chain and to improve its CSR brand image. In 2005, Nike introduced the Considered Boot for both men and women, priced at $110 a pair. The Considered Boot was Nike's response to consumer demand for a more environmentally sustainable shoe. At the same time, it represented Nike's efforts to get out in front of sustainability issues after spending a decade playing defense in response to public concerns about its labor practices.[2]

From its outward appearance, the Considered Boot certainly signaled a change in direction for Nike. Most Nike shoes come in bright, clean colors and sleek styling that signals a shoe designed for high-performance athletes. The Considered Boot looked very different. The boot's upper part included a long string of hemp, woven into a grid and sewn into the shoe's leather parts, which were visibly sewn to the

[1] Nike's sustainability practices have been described in several case studies (Carroll et al. 2013; Henderson et al. 2009; Paine et al. 2013).
[2] In 2009, Nike released the "Trash Talk" basketball shoe in partnership with NBA star Steve Nash, a committed environmentalist. The Trash Talk was made with recycled materials and used many Considered materials and production practices. The Trash Talk, which apparently never captured another nickname, was produced in limited quantities and sold in a few stores in New Orleans and New York.

sole. This rugged, hand-sewn look aimed to signal that these were sustainable shoes. They were made with more sustainable materials and were assembled with little glue or adhesives to be more easily disassembled for repair and recycling. The Considered Boot's manufacturing processes produced less waste, required less energy, and yielded fewer waste by-products (Industrial Designers Society of America 2010). For the first time in its history of making shoes, Nike was offering a green product.

The Considered Boot's design was as admired as it was environmentally sound. The Industrial Designers Society of America recognized the boots with a Gold Industrial Design Excellence recognition and a Best in Show award at its 2010 annual showcase. The award announcement praised Nike's design achievements: "The Nike Considered Boot is a performance shoe that combines subtle styling with unique environmental benefits without sacrificing Nike's commitment to design innovation" (Industrial Designers Society of America 2010). But Nike's Considered Boot did not catch on with consumers – one critic derisively called the walking boots "Air Hobbits." Sales were tepid and Nike quietly removed the Considered Boot from its product offerings.

The Considered Boot was part of a broader Nike program aimed at creating procedures and practices to embed sustainability into the design and manufacturing of Nike's mainstream shoes and apparel products. Nike produced a series of measurement tools to help designers measure the products' impacts of Nike's products as they were being designed and redesigned. The scores from each tool were aggregated into the Considered Index, which measured products' environmental performance along multiple dimensions. This internal Nike system then awarded points for achieving higher sustainability levels in materials, solvents, and waste, plus extra points for innovation. Nike's sustainability team began working with its product development teams to help them use the Considered Index even earlier in design processes.

In 2008, Nike announced that its Air Jordan basketball shoes had been produced with input from the Considered Index and used Considered Design Principles. Mr. Jordan was impressed, telling Nike brand managers, "I want all my shoes made this way" (Henderson et al. 2009: 2). Nike began to lay out goals and timelines for meeting Considered Index standards in all its consumer products. In 2010, Nike publicly released the "Considered Design Tool," a software program to help other companies – and perhaps vigilant environmental NGOs – report and monitor the environmental issues in supply chains throughout the apparel industry (Nike 2010).

Nike's experience with its Considered Boot suggests that even well-planned environmental initiatives may fail to deliver their financial promise. On the other hand, Nike has continued its Considered Design practices, using measurement and standards to steadily increase its apparel's environmental features. What explains the difference in Nike's response to its Considered Boot and its Considered Design Principles? Why did it let the boots fall by the wayside while it continued to study sustainable design and manufacturing practices and implement them quietly in so many of its consumer product offerings?

9.1 Environmental Strategy Overview

When a company adopts and manages an effective sustainability initiative, the value created is healthy for the planet's ecosystems, the company's stakeholders, and its own bottom line: what we have been calling the triple bottom line (Elkington 2018). An environmental strategy answers the question, "how can we improve our environmental performance in ways that enhance the long-term value of the company?" This book proposes a strategic framework for how companies can create and capture value by improving their environmental performance. The framework is based on the idea that a company's environmental impacts are negative externalities and are thus opportunities for value-enhancing environmental improvements. The company reduces its production of negative environmental externalities, and stakeholders respond by bestowing it with financial and nonfinancial value. Bringing these exchanges to fruition requires overcoming transaction costs: search and screening costs grounded in not knowing opportunities and stakeholders, bargaining and transfer costs that stem from the challenges of collective goods and nonfinancial value exchange, and monitoring and enforcement costs that arise from insufficient credibility about the terms of the exchange.

The components of an environmental strategy help companies identify the environmental improvements and their costs, the stakeholders that value them, and how to structure the value of environmental improvements. The steps may give the impression that creating an environmental strategy involves a rigid work-step sequence. As is often the case with such frameworks, and as the case studies suggest, considerable judgment and flexibility are required. For example, environmental initiatives that cost little or nothing do not require detailed environmental impact analysis. Firms that have the power to pass costs on to suppliers may not need to quantify the benefits of environmental initiatives with great precision. Companies threatened by environmental activists often choose to address the immediate threat, but had they earlier stepped back and conducted a thorough environmental impact study, they may have identified and addressed a deeper source of the activists' complaints.

Table 9.1 distills the processes described in this book into key questions that companies must answer to develop an effective environmental strategy.

In each of these areas, companies confront questions and challenges toward developing an environmental strategy that delivers on the promise of environmental improvements. Throughout this book, we have seen how Coasian exchanges, coupled with a focus on mitigating transaction costs, can be the foundations for a framework on corporate environmental strategy. There are circumstances where these challenges are more severe and perhaps insurmountable – even Nike's considerable marketing talents could not ensure efficient sales for the Considered Boot.

The goal of an environmental strategy is to identify environmental improvements that also increase revenues, lower costs, or manage risks, helping companies achieve the promise of environmental improvements. Chapters 3–5 described a framework for how companies can identify these opportunities, using transaction costs theory to identify the challenges that must be overcome to realize those opportunities. There must also be sufficient and adequate stakeholder demand for the improvement, channels for transferring value from the stakeholders to the company, and credibility to ensure the company and stakeholders will uphold their obligations in the deal. A sustainability initiative may fail to generate triple bottom line value if any of these problems remain unsolved. Chapters 6–8 respectively apply the strategic framework to market, employee relations, and NGO relations.

Not every environmental improvement is successful, even if the improvement can be achieved with manageable costs and stakeholders demand it. A goal of this book is to help scholarship on business and sustainability study when and how companies' sustainability

Table 9.1 *Environmental strategy framework*

Environmental strategy elements	Key questions	Potential work steps
Identifying which dimensions of environmental performance improvements can create business value	What alternatives do we have to reduce our environmental impact? What environmental benefits do they produce? What are their costs? Which stakeholders value environmental improvements? How might those stakeholders affect the value of our business?	Evaluate the life cycle impact of products and services on the environment Generate alternatives Identify stakeholders, their demands for environmental improvement, and their resources for influence Evaluate how stakeholders will perceive the impact of the potential initiatives Evaluate the risk of being targeted by NGOs and activists
Ensuring channel for value transfer	What mechanisms are available for transferring value?	Identify market or nonmarket channels to ensure the flow of resources back to the company
Ensuring credibility	How can we communicate the impact of our environmental initiatives to stakeholders in a credible way?	Produce "costly signals" of quality Evaluate the risk of charges of "greenwashing"
Capturing value from environmental improvements	Does the environmental improvement contribute to competitive advantage?	Evaluate opportunities to create or leverage market power to capture benefits or pass on costs to others Evaluate alignment of environmental strategy with competitive strategy and competitive advantage

Table 9.1 *(cont.)*

Environmental strategy elements	Key questions	Potential work steps
Engaging institutions	Would changes in the institutional context facilitate the achievement of environmental goals?	How do institutions influence the distribution of costs and benefits from environmental improvements? How do these costs and benefits influence other stakeholders' incentives for institutional change

improvements are successful. For example, the transaction cost obstacles to Coasian exchanges influence the conditions under which an environmental improvement can generate environmental and business value. Even when a transaction cost obstacle is higher, a company may possess a resource that can lower the cost of overcoming it. Identifying and measuring the transaction cost obstacles, along with companies' resources for overcoming them, can help advance scholarship on when companies' environmental improvements will be successful.

Environmental improvements are more likely to be successful when the company can easily identify external stakeholders and the stakeholders have strong demand for the environmental improvements the company can deliver. For Glassman's employee engagement programs at TD Bank, the stakeholders were the bank's employees, particularly younger employees. Glassman could easily learn about what these employees wanted through direct interaction and TD Bank's employee surveys. Swartz faced a clear and forceful set of stakeholder demands because Greenpeace had successfully mobilized stakeholders into vocal activists. We also saw in this book examples where the company was unable to accurately gauge stakeholder demand. Prior to the protest, Timberland's environmental issues, and stakeholders' potential concerns about them, were obscured in the depths of its supply chain. Coca-Cola's water troubles in Kerala, India stemmed in part from its misunderstanding of the local water system and residents' dependence on it.

Companies sometimes have relatively easy access to effective channels for transferring value. This can also help companies implement successful environmental improvements. Stonyfield could capture financial returns from its consumers by selling organic yogurt in retail outlets, from specialty natural food stores to supermarkets. Nike's Considered Design Principles contributed to its nonmarket strategy and thereby facilitated an indirect channel for value capture. The principles made it easier for stakeholders to compare Nike's environmental practices to those of its competitors. Nike anticipated that stakeholders would then pressure its competitors to improve their performance to the levels Nike had already achieved, thereby helping Nike's competitive position by raising its competitors' costs.

In some cases, there are no easy ways to capture value from environmental improvements. Many of the world's largest companies have publicly pronounced greenhouse gas reduction programs, including some with ambitious and measurable goals (Gelles & Sengupta 2020). But overall, the results have generally fallen far short of the rhetoric (Eavis & Krauss 2021). One explanation is the challenges companies face in capturing value from their stakeholders. In the aggregate, there maybe plenty of stakeholders who demand the improvements at least to some degree, but they are spread out and do not have any easy way to transfer value back to the companies. Microsoft, for example, is struggling to meet its ambitious and detailed timeline to become carbon negative by 2030. Part of the problem is that costs have not fallen as rapidly as anticipated, though costs would not be such a concern if Microsoft could capture more of the value its reductions produce. Lucas Joppa, Microsoft's chief environmental officer, suggested that the incentives from such voluntary initiatives would not be enough to solve the problem. He said, "if we are going to achieve a net-zero carbon economy for real, we will need everyone to act. And that means action can't be voluntary. We need requirements and standards that everyone is expected to meet" (quoted in Eavis & Krauss 2021).

The cost of ensuring credibility can also vary across circumstances. In Stonyfield's early years, Hirshberg struggled to convey his yogurt's sustainability features. "Organic" was not a term people readily understood and terms like "all-natural" did not precisely distinguish Stonyfield's yogurt from its competitors' offerings. Stonyfield's marketing efforts, and Hirshberg's supermarket aisle sales pitches, needed to spend more time educating consumers. Years later, circumstances had changed such that it was easier for companies to establish credibility for their environmental features. Organic certification was well established and recognized, and many consumers understood the meaning of Stonyfield's additional sustainability features, like its support of local dairy farmers.

Companies may also possess resources that help overcome the costs and capture value from their environmental improvements. An important resource is the ability to share information and expertise across organizational boundaries within the company. With her broad training and expertise, Glassman could speak the languages of finance, operations, and human resources to managers working in those areas across TD Bank. By translating her engagement programs to terms understandable among diverse audiences, Glassman received broad organizational acceptance, which helped her program succeed. When Stonyfield was aiming to expand its yogurt sales to national supermarket chains, it found it lacked expertise in the types of marketing and promotions such stores required. Its merger with Danone helped provide the expertise it needed to sell organic yogurt more broadly.

Institutions such as government regulations, industry associations, and a company's social license to operate influence the costs and benefits of environmental improvements. Huawei's efforts to improve social and environmental performance in its own supply chain were aided by the JAC's programs to organize standards and audits throughout the telecommunications industry. Understanding the distribution of these costs and benefits can help identify opportunities for institutional change and potential participants to engage in collective action to the make the institutional change happen.

This book aims to make several contributions. First, it presents a framework to help identify the opportunities and challenges for any company looking to manage its environmental performance. The opportunity lies in capturing a portion of the value created through its environmental improvements. The challenges stem from transaction cost obstacles such as incomplete information and property rights, holdup problems, and search and screening costs. The book shows that these problems are not unique to environmental strategy but appear in other areas as well, including competitive strategy. Many of the tools available for solving core business problems are thus available for overcoming the obstacles to a successful environmental strategy. Just as a company needs to convince consumers about the superior quality of its products, so to must it assure stakeholders about the superior quality of its environmental performance.

The framework can also help guide scholarly research. The framework highlights the range of factors that can influence a company's choices about its environmental performance:

- The company's own resources, capabilities, and competitive strategy.
- Exogenous factors such as the degree to which stakeholders can accurately assess a company's environmental improvements, the distribution of the costs and benefits of environmental improvements, and the improvements' financial costs.
- The institutional environment, including the strength of market and nonmarket stakeholders and the institutions that shape the distribution of environmental costs and benefits.

The framework connects these factors to concepts widely used throughout the social sciences, and the book's case studies shows how they can be grounded in real-world research settings. The framework then allows for more integrated research across a range of questions.

For example, a key research question in this area is on whether companies can increase profits through their environmental performance. The literature so far has not converged on a clear conclusion, most likely because there is not a simple answer that applies to all companies, for all environmental improvements, in all settings. Future research on businesses' sustainability strategies and practices can draw on this book's framework to investigate how these different factors, and interactions among them, influence the success of companies' environmental performance.

9.2 Nike, Environmental Apparel, Production, and Design

What alternatives do we have to reduce our environmental impact? To develop alternatives, a company first needs to understand its impact on the environment. Identifying a company's opportunities for environmental improvements should begin with an assessment of its environmental impacts, from inputs, through production, to product use and disposal. An environmental strategy also needs to estimate the costs of achieving these impacts.

Nike knew it needed to assess its environmental impacts across the life cycle of its product. After all, Nike had seen that controversy about its labor practices stemmed from issues at factories deep in its supply chain and therefore wanted to identify potential supply chain environmental problems. Among Nike's options, it could develop a new green product line, and it would build programs to embed greener production practices into its conventional products. Both its Considered Boot and Considered Index were developed using the principles of life cycle analysis to take into account the full range of potential environmental impacts and improvements. While they did not last long in consumer markets, Nike's Considered Boot generated innovative ways that Nike could improve the environmental features of its shoes. These lessons were instrumental to the Considered Index and Nike's later programs for sustainable apparel design and production. The product teams responsible for apparel design, manufacturing, and marketing were responsible for assessing the costs and business case for the environmental improvements.

What is our stakeholders' demand for these environmental impacts and improvements? To understand how different alternatives might affect stakeholders, a company has to identify stakeholders and understand what they care about. Companies do not always know how stakeholders will respond to an environmental problem or improvement. Environmental NGOs, local community groups, and other stakeholders can help companies understand the environmental issues that concern them.

Nike's sustainability efforts identified both market and nonmarket stakeholders. Research suggested there was a market segment of consumers willing to pay for shoes with environmental features. Nike's Considered Boot appeared to be in a promising position when it was introduced to the market, though the shoes ended up not selling well. Nike also anticipated significant nonmarket stakeholder demand for environmental improvements in the apparel industry, with activists becoming more concerned about the environmental harms generated in the company's supply chains. NGOs like Greenpeace were closely studying companies' supply chains and, as we saw with Timberland in Chapter 8, were ready to launch protests when they found the opportunity. Nonmarket stakeholders could mobilize activists' labor protests at Nike stores and with students at US colleges and universities where Nike had important business ties. Nike adjusted its environmental strategy to focus on the nonmarket stakeholders where demand for improvements was strongest.

What are the mechanisms for transferring value? Stakeholders can influence the value of a company, both positively and negatively. To assess stakeholders' potential impacts, a company needs to understand stakeholders' sources of leverage and how they can influence the company. Different stakeholders have different access to market and nonmarket channels through which the company can capture value. Attractive environmental improvements are those for which other people pay and from which the firm can capture some of the value. Other environmental improvements include creating value through reducing costs and risks, improving the company's social license to operate, or raising competitors' costs.

For Nike's Considered Boot, there appeared to be a ready channel for value transfer: Nike would use its regular market channels to sell sustainable shoes to the consumers willing to pay for them. The shoes might appeal to customers who would not otherwise purchase Nikes for their hiking boot needs. But when consumer demand turned out to be weak, Nike pivoted to target nonmarket stakeholders. While the 2008 Air Jordan basketball shoes received favorable press coverage for their sustainable design features, they were not directly marketed to consumers as a green consumer product. The Considered Index and design principles contributed to Nike's nonmarket strategy, where Nike's legacy of labor issues remained a burden. The Considered Design Principles aimed to show NGOs that Nike was an emerging sustainability leader in the apparel industry, thereby helping to fend off boycotts and protests such as those that arose from NGOs' concerns about labor practices and policies in Nike's supply chain. Nike's public release of the Considered Index had a strategic component: the index would help NGOs evaluate the sustainability practices of Nike's competitors, many of whom might struggle to match the sustainability practices that Nike had developed in-house for its own apparel and production processes.

The Considered Index could contribute to a nonmarket strategy that improved Nike's competitive position by raising rivals' costs. Now that Nike had raised its own costs in response to stakeholder pressures, it was in Nike's interest to share the technology with its competitors and to let its competitors' stakeholders know that those environmental improvements were available to all companies in the industry, therefore putting more pressure on the other companies to make these costly improvements as well. A Nike manager explained the company's willingness to share its water-based adhesives with competitors. Nike had created water-based adhesives in response to stakeholder pressures to improve the sustainability of its products and manufacturing products. These adhesives were an environmental improvement because they reduced volatile organic compounds during production. "We shared it with industry because our competitive advantage isn't in how the shoes are bonded. [It] is in how they are engineered, how they're designed, how they perform" (Paine et al. 2013: 12). Though Nike invested time and resources to improve its environmental practices, spreading this knowledge throughout the industry helped contribute to the company's nonmarket strategy.

How could we communicate the impact of our environmental initiatives to stakeholders in a credible way? To communicate credibly, a company has to find ways to produce "costly signals" of quality. Simply providing examples of environmental initiatives in a corporate sustainability report is unlikely to be credible, as stakeholders may suspect the company can cherry-pick examples at little cost or describe trivial changes in technically true but misleading terms. Reliable measurement systems and external verification can improve credibility.

Nike seemed to have solved the credibility challenge with its Considered Boot. The boot's "rugged look" suggested its sustainability features, and the backing of the Nike brand gave credibility to its sustainability claims. And, of course, the design awards noted the boot's sustainability, further burnishing the credibility of Nike's sustainability claims. If the shoes failed to catch on with consumers, the culprit was not a lack of credibility. Meanwhile, Nike was publicly releasing the Considered Index along with much of what it had learned about designing and producing sustainable apparel. Nike sought credibility through transparency; making public information about the sustainability practices it was using increased its environmental improvement credibility. Nike also made it well known that the Considered Index was publicly available for its competitors to evaluate and improve their own environmental practices. Transparency such as this can improve credibility with stakeholders.

How can we integrate environmental strategy with our broader strategy? An important concept for an environmental strategy is the extent to which an environmental improvement contributes to a company's competitive advantage. A company has a competitive advantage when it can meet customer demand more effectively than its

competitors, either by producing products at a lower cost or by producing products consumers are willing to pay more for, in ways that
are difficult for competitors to imitate over the long run. To evaluate
its ability to capture value from environmental initiatives, a company
needs to assess how its environmental improvements will increase the
company's value over the long run. A company's environmental programs can produce new sources of competitive advantage or reinforce
existing ones.

Nike's experience with its Considered Boot, Considered Index,
and design principles suggest the importance of aligning a company's environmental strategy with its broader competitive strategy.
The Considered Boot was not well aligned with Nike's competitive
strategy. Nike's brand image, carefully cultivated over many years,
promised that its product would offer sleek styling and meet the performance needs of elite athletes, while regular folks could "just do it"
and train like elite athletes. As one product designer explained, "[w]e
try to make designs look cool first, then run it by other filters like cost
and Considered. We design in response to a lot of constraints, like price
and performance requirements, and goals like cool looks and feel"
(quoted in Henderson et al. 2009: 12). Nike's brand set its products
apart from competitors and positioned the company to capture loyal
customers' sales. A consumer looking for high-performance boots was
not likely to see much in the Considered Boot, which appeared more
suitable for a leisurely stroll through the farmers' market. Participants
in a consumer focus group conducted by Nike were receptive to a
sustainable running shoe, but when told of the strengths of its environmental features, they stated their belief that the shoe would not
perform as effectively (Henderson et al. 2009). Consumers looking for
sustainable shoes had plenty of other options, including offerings from
Patagonia, a company with a well-established brand for high-quality
and environmentally sustainable products. In Nike's case, a potential
explanation for the Considered Boot's weak sales is that it didn't align
with Nike's brand image.

Fortunately, the Considered Index and design principles were aligned
with Nike's nonmarket strategy in other areas, particularly with labor
practices among its suppliers. Faced with strong stakeholder pressures
around such practices, Nike shifted its approach in the latter 1990s.
Nike engaged more proactively with activists to identify and fix labor
issues in its supply chain and then would publicly release the results

of its efforts. A goal of this transparency was to raise expectations for its competitors: if Nike could achieve these labor practices, activists could pressure its competitors to do so as well. Publicly releasing the Considered Index and design principles applied this approach to environmental issues: the lower-polluting adhesives Nike was using in its shoes were readily available to its competitors (Winston 2014). Nike could use the Considered Index as it worked with other companies, NGOs, and apparel associations to develop products, reports, and certification standards for the industry. Nike would have a hand in creating the evaluative yardsticks against which it, and its competitors, would be judged.

Nike reorganized its company structure in 2009 to empower those working on its sustainability efforts. For a decade, Phil Knight, Nike's founder and leader, spoke publicly about Nike's ambition to be a leader in labor and sustainability issues. Its board had a permanent corporate responsibility member, and now there was a vice president of sustainability, business, and innovation (SB&I) reporting directly to the CEO. It created what we might call a "senior green team," the Committee on Sustainable Innovation, whose members included the CEO and vice presidents for strategy, design, and marketing. Grounding these initiatives in Nike's formal organizational structure helped signal Nike's commitment to continuing its environmental improvements.

The reorganization also helped Nike channel strategic resources toward its sustainability programs. Nike had considerable expertise in innovative apparel design and production, resources that it dedicated toward designing and producing shoes with leading-edge sustainability features. Nike's Considered Boot had been produced as a separate effort, designed from the sole up by a carefully selected team charged with producing a signature sustainable shoe. Implementation of the Considered Index and design and manufacturing practices were integrated throughout the company. Most Nike products were overseen by three-person teams made up of managers from marketing, production, and design. Members of Nike's SB&I team, many of whom had backgrounds in design, product development, engineering, and the sciences, would work with the product teams to find ways to integrate the Considered principles into the product and its manufacturing. In addition to providing guidance on how to be sustainable, the Considered Index fit with Nike's culture and top management objectives to provide product teams with incentives for implementing Considered practices. The Considered Index's bronze, silver, and gold designations allowed for recognition of the product teams' environmental achievements. And, as one Nike manager explained, "[b]ecause Nike is Nike, it got competitive [among product teams.] So we made it a race and said, 'by the way, let us make sure that everyone hits bronze footwear by 2011'" (Carroll et al. 2013: 9). The SB&I managers were also able to get the Considered Index's language incorporated into the Nike lexicon, with one manager saying, "what's amazing is, once we educate the designers, they use words like 'VOCs' [volatile organic compounds]. We know we're making progress, because before, people didn't have it in their vocabulary" (Henderson et al. 2009: 13).

These days, Nike has lofty goals for sustainability in areas such as climate impact, eliminating waste, and sustainable sourcing. The Considered Design Principles and measurement are at the backbone of its sustainability efforts. Nike's CSR practices still receive NGO scrutiny, however, which sometimes yields negative publicity. In 2016, Greenpeace called out Nike and other apparel companies for failing to make sufficient progress in removing toxic chemicals from their supply chains (Greenpeace International 2016).

References

Aguinis, H., & Glavas, A. (2012). What We Know and Don't Know about Corporate Social Responsibility: A Review and Research Agenda. *Journal of Management*, 38(4), 932–968.

Akerlof, G. A. (1970). The Market for "Lemons": Quality Uncertainty and the Market Mechanism. *The Quarterly Journal of Economics*, 84(3), 488–500.

Akerlof, G. A., & Kranton, R. E. (2005). Identity and the Economics of Organizations. *Journal of Economic Perspectives*, 19(1), 9–32.

Albino, V., Dangelico, R. M., & Pontrandolfo, P. (2012). Do Inter-organizational Collaborations Enhance a Firm's Environmental Performance? A Study of the Largest US Companies. *Journal of Cleaner Production*, 37, 304–315.

Aldashev, G., & Verdier, T. (2010). Goodwill Bazaar: NGO Competition and Giving to Development. *Journal of Development Economics*, 91(1), 48–63.

Amel-Zadeh, A., & Serafeim, G. (2018). Why and How Investors Use ESG Information: Evidence from a Global Survey. *Financial Analysts Journal*, 74(3), 87–103.

Amrutha, V. N., & Geetha, S. N. (2020). A Systematic Review on Green Human Resource Management: Implications for Social Sustainability. *Journal of Cleaner Production*, 247, 1–15.

Amui, L. B. L., Jabbour, C. J. C., de Sousa Jabbour, A. B. L., & Kannan, D. (2017). Sustainability as a Dynamic Organizational Capability: A Systematic Review and a Future Agenda toward a Sustainable Transition. *Journal of Cleaner Production*, 142, 308–322.

Ando, A. W., & Langpap, C. (2018). The Economics of Species Conservation. *Annual Review of Resource Economics*, 10(1), 445–467.

Andreoni, J. (1990). Impure Altruism and Donations to Public Goods: A Theory of Warm-Glow Giving. *The Economic Journal*, 100(401), 464–477.

Andrews, K. T., Ganz, M., Baggetta, M., Han, H., & Lim, C. (2010). Leadership, Membership, and Voice: Civic Associations That Work. *American Journal of Sociology*, 115(4), 1191–1242.

Antonetti, P., & Maklan, S. (2014). Feelings That Make a Difference: How Guilt and Pride Convince Consumers of the Effectiveness of Sustainable Consumption Choices. *Journal of Business Ethics*, 124(1), 117–134.

Aragón-Correa, J. A., Marcus, A. A., & Vogel, D. (2020). The Effects of Mandatory and Voluntary Regulatory Pressures on Firms' Environmental Strategies: A Review and Recommendations for Future Research. *Academy of Management Annals*, 14(1), 339–365.

Aragón-Correa, J. A., & Sharma, S. (2003). A Contingent Resource-Based View of Proactive Corporate Environmental Strategy. *Academy of Management Review*, 28(1), 71–88.

Ariely, D., Kamenica, E., & Prelec, D. (2008). Man's Search for Meaning: The Case of Legos. *Journal of Economic Behavior & Organization*, 67(3–4), 671–677.

Attridge, M. (2009). Measuring and Managing Employee Work Engagement: A Review of the Research and Business Literature. *Journal of Workplace Behavioral Health*, 24(4), 383–398.

Austin, J. E., & Seitanidi, M. M. (2012a). Collaborative Value Creation: A Review of Partnering between Nonprofits and Businesses: Part I. Value Creation Spectrum and Collaboration Stages. *Nonprofit and Voluntary Sector Quarterly*, 41(5), 726–758.

Austin, J. E., & Seitanidi, M. M. (2012b). Collaborative Value Creation: A Review of Partnering between Nonprofits and Businesses. Part 2: Partnership Processes and Outcomes. *Nonprofit and Voluntary Sector Quarterly*, 41(6), 929–968.

Auyero, J., Hernandez, M., & Stitt, M. E. (2019). Grassroots Activism in the Belly of the Beast: A Relational Account of the Campaign against Urban Fracking in Texas. *Social Problems*, 66(1), 28–50.

Bachmann, R., Ehrlich, G., Fan, Y., & Ruzic, D. (2019). Firms and Collective Reputation: A Study of the Volkswagen Emissions Scandal. NBER Working Paper No. 26117. Retrieved August 9, 2022 from https://doi.org/10.3386/w26117.

Baker, G., Gibbons, R., & Murphy, K. J. (2002). Relational Contracts and the Theory of the Firm. *The Quarterly Journal of Economics*, 117(1), 39–84.

Bansal, P. (2003). From Issues to Actions: The Importance of Individual Concerns and Organizational Values in Responding to Natural Environmental Issues. *Organization Science*, 14(5), 510–527.

Barnett, M. L. (2007). Stakeholder Influence Capacity and the Variability of Financial Returns to Corporate Social Responsibility. *The Academy of Management Review*, 32(3), 794–816.

Barnett, M. L., Henriques, I., & Husted, B. W. (2020). Beyond Good Intentions: Designing CSR Initiatives for Greater Social Impact. *Journal of Management*, 46(6), 937–964.

Barney, J. B. (1986). Organizational Culture: Can It Be a Source of Sustained Competitive Advantage? *The Academy of Management Review*, 11(3), 656–665.

Barney, J. B. (1991). Firm Resources and Sustained Competitive Advantage. *Journal of Management*, 17(1), 99–120.

Baron, D. P., & Diermeier, D. (2007). Strategic Activism and Nonmarket Strategy. *Journal of Economics & Management Strategy*, 16(3), 599–634.

Barrage, L., Chyn, E., & Hastings, J. (2020). Advertising and Environmental Stewardship: Evidence from the BP Oil Spill. *American Economic Journal: Economic Policy*, 12(1), 33–61.

Barrett, S. (1991). Environmental Regulation for Competitive Advantage. *Business Strategy Review*, 2(1), 1–15.

Bartley, T., & Child, C. (2011). Movements, Markets and Fields: The Effects of Anti-sweatshop Campaigns on U.S. Firms, 1993–2000. *Social Forces*, 90(2), 425–451.

Bartley, T., & Child, C. (2014). Shaming the Corporation: The Social Production of Targets and the Anti-sweatshop Movement. *American Sociological Review*, 79(4), 653–679.

Bauman, C. W., & Skitka, L. J. (2012). Corporate Social Responsibility as a Source of Employee Satisfaction. *Research in Organizational Behavior*, 32, 63–86.

Bavadam, L. (2021). Protests in Gujarat against Corporate Projects That Threaten People's Livelihoods and Damage the Environment. *The Hindu*, September 10. Retrieved April 14, 2022 from https://frontline.thehindu.com/environment/protests-in-gujarat-against-corporate-projects-that-threaten-peoples-livelihoods-and-damage-the-environment/article36039532.ece.

Beaudoin, C. A., Cianci, A. M., Hannah, S. T., & Tsakumis, G. T. (2019). Bolstering Managers' Resistance to Temptation via the Firm's Commitment to Corporate Social Responsibility. *Journal of Business Ethics*, 157(2), 303–318.

Bhattacharya, C. B., Sen, S., & Korschun, D. (2011). *Leveraging Corporate Responsibility: The Stakeholder Route to Maximizing Business and Social Value*, Cambridge University Press.

Bhide, A. V., & Thurber, M. (1995). *Stonyfield Farm: September 1994* (No. 395157), Harvard Business School Press. Retrieved August 9, 2022 from https://hbsp.harvard.edu/product/395157-PDF-ENG?Ntt=Stonyfield&itemFindingMethod=Search.

Blackburn, W. R. (2007). *The Sustainability Handbook: The Complete Management Guide to Achieving Social, Economic, and Environmental Sustainability*. Environmental Law Institute.

Blackrock. (2021). BlackRock Client Letter. Retrieved August 31, 2021 from www.blackrock.com/corporate/investor-relations/larry-fink-ceo-letter.

Bode, C., Singh, J., & Rogan, M. (2015). Corporate Social Initiatives and Employee Retention. *Organization Science*, 26(6), 1702–1720.

Bomey, N., & Snavely, B. (2016). Volkswagen CEO: "We Are Not a Criminal Brand." *USA Today*, January 10. Retrieved July 22, 2020 from www.usatoday.com/story/money/cars/2016/01/10/volkswagen-detroit-auto-show-naias-matthias-mueller-emissions-scandal/78603744/.

Bourgeois, L. J. (1981). On the Measurement of Organizational Slack. *The Academy of Management Review*, 6(1), 29–39.

Bowen, F. E., Cousins, P. D., Lamming, R. C., & Farukt, A. C. (2001). The Role of Supply Management Capabilities in Green Supply. *Production and Operations Management*, 10(2), 174–189.

Brewer, G., Carceres, H., Cartmill, M., Doh, J., Dubin, J., Iott, S., Lin, H., Reyna, E., Rivera, J., Sanchez, J., Sauers, L., Tredennick, C., & Wyeth, G. (2013). *Report, Gold and Green Together*. Pacific Basin Research Center, Soka University of America. Retrieved March 22, 2022 from https://docs.google.com/viewer?a=v&pid=sites&srcid=ZGVmYXVsdGRvbWFpbnxqb3JnZXXJpdmVyYYWd3dXxneDozZmRkMzg5MjQ4YTI5N2I0.

Bryson, J. M. (2004). What to Do When Stakeholders Matter. *Public Management Review*, 6(1), 21–53.

Bryson, J. M. (2018). *Strategic Planning for Public and Nonprofit Organizations: A Guide to Strengthening and Sustaining Organizational Achievement*, John Wiley & Sons.

Burbano, V. C. (2016). Social Responsibility Messages and Worker Wage Requirements: Field Experimental Evidence from Online Labor Marketplaces. *Organization Science*, 27(4), 1010–1028.

Burbano, V. C. (2019). Getting Gig Workers to Do More by Doing Good: Field Experimental Evidence from Online Platform Labor Marketplaces. *Organization & Environment*, 34(3), 387–412.

Burbano, V. C., Mamer, J., & Snyder, J. (2018). Pro Bono as a Human Capital Learning and Screening Mechanism: Evidence from Law Firms. *Strategic Management Journal*, 39(11), 2899–2920.

Butler, R. (2020). Putting Sustainability at the Center of Business Strategy: An Interview with Paul Polman. Mongabay.com, October 19. Retrieved April 14, 2022 from https://news.mongabay.com/2020/10/putting-sustainability-at-the-center-of-business-strategy-an-interview-with-paul-polman/.

Cain, C. (2014). Negotiating with the Growth Machine: Community Benefits Agreements and Value-Conscious Growth. *Sociological Forum*, 29(4), 937–958.

Caligiuri, P., Mencin, A., & Jiang, K. (2013). Win–Win–Win: The Influence of Company-Sponsored Volunteerism Programs on Employees, NGOs, and Business Units. *Personnel Psychology*, 66(4), 825–860.

Callery, P. J., & Perkins, J. (2020). Detecting False Accounts in Intermediated Voluntary Disclosure. *Academy of Management Discoveries*, 7(1), 40–56.

Carnahan, S., Kryscynski, D., & Olson, D. (2017). When Does Corporate Social Responsibility Reduce Employee Turnover? Evidence from Attorneys before and after 9/11. *Academy of Management Journal*, 60(5), 1932–1962.

Carroll, A. B. (1999). Corporate Social Responsibility: Evolution of a Definitional Construct. *Business & Society*, 38(3), 268–295.

Carroll, G., Shifrin, D., & Brady, D. (2013). Nike: Sustainability and Labor Practices 1998–2013. Case Study, Stanford Graduate School of Business.

Casadesus-Masanell, R., Crooke, M., Reinhardt, F., & Vasishth, V. (2009). Households' Willingness to Pay for "Green" Goods: Evidence from Patagonia's Introduction of Organic Cotton Sportswear. *Journal of Economics & Management Strategy*, 18(1), 203–233.

CGS. (2019). CGS Survey Reveals "Sustainability" Is Driving Demand and Customer Loyalty. January 8. Retrieved July 11, 2020 from www.cgsinc .com/en/infographics/cgs-survey-reveals-sustainability-is-driving-demand-and-customer-loyalty.

Chandler, D., & Kapelner, A. (2013). Breaking Monotony with Meaning: Motivation in Crowdsourcing Markets. *Journal of Economic Behavior & Organization*, 90, 123–133.

Chatterji, A. K., Levine, D. I., & Toffel, M. W. (2009). How Well Do Social Ratings Actually Measure Corporate Social Responsibility? *Journal of Economics & Management Strategy*, 18(1), 125–169.

Cheng, B., Ioannou, I., & Serafeim, G. (2014). Corporate Social Responsibility and Access to Finance. *Strategic Management Journal*, 35(1), 1–23.

Chernev, A., & Blair, S. (2015). Doing Well by Doing Good: The Benevolent Halo of Corporate Social Responsibility. *Journal of Consumer Research*, 41(6), 1412–1425.

Chiroleu-Assouline, M., & Lyon, T. P. (2020). Merchants of Doubt: Corporate Political Action when NGO Credibility Is Uncertain. *Journal of Economics & Management Strategy*, 29(2), 439–461.

Christensen, C. M. (1997). *The Innovator's Dilemma: When New Technologies Cause Great Firms to Fail*, Harvard Business Review Press.

Christian, M. S., Garza, A. S., & Slaughter, J. E. (2011). Work Engagement: A Quantitative Review and Test of Its Relations with Task and Contextual Performance. *Personnel Psychology*, 64(1), 89–136.

Christmann, P. (2000). Effects of "Best Practices" of Environmental Management on Cost Advantage: The Role of Complementary Assets. *Academy of Management Journal*, 43(4), 663–680.

Chrun, E., Dolšak, N., & Prakash, A. (2016). Corporate Environmentalism: Motivations and Mechanisms. *Annual Review of Environment and Resources*, 41(1), 341–362.

Chua, W. Y., Lee, A., & Sadeque, S. (2010). Why Do People Buy Hybrid Cars? In *Proceedings of Social Marketing Forum*, University of Western Australia, Perth, Western Australia, Edith Cowan University, Churchlands, pp. 1–13.

Clancy, H. (2013). *TD Bank: Where Green Is Going Viral*, Net Impact. Retrieved August 20, 2019 from www.td.com/document/PDF/corporateresponsibility/publications/td-bank-where-going-green-is-going-viral.pdf.

Coase, R. H. (1960). The Problem of Social Cost. *The Journal of Law and Economics*, 3(4), 1–44.

Coca-Cola Company. (2018). Improving Our Water Efficiency. August 28. Retrieved January 21, 2021 from www.coca-colacompany.com/news/improving-our-water-efficiency.

Cohen, M. A., & Tubb, A. (2018). The Impact of Environmental Regulation on Firm and Country Competitiveness: A Meta-analysis of the Porter Hypothesis. *Journal of the Association of Environmental and Resource Economists*, 5(2), 371–399.

Cone Communications. (2016). *2016 Cone Communications Employee Engagement Study*. Retrieved June 4, 2018 from www.conecomm.com/research-blog/2016-employee-engagement-study.

Cordano, M., & Frieze, I. H. (2000). Pollution Reduction Preferences of U.S. Environmental Managers: Applying Ajzen's Theory of Planned Behavior. *The Academy of Management Journal*, 43(4), 627–641.

Cowell, R., Bristow, G., & Munday, M. (2011). Acceptance, Acceptability and Environmental Justice: The Role of Community Benefits in Wind Energy Development. *Journal of Environmental Planning and Management*, 54(4), 539–557.

CRE Finance Council. (2021). Glasgow Financial Alliance for Net Zero Pledges Trillions in Climate Investment. Retrieved April 14, 2022 from www.crefc.org/cre/content/News/Items/advocacy-items/Glasgow_Financial_Alliance_for_Net_Zero_Pledges_Trillions_in_Climate_Investment.aspx.

Crilly, D., & Sloan, P. (2014). Autonomy or Control? Organizational Architecture and Corporate Attention to Stakeholders. *Organization Science*, 25(2), 339–355.

Csaszar, F. A. (2012). An Efficient Frontier in Organization Design: Organizational Structure as a Determinant of Exploration and Exploitation. *Organization Science*, 24(4), 1083–1101.

Cummings, J. L., & Doh, J. P. (2000). Identifying Who Matters: Mapping Key Players in Multiple Environments. *California Management Review*, 42(2), 83–104.

Dahan, N. M., Doh, J. P., Oetzel, J., & Yaziji, M. (2010). Corporate–NGO Collaboration: Co-creating New Business Models for Developing Markets. *Long Range Planning*, 43(2), 326–342.

Dangelico, R. M. (2015). Improving Firm Environmental Performance and Reputation: The Role of Employee Green Teams. *Business Strategy and the Environment*, 24(8), 735–749.

Dangelico, R. M., & Pujari, D. (2010). Mainstreaming Green Product Innovation: Why and How Companies Integrate Environmental Sustainability. *Journal of Business Ethics*, 95(3), 471–486.

Dangelico, R. M., Pujari, D., & Pontrandolfo, P. (2017). Green Product Innovation in Manufacturing Firms: A Sustainability-Oriented Dynamic Capability Perspective. *Business Strategy and the Environment*, 26(4), 490–506.

Darnall, N., & Edwards, D. (2006). Predicting the Cost of Environmental Management System Adoption: The Role of Capabilities, Resources and Ownership Structure. *Strategic Management Journal*, 27(4), 301–320.

Darnall, N., Ji, H., & Potoski, M. (2017). Institutional Design of Ecolabels: Sponsorship Signals Rule Strength. *Regulation & Governance*, 11(4), 438–450.

Darnall, N., Potoski, M., & Prakash, A. (2010). Sponsorship Matters: Assessing Business Participation in Government- and Industry-Sponsored Voluntary Environmental Programs. *Journal of Public Administration Research and Theory*, 20(2), 283–307.

Dauvergne, P., & Lister, J. (2012). Big Brand Sustainability: Governance Prospects and Environmental Limits. *Global Environmental Change*, 22(1), 36–45.

Davies, J. (2014). The 2014 GreenBiz NGO Report. Greenbiz.com. Retrieved June 22, 2020 from http://info.greenbiz.com/rs/greenbizgroup/images/greenbiz-ngo-report.pdf.

Delmas, M. A., & Burbano, V. C. (2011). The Drivers of Greenwashing. *California Management Review*, 54(1), 64–87.

Delmas, M. A., & Colgan, D. (2018). *The Green Bundle: Pairing the Market with the Planet*, Stanford University Press.

Delmas, M. A., & Pekovic, S. (2013). Environmental Standards and Labor Productivity: Understanding the Mechanisms that Sustain Sustainability. *Journal of Organizational Behavior*, 34(2), 230–252.

Delmas, M. A., & Toffel, M. W. (2008). Organizational Responses to Environmental Demands: Opening the Black Box. *Strategic Management Journal*, 29(10), 1027–1055.

Den Hond, F., & de Bakker, F. G. A. (2007). Ideologically Motivated Activism: How Activist Groups Influence Corporate Social Change Activities. *Academy of Management Review*, 32(3), 901–924.

Deryugina, T., Moore, F., & Tol, R. S. (2020). Applications of the Coase Theorem. *ArXiv: General Economics*. http://arxiv.org/pdf/2004.04247.

Deryugina, T., Moore, F., & Tol, R. S. J. (2021). Environmental Applications of the Coase Theorem. *Environmental Science & Policy*, 120, 81–88.

Diani, M. (2007). Networks and Participation. In D. A. Snow & S. A. Soule (eds.), *The Blackwell Companion to Social Movements*, John Wiley & Sons, Ltd, pp. 339–359.

Donia, M. B., Ronen, S., Sirsly, C.-A. T., & Bonaccio, S. (2017). CSR by Any Other Name? The Differential Impact of Substantive and Symbolic CSR Attributions on Employee Outcomes. *Journal of Business Ethics, 2*, 1–21.

Donia, M. B., & Sirsly, C.-A. T. (2016). Determinants and Consequences of Employee Attributions of Corporate Social Responsibility as Substantive or Symbolic. *European Management Journal*, 34(3), 232–242.

Dorobantu, S., Henisz, W. J., & Nartey, L. (2017a). Not All Sparks Light a Fire: Stakeholder and Shareholder Reactions to Critical Events in Contested Markets. *Administrative Science Quarterly*, 62(3), 561–597.

Dorobantu, S., Kaul, A., & Zelner, B. (2017b). Nonmarket Strategy Research through the Lens of New Institutional Economics: An Integrative Review and Future Directions. *Strategic Management Journal*, 38(1), 114–140.

Dorobantu, S., & Odziemkowska, K. (2017). Valuing Stakeholder Governance: Property Rights, Community Mobilization, and Firm Value. *Strategic Management Journal*, 38(13), 2682–2703.

Eavis, P., & Krauss, C. (2021). What's Really behind Corporate Promises on Climate Change? *The New York Times*, February 22. Retrieved March 21, 2022 from www.nytimes.com/2021/02/22/business/energy-environment/corporations-climate-change.html.

Eden, S. (2004). Greenpeace. *New Political Economy*, 9(4), 595–610.

Edinger-Schons, L. M., Lengler-Graiff, L., Scheidler, S., & Wieseke, J. (2019). Frontline Employees as Corporate Social Responsibility (CSR) Ambassadors: A Quasi-Field Experiment. *Journal of Business Ethics*, 157(2), 359–373.

Edmans, A. (2011). Does the Stock Market Fully Value Intangibles? Employee Satisfaction and Equity Prices. *Journal of Financial Economics*, 101(3), 621–640.

Edwards-Jones, G. (2010). Does Eating Local Food Reduce the Environmental Impact of Food Production and Enhance Consumer Health? *Proceedings of the Nutrition Society*, 69(4), 582–591.

Eesley, C., Decelles, K. A., & Lenox, M. (2016). Through the Mud or in the Boardroom: Examining Activist Types and Their Strategies in Targeting Firms for Social Change. *Strategic Management Journal*, 37(12), 2425–2440.

Eesley, C., & Lenox, M. J. (2006). Firm Responses to Secondary Stakeholder Action. *Strategic Management Journal*, 27(8), 765–781.

Effron, D. A., O'Connor, K., Leroy, H., & Lucas, B. J. (2018). From Inconsistency to Hypocrisy: When Does "Saying One Thing but Doing Another" Invite Condemnation? *Research in Organizational Behavior*, 38, 61–75.

Elkington, J. (2018). 25 Years Ago I Coined the Phrase "Triple Bottom Line." Here's Why It's Time to Rethink It. *Harvard Business Review*, June 25. Retrieved January 11, 2021 from https://hbr.org/2018/06/25-years-ago-i-coined-the-phrase-triple-bottom-line-heres-why-im-giving-up-on-it.

Ellen, P. S., Webb, D. J., & Mohr, L. A. (2006). Building Corporate Associations: Consumer Attributions for Corporate Socially Responsible Programs. *Journal of the Academy of Marketing Science*, 34(2), 147–157.

Environmental Defense Fund. (2010). McDonald's and Environmental Defense Fund Mark 20 Years of Partnerships for Sustainability. Retrieved June 25, 2020 from www.edf.org/news/mcdonald%E2%80%99s-and-environmental-defense-fund-mark-20-years-partnerships-sustainability.

Environmental Defense Fund. (2014). Poland Spring Reduces Idling to Curb Emissions. Retrieved July 22, 2015 from http://business.edf.org/files/2014/03/poland-spring.pdf.

Environmental Defense Fund. (2018, November). McDonald's saves billions cutting waste. Retrieved September 14, 2021 from www.edf.org/partnerships/mcdonalds.

Esty, D. C., & Winston, A. (2009). *Green to Gold: How Smart Companies Use Environmental Strategy to Innovate, Create Value, and Build Competitive Advantage*. John Wiley & Sons.

Farooq, O., Payaud, M., Merunka, D., & Valette-Florence, P. (2014). The Impact of Corporate Social Responsibility on Organizational Commitment: Exploring Multiple Mediation Mechanisms. *Journal of Business Ethics*, 125(4), 563–580.

Fiol, C. M. (1991). Managing Culture as a Competitive Resource: An Identity-Based View of Sustainable Competitive Advantage. *Journal of Management*, 17(1), 191–211.

Flammer, C., Hong, B., & Minor, D. (2019). Corporate Governance and the Rise of Integrating Corporate Social Responsibility Criteria in Executive Compensation: Effectiveness and Implications for Firm Outcomes. *Strategic Management Journal*, 40(7), 1097–1122.

Flammer, C., & Luo, J. (2017). Corporate Social Responsibility as an Employee Governance Tool: Evidence from a Quasi-Experiment. *Strategic Management Journal*, 38(2), 163–183.

Franks, D. M., Davis, R., Bebbington, A. J., Ali, S. H., Kemp, D., & Scurrah, M. (2014). Conflict Translates Environmental and Social Risk into Business Costs. *Proceedings of the National Academy of Sciences*, 111(21), 7576–7581.

Freeman, R. E. (2010). *Strategic Management: A Stakeholder Approach*, Cambridge University Press.

Friede, G., Busch, T., & Bassen, A. (2015). ESG and Financial Performance: Aggregated Evidence from More than 2000 Empirical Studies. *Journal of Sustainable Finance & Investment*, 5(4), 210–233.

Friedman, M. (1970). The Social Responsibility of Business Is to Increase Its Profits. *The New York Times*, September 13. Retrieved June 18, 2020 from www.nytimes.com/1970/09/13/archives/article-15-no-title.html.

Frooman, J. (1999). Stakeholder Influence Strategies. *Academy of Management Review*, 24(2), 191–205.

Fu, R., Tang, Y., & Chen, G. (2020). Chief Sustainability Officers and Corporate Social (Ir)responsibility. *Strategic Management Journal*, 41(4), 656–680.

Gabriel, T. (1990). If a Tree Falls in the Forest, They Hear It. *New York Times*, November 4. Retrieved June 21, 2020 from www.nytimes.com/1990/11/04/magazine/if-a-tree-falls-in-the-forest-they-hear-it.html.

Gallup Inc. (2020). Environment. Retrieved July 11, 2020 from https://news.gallup.com/poll/1615/Environment.aspx.

Garicano, L., & Posner, R. A. (2005). Intelligence Failures: An Organizational Economics Perspective. *Journal of Economic Perspectives*, 19(4), 151–170.

Gatignon-Turnau, A.-L., & Mignonac, K. (2015). (Mis) Using Employee Volunteering for Public Relations: Implications for Corporate Volunteers' Organizational Commitment. *Journal of Business Research*, 68(1), 7–18.

Gehman, J., Grimes, M. G., & Cao, K. (2019). Why We Care about Certified B Corporations: From Valuing Growth to Certifying Values Practices. *Academy of Management Discoveries*, 5(1), 97–101.

Gelles, D., & Sengupta, S. (2020). Big Business Says It Will Tackle Climate Change, but Not How or When. *The New York Times*, January 23. Retrieved June 18, 2020 from www.nytimes.com/2020/01/23/business/corporate-climate-davos.html.

Geneva: International Organization for Standardization. (2015). *Environmental Management Systems – Requirements with Guidance for Use [ISO 14001: 2015(E)]*. International Organization for Standardization.

Georgeson, L., & Maslin, M. (2019). Estimating the Scale of the US Green Economy within the Global Context. *Palgrave Communications*, 5(1), 1–12.

Geyer, R. (2021). *The Business of Less: The Role of Companies and Households on a Planet in Peril*. New York. Routledge.

Geyer, R., Kuczenski, B., Zink, T., & Henderson, A. (2016). Common Misconceptions about Recycling. *Journal of Industrial Ecology*, 20(5), 1010–1017.

Gibbons, R. (2005). Incentives between Firms (and within). *Management Science*, 51(1), 2–17.

Gibbons, R., & Henderson, R. (2012). Relational Contracts and Organizational Capabilities. *Organization Science*, 23(5), 1350–1364.

Glavas, A., & Piderit, S. K. (2009). How Does Doing Good Matter? *Journal of Corporate Citizenship*, 36(3), 51–70.

Gold, A. H., Malhotra, A., & Segars, A. H. (2001). Knowledge Management: An Organizational Capabilities Perspective. *Journal of Management Information Systems: JMIS*, 18(1), 185–214.

Goldstein, N. J., Cialdini, R. B., & Griskevicius, V. (2008). A Room with a Viewpoint: Using Social Norms to Motivate Environmental Conservation in Hotels. *Journal of Consumer Research*, 35(3), 472–482.

Gond, J.-P., El Akremi, A., Swaen, V., & Babu, N. (2017). The Psychological Microfoundations of Corporate Social Responsibility: A Person-Centric Systematic Review. *Journal of Organizational Behavior*, 38(2), 225–246.

Grant, A. M. (2008a). Employees without a Cause: The Motivational Effects of Prosocial Impact in Public Service. *International Public Management Journal*, 11(1), 48–66.

Grant, A. M. (2008b). The Significance of Task Significance: Job Performance Effects, Relational Mechanisms, and Boundary Conditions. *Journal of Applied Psychology*, 93(1), 108.

Grant, A. M. (2012). Giving Time, Time after Time: Work Design and Sustained Employee Participation in Corporate Volunteering. *Academy of Management Review*, 37(4), 589–615.

Grant, A. M., Fried, Y., & Juillerat, T. (2011). Work Matters: Job Design in Classic and Contemporary Perspectives. In *APA Handbook Of industrial and Organizational Psychology*, Vol. 1, *Building and Developing the Organization*. American Psychological Association, pp. 417–453.

Grant, L. E., & Potoski, M. (2015). Collective Reputations Affect Donations to Nonprofits. *Journal of Policy Analysis and Management*, 34(4), 835–852.

Grant, R. M. (1991). The Resource-Based Theory of Competitive Advantage: Implications for Strategy Formulation. *California Management Review*, 33(3), 114–135.

Grant, R. M. (1996). Toward a Knowledge-Based Theory of the Firm. *Strategic Management Journal*, 17(S2), 109–122.

Greenbiz. (2016). *The State of the Profession 2016*. Retrieved June 20, 2022 from www.greenbiz.com/report/state-profession-2016.

Greenpeace. (2010). Greenpeace Praises Timberland's Policy on Amazon Leather. July 6. Retrieved June 15, 2020 from www.greenpeace.org/usa/news/greenpeace-praises-timberland/.

Greenpeace International. (2009). *Slaughtering the Amazon*. Retrieved February 23, 2021 from www.greenpeace.org/usa/wp-content/uploads/legacy/Global/usa/planet3/PDFs/slaughtering-the-amazon.pdf.

Greenpeace International. (2016). Greenpeace: Nike, Esprit, Victoria's Secret and LiNing fail toxic-free fashion ranking. July 5. Retrieved February 23, 2021 from www.greenpeace.org/international/press-release/7357/greenpeace-nike-esprit-victorias-secret-and-lining-fail-toxic-free-fashion-ranking.

Greenpeace International. (n.d.-a). Greenpeace: Ask Nestle to Give Rainforests a Break. Retrieved July 22, 2020 from https://wayback.archive-it.org/9650/20200406223212/http://p3-raw.greenpeace.org/international/en/campaigns/climate-change/kitkat/.

Greenpeace International. (n.d.-b). McVictory. Retrieved July 22, 2020 from http://p3-raw.greenpeace.org/international/en/news/features/McVictory-200706/.

Griskevicius, V., Tybur, J. M., & Van den Bergh, B. (2010). Going Green to Be Seen: Status, Reputation, and Conspicuous Conservation. *Journal of Personality and Social Psychology*, 98(3), 392.

Gromet, D. M., Kunreuther, H., & Larrick, R. P. (2013). Political Ideology Affects Energy-Efficient Attitudes and Choices. *Proceedings of the National Academy of Sciences*, 110(23), 9314–9319.

Gulbrandsen, L. H. (2009). The Emergence and Effectiveness of the Marine Stewardship Council. *Marine Policy*, 33(4), 654–660.

Gunningham, N., Kagan, R. A., & Thornton, D. (2004). Social License and Environmental Protection: Why Businesses Go beyond Compliance. *Law & Social Inquiry*, 29(2), 307–341.

Gupta, S. (2014). *Marketing Reading: Creating Customer Value*, Harvard Business Publishing. https://hbsp.harvard.edu/product/8176-PDF-ENG.

Hafenbrädl, S., & Waeger, D. (2017). Ideology and the Micro-foundations of CSR: Why Executives Believe in the Business Case for CSR and How This Affects Their CSR Engagements. *Academy of Management Journal*, 60(4), 1582–1606.

Hallstein, E., & Miller, M. L. (2014). A Renter's Market: Bird Returns Offers Innovative Conservation. *Nature*, August 6. Retrieved April 20, 2021 from https://blog.nature.org/science/2014/08/06/birds-birdreturns-innovative-lands-conservation-science/.

Hamilton, J. T. (1995). Pollution as News: Media and Stock Market Reactions to the Toxics Release Inventory Data. *Journal of Environmental Economics and Management*, 28(1), 98–113.

Han, H. (2016). The Organizational Roots of Political Activism: Field Experiments on Creating a Relational Context. *American Political Science Review*, 110(2), 296–307.

Hanson, D. J. (1985). Congress Ponders US Chemical Releases Survey, Bhopal Accident. *Chemical and Engineering News*, April 8, 20–21.

Hart, S. L. (1995). A Natural-Resource-Based View of the Firm. *Academy of Management Review*, 20(4), 986–1014.

Hart, S. L., & Dowell, G. (2011). Invited Editorial: A Natural-Resource-Based View of the Firm: Fifteen Years after. *Journal of Management*, 37(5), 1464–1479.

Harter, J. K., Schmidt, F. L., & Hayes, T. L. (2002). Business-Unit-Level Relationship between Employee Satisfaction, Employee Engagement, and Business Outcomes: A Meta-analysis. *Journal of Applied Psychology*, 87(2), 268–279.

Henderson, R., Locke, R. M., Lyddy, C., & Reavis, C. (2009). Nike Considered: Getting Traction on Sustainability. MIS Sloan Management School of Management. Retrieved September, 12, 2022 from https://mitsloan.mit.edu/sites/default/files/2020-03/Nike%20Considered.IC_.pdf.

Henisz, W. J., Dorobantu, S., & Nartey, L. J. (2014). Spinning Gold: The Financial Returns to Stakeholder Engagement. *Strategic Management Journal*, 35(12), 1727–1748.

Henriques, I., & Sadorsky, P. (1999). The Relationship between Environmental Commitment and Managerial Perceptions of Stakeholder Importance. *Academy of Management Journal*, 42(1), 87–99.

Hewlett-Packard. (2019). *HP Workforce Sustainability Survey Global Insights Report*. Retrieved October 29, 2021 from https://press.hp.com/content/dam/hpi/press/press-kits/2019/earth-day-2019/HP%20Workforce%20Sustainability%20Survey.pdf.

Heyes, A., & King, B. (2020). Understanding the Organization of Green Activism: Sociological and Economic Perspectives. *Organization & Environment*, 33(1), 7–30.

Heyes, A., & Martin, S. (2015). NGO Mission Design. *Journal of Economic Behavior & Organization*, 119, 197–210.

Hirshberg, G. (2008). *Stirring It up: How to Make Money and Save the World*, Hyperion.

Hoffman, A. J. (2000). *Competitive Environmental Strategy: A Guide to the Changing Business Landscape*, Island Press.

Holt, D. B. (2003). *Brands and Branding*, Harvard Business School Press.

Hsieh, N. (2017). The Responsibilities and Role of Business in Relation to Society: Back to Basics? *Business Ethics Quarterly*, 27(2), 293–314.

Hur, W.-M., Moon, T.-W., & Ko, S.-H. (2018). How Employees' Perceptions of CSR Increase Employee Creativity: Mediating Mechanisms of Compassion at Work Intrinsic Motivation. *Journal of Business Ethics*, 153(3), 629–644.

Industrial Designers Society of America. (2010). Nike Considered Boot. May 23. Retrieved July 13, 2020 from www.idsa.org/awards/idea/computer-equipment/nike-considered-boot.

Ingram, P., Yue, L. Q., & Rao, H. (2010). Trouble in Store: Probes, Protests, and Store Openings by Wal-Mart, 1998–2007. *American Journal of Sociology*, 116(1), 53–92.

Inkpen, A. C. (2005). Learning through Alliances: General Motors and Nummi. *California Management Review*, 47(4), 114–136.

Innes, R. (2006). A Theory of Consumer Boycotts under Symmetric Information and Imperfect Competition. *The Economic Journal*, 116(511), 355–381.

Irmak, C., Sen, S., & Bhattacharya, C. B. (2015). Consumer Reactions to Business–Nonprofit Alliances: Who Benefits and When? *Marketing Letters*, 26(1), 29–42.

Isidore, C. (2016). Coca-Cola: We're Replenishing All of the Water We Use. *CNN*, August 29. Retrieved July 22, 2020 from https://money.cnn.com/2016/08/29/news/companies/coca-cola-water/index.html.

Jones, D., Molitor, D., & Reif, J. (2019). What Do Workplace Wellness Programs Do? Evidence from the Illinois Workplace Wellness Study. *The Quarterly Journal of Economics*, 134(4), 1747–1791.

Jones, D. A. (2010). Does Serving the Community Also Serve the Company? Using Organizational Identification and Social Exchange Theories to Understand Employee Responses to a Volunteerism Programme. *Journal of Occupational and Organizational Psychology*, 83(4), 857–878.

Jones, D. A. (2016). Widely Assumed but Thinly Tested: Do Employee Volunteers' Self-reported Skill Improvements Reflect the Nature of Their Volunteering Experiences? *Frontiers in Psychology*, 7, 495.

Jones, D. A., Willness, C. R., & Heller, K. W. (2016). Illuminating the Signals Job Seekers Receive from an Employer's Community Involvement and Environmental Sustainability Practices: Insights into Why Most Job Seekers Are Attracted, Others Are Indifferent, and a Few Are Repelled. *Frontiers in Psychology*, 7, 426.

Jones, D. A., Willness, C. R., & Madey, S. (2014). Why Are Job Seekers Attracted by Corporate Social Performance? Experimental and Field Tests of Three Signal-Based Mechanisms. *Academy of Management Journal*, 57(2), 383–404.

Joseph, J., & Wilson, A. J. (2018). The Growth of the Firm: An Attention-Based View. *Strategic Management Journal*, 39(6), 1779–1800.

Kanashiro, P., & Rivera, J. (2019). Do Chief Sustainability Officers Make Companies Greener? The Moderating Role of Regulatory Pressures. *Journal of Business Ethics*, 155(3), 687–701.

Kaplan, R. S., & Norton, D. P. (2006). *Alignment: Using the Balanced Scorecard to Create Corporate Synergies*, Harvard Business Press.

Kaufman, L. (2010). Ad for a Dish Detergent Becomes Part of a Story. *New York Times*, June 16. Retrieved October 5, 2021 from www.nytimes .com/2010/06/16/science/earth/16dawn.html.

Khanna, M. (2020). *Growing Green Business Investments in Asia and the Pacific: Trends and Opportunities*, Asian Development Bank. Retrieved February 23, 2022 from www.adb.org/publications/ green-business-investments-asia-pacific-trends.

Kim, A., Kim, Y., Han, K., Jackson, S. E., & Ployhart, R. E. (2017). Multilevel Influences on Voluntary Workplace Green Behavior: Individual Differences, Leader Behavior, and Coworker Advocacy. *Journal of Management*, 43(5), 1335–1358.

King, A. (1995). Innovation from Differentiation: Pollution Control Departments and Innovation in the Printed Circuit Industry. *IEEE Transactions on Engineering Management*, 42(3), 270–277.

King, A. (1999). Retrieving and Transferring Embodied Data: Implications for the Management of Interdependence within Organizations. *Management Science*, 45(7), 918–935.

King, A. (2007). Cooperation between Corporations and Environmental Groups: A Transaction Cost Perspective. *Academy of Management Review*, 32(3), 889–900.

King, A. A., & Lenox, M. J. (2000). Industry Self-regulation without Sanctions: The Chemical Industry's Responsible Care Program. *Academy of Management Journal*, 43(4), 698–716.

King, B. G., Bentele, K. G., Soule, S. A., Bentele, K. G., & Soule, S. A. (2007). Protest and Policymaking: Explaining Fluctuation in Congressional Attention to Rights Issues, 1960–1986. *Social Forces*, 86(1), 137–163.

King, B. G., & Carberry, E. J. (2018). Reversed Riches and Matthew's Curse: The Liability of Status When Organizations Misbehave. *Journal of Management Inquiry*, 27(4), 365–367.

King, B. G., & McDonnell, M. (2015). Good Firms, Good Targets: The Relationship among Corporate Social Responsibility, Reputation, and Activist Targeting. In K. Tsutsui & A. Lim (eds.), *Corporate Social Responsibility in a Globalizing World*, Cambridge University Press, pp. 430–454.

King, B. G., & Soule, S. A. (2007). Social Movements as Extra-institutional Entrepreneurs: The Effect of Protests on Stock Price Returns. *Administrative Science Quarterly*, 52(3), 413–442.

Klandermans, B. (2007). The Demand and Supply of Participation: Social-Psychological Correlates of Participation in Social Movements. In D. A. Snow & S. A. Soule (eds.), *The Blackwell Companion to Social Movements*, John Wiley & Sons, Ltd., pp. 360–379.

Klein, J., & Dawar, N. (2004). Corporate Social Responsibility and Consumers' Attributions and Brand Evaluations in a Product–Harm Crisis. *International Journal of Research in Marketing*, 21(3), 203–217.

Kleindorfer, P. R., Singhal, K., & Van Wassenhove, L. N. (2005). Sustainable Operations Management. *Production and Operations Management*, 14(4), 482–492.

Knoke, D. (1988). Incentives in Collective Action Organizations. *American Sociological Review*, 53(3), 311–329.

Koehn, N. F., Kahn, N. N., & Legris, E. (2012). *Gary Hirshberg and Stonyfield Farm,* Case Study No. 9–312–122, Harvard Business School Press. Retrieved August 5, 2017 from https://hbsp.harvard.edu/product/312122-PDF-ENG ?Ntt=Stonyfield&itemFindingMethod=Search.

Koh, P.-S., Qian, C., & Wang, H. (2014). Firm Litigation Risk and the Insurance Value of Corporate Social Performance. *Strategic Management Journal*, 35(10), 1464–1482.

Koku, P. S., Akhigbe, A., & Springer, T. M. (1997). The Financial Impact of Boycotts and Threats of Boycott. *Journal of Business Research*, 40(1), 15–20.

Kotchen, M. J. (2006). Green Markets and Private Provision of Public Goods. *Journal of Political Economy*, 114(4), 816–834.

Kotler, P., & Keller, K. L. (2015). *Marketing Management, Global Edition*, Pearson Education UK.

Kramer, M. R., & Pfitzer, M. W. (2016). The Ecosystem of Shared Value. *Harvard Business Review*, 94(10), 80–89.

Kristof, A. L. (1996). Person–Organization Fit: An Integrative Review of Its Conceptualizations, Measurement, and Implications. *Personnel Psychology*, 49(1), 1–49.

Lam, A. (2000). Tacit Knowledge, Organizational Learning and Societal Institutions: An Integrated Framework. *Organization Studies*, 21(3), 487–513.

Lenox, M. J., & Eesley, C. E. (2009). Private Environmental Activism and the Selection and Response of Firm Targets. *Journal of Economics & Management Strategy*, 18(1), 45–73.

Leonard, D., & Sensiper, S. (1998). The Role of Tacit Knowledge in Group Innovation. *California Management Review*, 40(3), 112–132.

Lin, Y.-C., & Chang, C. A. (2012). Double Standard: The Role of Environmental Consciousness in Green Product Usage. *Journal of Marketing*, 76(5), 125–134.

Livesey, S. M. (1999). McDonald's and the Environmental Defense Fund: A Case Study of a Green Alliance. *The Journal of Business Communication*, 36(1), 5–39.

Lotz, S., Christandl, F., & Fetchenhauer, D. (2013). What Is Fair Is Good: Evidence of Consumers' Taste for Fairness. *Food Quality and Preference*, 30(2), 139–144.

Luchs, M. G., Naylor, R. W., Irwin, J. R., & Raghunathan, R. (2010). The Sustainability Liability: Potential Negative Effects of Ethicality on Product Preference. *Journal of Marketing*, 74(5), 18–31.

Lyon, T. P. (2020). Introduction to the Special Issue on "Social Movements and Private Environmental Governance." *Organization & Environment*, 33(1), 3–6.

Marcus, A. A, & Anderson, M. H. (2006). A General Dynamic Capability: Does It Propagate Business and Social Competencies in the Retail Food Industry? *Journal of Management Studies*, 43(1), 19–46.

Max, D. T. (2014). Green Is Good. *New Yorker*, May 5. Retrieved from September 23, 2020 from www.newyorker.com/magazine/2014/05/12/green-is-good.

Maynard, M. (2007). Say "Hybrid" and Many People Will Hear "Prius." *New York Times*, July 4. Retrieved February 23, 2022 from www.nytimes.com/2007/07/04/business/04hybrid.html.

McCarthy, J. D., & Zald, M. N. (1977). Resource Mobilization and Social Movements: A Partial Theory. *American Journal of Sociology*, 82(6), 1212–1241.

McDonnell, M.-H., & King, B. (2013). Keeping up Appearances: Reputational Threat and Impression Management after Social Movement Boycotts. *Administrative Science Quarterly*, 58(3), 387–419.

McDonnell, M.-H., King, B. G., & Soule, S. A. (2015). A Dynamic Process Model of Private Politics: Activist Targeting and Corporate Receptivity to Social Challenges. *American Sociological Review*, 80(3), 654–678.

McDonnell, M.-H., & Werner, T. (2016). Blacklisted Businesses: Social Activists' Challenges and the Disruption of Corporate Political Activity. *Administrative Science Quarterly*, 61(4), 584–620.

McKinsey. (2020). The ESG Premium: New Perspectives on Value and Performance. Retrieved April 4, 2022 from www.mckinsey.com/business-functions/sustainability/our-insights/the-esg-premium-new-perspectives-on-value-and-performance.

McShane, L., & Cunningham, P. (2012). To Thine Own Self Be True? Employees' Judgments of the Authenticity of Their Organization's Corporate Social Responsibility Program. *Journal of Business Ethics*, 108(1), 81–100.

McWilliams, A., & Siegel, D. S. (2011). Creating and Capturing Value: Strategic Corporate Social Responsibility, Resource-Based Theory, and Sustainable Competitive Advantage. *Journal of Management*, 37(5), 1480–1495.

McWilliams, A., Van Fleet, D. D., & Cory, K. D. (2002). Raising Rivals' Costs through Political Strategy: An Extension of Resource-Based Theory. *Journal of Management Studies*, 39(5), 707–724.

Memarzadeh, M., Britten, G. L., Worm, B. and Boettiger, C., 2019. Rebuilding Global Fisheries under Uncertainty. *Proceedings of the National Academy of Sciences*, 116(32), 15985–15990.

Merritt, A. C., Effron, D. A., & Monin, B. (2010). Moral Self-licensing: When Being Good Frees Us to Be Bad. *Social and Personality Psychology Compass*, 4(5), 344–357.

Miles, S. (2017). Stakeholder Theory Classification: A Theoretical and Empirical Evaluation of Definitions. *Journal of Business Ethics*, 142(3), 437–459.

Minkoff, D. C. (1997). The Sequencing of Social Movements. *American Sociological Review*, 62(5), 779–799.

Minor, D., & Morgan, J. (2011). CSR as Reputation Insurance: Primum Non Nocere. *California Management Review*, 53(3), 40–59.

Mirvis, P. (2012). Employee Engagement and CSR: Transactional, Relational, and Developmental Approaches. *California Management Review*, 54(4), 93–117.

Mishra, S., Charan Rath, C., & Das, A. P. (2019). Marine Microfiber Pollution: A Review on Present Status and Future Challenges. *Marine Pollution Bulletin*, 140, 188–197.

Mitchell, R. K., Agle, B. R., & Wood, D. J. (1997). Toward a Theory of Stakeholder Identification and Salience: Defining the Principle of Who and What Really Counts. *Academy of Management Review*, 22(4), 853–886.

Morgan, J. (2018). How Greenpeace Changed an Industry: 25 Years of GreenFreeze to Cool the Planet., March. Retrieved June 25, 2020 from www.greenpeace.org/international/story/15323/how-greenpeace-changed-an-industry-25-years-of-greenfreeze-to-cool-the-planet/.

Nestlé. 2013. Nestlé in Society. Retrieved April 14, 2020 from www.nestle.com/sites/default/files/asset-library/documents/library/documents/corporate_social_responsibility/nestle-csv-full-report-2013-en.pdf.

Nike. (2010). Nike Releases Environmental Design Tool. November 29. Retrieved March 18, 2021 from https://news.nike.com/news/nike-releases-environmental-design-tool-to-industry.

Nike. (2019). A Brief History of Nike Air. March 18. Retrieved July 13, 2020 from https://news.nike.com/news/history-of-nike-air.

Ocasio, W., & Joseph, J. (2018). The Attention-Based View of *Great* Strategies. *Strategy Science*, 3(1), 289–294.

Odziemkowska, K., & Dorobantu, S. (2020). *Contracting beyond the Market*, SSRN Scholarly Paper No. ID 3591227, Social Science Research Network. Retrieved June 14, 2020 from https://papers.ssrn.com/abstract=3591227.

Odziemkowska, K., & McDonnell, M.-H. (2019). *Ripple Effects: How Firm–Activist Collaborations Reduce Movement Contention*, SSRN Scholarly Paper No. ID 3428050, Social Science Research Network. Retrieved June 26, 2020 from https://papers.ssrn.com/abstract=3428050.

Oliver, C., & Holzinger, I. (2008). The Effectiveness of Strategic Political Management: A Dynamic Capabilities Framework. *Academy of Management Review*, 33(2), 496–520.

Olson, M. (2009). *The Logic of Collective Action: Public Goods and the Theory of Groups*, second printing with a new Preface and Appendix, Harvard University Press.

O'Reilly, C. (1989). Corporations, Culture, and Commitment: Motivation and Social Control in Organizations. *California Management Review*, 31(4), 9–25.

O'Reilly, C. A., & Chatman, J. A. (1996). Culture as Social Control: Corporations, Cults, and Commitment. In B. M. Staw & L. L. Cummings (eds.), *Research in Organizational Behavior: An Annual Series of Analytical Essays and Critical Reviews*, Vol. 18, Elsevier Science/JAI Press, pp. 157–200.

Organic Trade Association. (2019). COVID-19 Will Shape Organic Industry in 2020 after Banner Year in 2019. Retrieved April 2, 2021 from https://ota.com/news/press-releases/21328.

Ostrom, E. (1990). *Governing the Commons: The Evolution of Institutions for Collective Action*, Cambridge University Press.

Ostrom, E. (1996). Crossing the Great Divide: Coproduction, Synergy, and Development. *World Development*, 24(6), 1073–1087.

Ostrom, E. (2007). A Diagnostic Approach for Going Beyond Panaceas. *Proceedings of the National Academy of Sciences*, 104(39), 15181–15187.

Ostrom, E., & Cox, M. (2010). Moving beyond Panaceas: A Multi-tiered Diagnostic Approach for Social-Ecological Analysis. *Environmental Conservation*, 37(40), 451–463.

Ostrom, E., Janssen, M. A., & Anderies, J. M. (2007). Going beyond Panaceas. *Proceedings of the National Academy of Sciences*, 104(39), 15176–15178.

Ottman, J. A., Stafford, E. R., & Hartman, C. L. (2006). Avoiding Green Marketing Myopia: Ways to Improve Consumer Appeal for Environmentally Preferable Products. *Environment: Science and Policy for Sustainable Development*, 48(5), 22–36.

Padel, S., & Foster, C. (2005). Exploring the Gap between Attitudes and Behaviour: Understanding Why Consumers Buy or Do Not Buy Organic Food. *British Food Journal*, 107(8), 606–625.

Paine, L. S., Hsieh, N.-H., & Adamsons, L. (2013). *Governance and Sustainability at Nike (A)*, Harvard Business Publishing. Retrieved March 18, 2020 from https://hbsp.harvard.edu/product/313146-PDF-ENG.

Palazzo, J., Geyer, R., & Suh, S. (2020). A Review of Methods for Characterizing the Environmental Consequences of Actions in Life Cycle Assessment. *Journal of Industrial Ecology*, 24(4), 815–829.

Pankaj, G., & Rivkin, J. W. (2014). *Strategy Reading: Competitive Advantage*, Harvard Business School Press. Retrieved March 18, 2020 from https://hbsp .harvard.edu/product/8105-PDF-ENG?itemFindingMethod=Collections.

Patagonia. (n.d.). Environmental & Social Footprint – Patagonia. Retrieved July 22, 2020 from www.patagonia.com/our-footprint/.

Peloza, J., & Hassay, D. N. (2006). Intra-organizational Volunteerism: Good Soldiers, Good Deeds and Good Politics. *Journal of Business Ethics*, 64(4), 357–379.

Peloza, J., Ye, C., & Montford, W. J. (2015). When Companies Do Good, Are Their Products Good for You? How Corporate Social Responsibility Creates a Health Halo. *Journal of Public Policy & Marketing*, 34(1), 19–31.

Plambeck, E. L., & Denend, L. (2008). The Greening of Wal-Mart. *Stanford Social Innovation Review*, 6(2), 52–59.

Polletta, F., & Jasper, J. M. (2001). Collective Identity and Social Movements. *Annual Review of Sociology*, 27(1), 283–305.

Polman, P., & Bhattacharya, C. (2016). Engaging Employees to Create a Sustainable Business. *Stanford Social Innovation Review*, 14(4), 34–39.

Porter, M. E. (2008). The Five Competitive Forces That Shape Strategy. *Harvard Business Review*, 86(1), 25–40.

Porter, M. E., & Kramer, M. R. (2011). Creating Shared Value. *Harvard Business Review* 89(1–2), 62–77.

Porter, M. E., & van der Linde, C. (1995). Toward a New Conception of the Environment–Competitiveness Relationship. *Journal of Economic Perspectives*, 9(4), 97–118.

Potoski, M., & Callery, P. J. (2018). Peer Communication Improves Environmental Employee Engagement Programs: Evidence from a Quasi-experimental Field Study. *Journal of Cleaner Production*, 172, 1486–1500.

Potoski, M., & Prakash, A. (2004). The Regulation Dilemma: Cooperation and Conflict in Environmental Governance. *Public Administration Review*, 64(2), 152–163.

Potoski, M., & Prakash, A. (2005). Green Clubs and Voluntary Governance: ISO 14001 and Firms' Regulatory Compliance. *American Journal of Political Science*, 49(2), 235–248.

Potoski, M., & Prakash, A. (2009). *Voluntary Programs: A Club Theory Perspective*, The MIT Press.

Potoski, M., & Prakash, A. (2013). Green Clubs: Collective Action and Voluntary Environmental Programs. *Annual Review of Political Science*, 16, 399–419.

Prakash, A., & Kollman, K. (2004). Policy Modes, Firms and the Natural Environment. *Business Strategy and the Environment*, 13(2), 107–128.

Prakash, A., & Potoski, M. (2006). *The Voluntary Environmentalists: Green Clubs, ISO 14001, and Voluntary Environmental Regulations*, Cambridge University Press.

Prakash, A., & Potoski, M. (2007). Collective Action through Voluntary Environmental Programs: A Club Theory Perspective. *Policy Studies Journal*, 35(4), 773–792.

Ramus, C. A. (2001). Organizational Support for Employees: Encourage Creative Ideas for Environmental Sustainability. *California Management Review*, 43(3), 85–105.

Ramus, C. A., & Killmer, A. B. C. (2007). Corporate Greening through Prosocial Extrarole Behaviours: A Conceptual Framework for Employee Motivation. *Business Strategy and the Environment*, 16(8), 554–570.

Ramus, C. A., & Steger, U. (2000). The Roles of Supervisory Support Behaviors and Environmental Policy in Employee "Ecoinitiatives" at Leading-Edge European Companies. *Academy of Management Journal*, 43(4), 605–626.

Rao, A. R., Qu, L., & Ruekert, R. W. (1999). Signaling Unobservable Product Quality through a Brand Ally. *Journal of Marketing Research*, 36(2), 258–268.

Reed, M. S., Graves, A., Dandy, N., Posthumus, H., Hubacek, K., Morris, J., Prell, C., Quinn, C. H., & Stringer, L. C. (2009). Who's in and Why? A Typology of Stakeholder Analysis Methods for Natural Resource Management. *Journal of Environmental Management*, 90(5), 1933–1949.

Rehbein, K., Waddock, S., & Graves, S. B. (2004). Understanding Shareholder Activism: Which Corporations Are Targeted? *Business & Society*, 43(3), 239–267.

Reinhardt, F. L. (1999). Bringing the Environment down to Earth. *Harvard Business Review*,77(4), 149–158.

Rivera, J. (2002). Assessing a Voluntary Environmental Initiative in the Developing World: The Costa Rican Certification for Sustainable Tourism. *Policy Sciences*, 35(4), 333–360.

Rivera, J., & De Leon, P. (2004). Is Greener Whiter? Voluntary Environmental Performance of Western Ski Areas. *Policy Studies Journal*, 32(3), 417–437.

Rivera, J. E. (2010). *Business and Public Policy: Responses to Environmental and Social Protection Processes*, Cambridge University Press.

Roberts, S. (2003). Supply Chain Specific? Understanding the Patchy Success of Ethical Sourcing Initiatives. *Journal of Business Ethics*, 44(2), 159–170.

Robertson, J. L., & Barling, J. (2013). Greening Organizations through Leaders' Influence on Employees' pro-Environmental Behaviors. *Journal of Organizational Behavior*, 34(2), 176–194.

Rodell, J. B. (2013). Finding Meaning through Volunteering: Why Do Employees Volunteer and What Does It Mean for Their Jobs? *Academy of Management Journal*, 56(5), 1274–1294.

Rodell, J. B., Breitsohl, H., Schröder, M., & Keating, D. J. (2016). Employee Volunteering: A Review and Framework for Future Research. *Journal of Management*, 42(1), 55–84.

Rodell, J. B., & Lynch, J. W. (2016). Perceptions of Employee Volunteering: Is It "Credited" or "Stigmatized" by Colleagues? *Academy of Management Journal*, 59(2), 611–635.

Rose-Ackerman, S. (1996). Altruism, Nonprofits, and Economic Theory. *Journal of Economic Literature*, 34(2), 701–728.

Rousseau, D. (1995). *Psychological Contracts in Organizations: Understanding Written and Unwritten Agreements*, SAGE.

Rugman, A. M., & Verbeke, A. (1998). Corporate Strategies and Environmental Regulations: An Organizing Framework. *Strategic Management Journal*, 19(4), 363–375.

Rupp, D. E., Shao, R., Skarlicki, D. P., Paddock, E. L., Kim, T.-Y., & Nadisic, T. (2018). Corporate Social Responsibility and Employee Engagement: The Moderating Role of CSR-Specific Relative Autonomy and Individualism. *Journal of Organizational Behavior*, 39(5), 559–579.

Rupp, D., & Mallory, D. (2015). Corporate Social Responsibility: Psychological, Person-Centric, and Progressing. *Annual Review of Organizational Psychology and Organizational Behavior*, 2, 211–236.

Russo, M. V., & Fouts, P. A. (1997). A Resource-Based Perspective on Corporate Environmental Performance and Profitability. *Academy of Management Journal*, 40(3), 534–559.

Russo, M. V., & Harrison, N. S. (2005). Organizational Design and Environmental Performance: Clues from the Electronics Industry. *Academy of Management Journal*, 48(4), 582–593.

Schechter, A. (2012). Meet the Jewish Billionaire Who Studies Torah Every Morning. *Haaretz*, March 16. Retrieved June 24, 2020 from www.haaretz.com/1.5205860.

Scheidler, S., Edinger-Schons, L. M., Spanjol, J., & Wieseke, J. (2019). Scrooge Posing as Mother Teresa: How Hypocritical Social Responsibility Strategies Hurt Employees and Firms. *Journal of Business Ethics*, 157(2), 339–358.

Schwartz, J. (2015). Coca-Cola Says It's Close to Water Replenishment Goal. *New York Times*, August 25. Retrieved November 13, 2020 from www.nytimes.com/2015/08/26/business/coca-cola-expects-to-reach-its-water-replenishment-goal-5-years-early.html.

Seitanidi, M. M., & Crane, A. (2009). Implementing CSR through Partnerships: Understanding the Selection, Design and Institutionalisation of Nonprofit–Business Partnerships. *Journal of Business Ethics*, 85(2), 413–429.

Sen, S., & Bhattacharya, C. B. (2001). Does Doing Good Always Lead to Doing Better? Consumer Reactions to Corporate Social Responsibility. *Journal of Marketing Research*, 38(2), 225–243.

Seuring, S., & Müller, M. (2008). From a Literature Review to a Conceptual Framework for Sustainable Supply Chain Management. *Journal of Cleaner Production*, 16(15), 1699–1710.

Sexton, S. E., & Sexton, A. L. (2014). Conspicuous Conservation: The Prius Halo and Willingness to Pay for Environmental Bona Fides. *Journal of Environmental Economics and Management*, 67(3), 303–317.

Shah, K. U., & Rivera, J. E. (2013). Do Industry Associations Influence Corporate Environmentalism in Developing Countries? Evidence from Trinidad and Tobago. *Policy Sciences*, 46(1), 39–62.

Shahbandeh, M. 2022. Worldwide Sales of Organic Foods. Retrieved April 4, 2022 from www.statista.com/statistics/273090/worldwide-sales-of-organic-foods-since-1999/.

Sharma, S., & Vredenburg, H. (1998). Proactive Corporate Environmental Strategy and the Development of Competitively Valuable Capabilities. *Strategic Management Journal*, 19(8), 729–753.

Shea, C. T., & Hawn, O. V. (2018). Microfoundations of Corporate Social Responsibility and Irresponsibility. *Academy of Management Journal*, 62(5), 1609–1642.

Sheel, R. C., & Vohra, N. (2016). Relationship between Perceptions of Corporate Social Responsibility and Organizational Cynicism: The Role of Employee Volunteering. *The International Journal of Human Resource Management*, 27(13), 1373–1392.

Shen, Y. (2015). Protest against Industrial Air Pollution: A Case from Hangzhou City, China. Mei.edu, December 15. Retrieved April 14, 2022 from www.mei.edu/publications/protest-against-industrial-air-pollution-case-hangzhou-city-china.

Shiu, Y. M., & Yang, S. L. (2017). Does Engagement in Corporate Social Responsibility Provide Strategic Insurance-like Effects? *Strategic Management Journal*, 38(2), 455–470.

Shook, J. (2010). How to Change a Culture: Lessons from NUMMI. *MIT Sloan Management Review*, 51(2), 63–68.

Shuck, B., & Wollard, K. (2010). Employee Engagement and HRD: A Seminal Review of the Foundations. *Human Resource Development Review*, 9(1), 89–110.

Siegel, D. S., & Vitaliano, D. F. (2007). An Empirical Analysis of the Strategic Use of Corporate Social Responsibility. *Journal of Economics & Management Strategy*, 16(3), 773–792.

Siemens Industry Inc., & McGraw-Hill Construction. (2009). 2009 Greening of Corporate America. Retrieved May 4, 2020 from http://construction .com/market_research/FreeReport/GreeningCorpAmerica/2009_GreeningCorpAmerica.pdf.

Smith, A. (2000). *The Wealth of Nations*, Modern Library Classics.

Sörqvist, P., Haga, A., Langeborg, L., Holmgren, M., Wallinder, M., Nöstl, A., Seager, P. B., & Marsh, J. E. (2015). The Green Halo: Mechanisms and Limits of the Eco-Label Effect. *Food Quality and Preference*, 43, 1–9.

Sorrel, C. (2000). Briton Invented iPod, DRM and On-Line Music in 1979. *Wired*, September 9. Retrieved April 9, 2021 from www.wired .com/2008/09/briton-invented/.

Spence, M. (1973). Job Market Signaling. *The Quarterly Journal of Economics*, 87(3), 355–374.

Spicer, A., & Hyatt, D. (2017). Walmart's Emergent Low-Cost Sustainable Product Strategy. *California Management Review*, 59(2), 116–141.

Stafford, E. R., Polonsky, M. J., & Hartman, C. L. (2000). Environmental NGO – Business Collaboration and Strategic Bridging: A Case Analysis of the Greenpeace–Foron Alliance. *Business Strategy and the Environment*, 9(2), 122–135.

Starik, M., & Marcus, A. A. (2000). Introduction to the Special Research Forum on the Management of Organizations in the Natural Environment: A Field Emerging from Multiple Paths, with Many Challenges Ahead. *Academy of Management Journal*, 43(4), 539–547.

Starik, M., & Rands, G. P. (1995). Weaving an Integrated Web: Multilevel and Multisystem Perspectives of Ecologically Sustainable Organizations. *The Academy of Management Review*, 20(4), 908–935.

Stein, M. A. (1990). "Redwood Summer": It Was Guerrilla Warfare. *LA Times*, September 2. Retrieved June 20, 2020 from www.latimes .com/archives/la-xpm-1990-09-02-mn-2050-story.html.

Strahilevitz, M., & Myers, J. G. (1998). Donations to Charity as Purchase Incentives: How Well They Work May Depend on What You Are Trying to Sell. *Journal of Consumer Research*, 24(4), 434–446.

Suh, S., & Huppes, G. (2005). Methods for Life Cycle Inventory of a Product. *Journal of Cleaner Production*, 13(7), 687–697.

Swanson, E. (2013). Poll Finds BP Public Image Still Tarnished 3 Years after Gulf Spill. *HuffPost*, May 20. Retrieved July 22, 2020 from www .huffpost.com/entry/bp-poll_n_3111551?guccounter=1.

Swartz, J. (2010). Timberland's CEO on Standing up to 65,000 Angry Activists. *Harvard Business Review*, 88(9), 39–43.

Tantalo, C., & Priem, R. L. (2016). Value Creation through Stakeholder Synergy. *Strategic Management Journal*, 37(2), 314–329.

Taylor, V., & Van dyke, N. (2004). "Get up, Stand up": Tactical Repertoires of Social Movements. In D. A. Snow & S. A. Soule (eds.), *The Blackwell Companion to Social Movements*, John Wiley & Sons, Ltd., pp. 262–293.

Teece, D. J. (2007). Explicating Dynamic Capabilities: The Nature and Microfoundations of (Sustainable) Enterprise Performance. *Strategic Management Journal*, 28(13), 1319–1350.

Teisl, M. F., Roe, B., & Hicks, R. L. (2000). Can Eco-Labels Tune a Market? Evidence from Dolphin-Safe Labeling. *Journal of Environmental Economics and Management*, 43(3), 339–359.

The Economic Times. (2007). Adding Fizz to the Fire. June 26. Retrieved January 21, 2021 from https://economictimes.indiatimes.com/adding-fizz-to-the-fire/articleshow/2152124.cms.

The Nature Conservancy. (n.d.). Program Overview. Retrieved April 20, 2021 from https://birdreturns.org/home-page/about/about/.

The Naturewatch Foundation. (2017). Boycott The Body Shop. Retrieved June 15, 2020 from https://naturewatch.org/campaign/previous/cruelty-free-shopping/boycott-the-body-shop-boycott.

Tompkins, A. (2016). *Ghostworkers and Greens: The Cooperative Campaigns of Farmworkers and Environmentalists for Pesticide Reform*, Cornell University Press.

Unilever. (2020). Partnerships for Transformational Change. Retrieved May 1, 2020 from www.unilever.com/sustainable-living/reducing-environmental-impact/sustainable-sourcing/transforming-the-palm-oil-industry/partnerships-for-transformational-change/.

United Nations Environment Programme. (2019). Environmental Rule of Law: First Global Report. January 24. Retrieved April 11, 2022 from www.unep .org/resources/assessment/environmental-rule-law-first-global-report.

US Federal Trade Commission. (2010). 16 C.F.R. Part 260: Guides for the Use of Environmental Marketing Claims: Request for Public Comment on Proposed, Revised Guides. Retrieved October 29, 2020 from www.ftc.gov/legal-library/browse/federal-register-notices/16-cfr-part-260-guides-use-environmental-marketing-claims-request-public-comment-proposed-revised.

US Federal Trade Commission. (2017). Re Moonling Slumber, LLC, No. C-4634 (Federal Trade Commission, December 11). Retrieved October 29, 2020 from www.ftc.gov/system/files/documents/cases/162_3128_c4634_moonlight_slumber_decision_order_final.pdf.

US SIF. (2020). US SIF Foundation Opens 2020 Survey on US Sustainable and Impact Investing Trends. April 1. Retrieved April 27, 2021 from www.ussif.org/blog_home.asp?display=138.

Van Hasselt, C. (2011). How Canada's TD Bank Is Invading U.S. Market. *Wall Street Journal*, August 1. Retrieved July 8, 2020 from www.wsj .com/articles/SB10001424053111904253204576510590825735486.

Van Tulder, R., Seitanidi, M., Crane, A., & Brammer, S. (2016). Enhancing the Impact of Cross-sector Partnerships. *Journal of Business Ethics*, 135(1), 1–7.

Vasi, I. B., & King, B. G. (2012). Social Movements, Risk Perceptions, and Economic Outcomes: The Effect of Primary and Secondary Stakeholder Activism on Firms' Perceived Environmental Risk and Financial Performance. *American Sociological Review*, 77(4), 573–596.

Vlachos, P. A., Tsamakos, A., Vrechopoulos, A. P., & Avramidis, P. K. (2009). Corporate Social Responsibility: Attributions, Loyalty, and the Mediating Role of Trust. *Journal of the Academy of Marketing Science*, 37(2), 170–180.

Vogel, D. (2007). *The Market for Virtue: The Potential and Limits of Corporate Social Responsibility*, Brookings Institution Press.

Vox Global. (2012). Making the Pitch: Selling Sustainability from Inside Corporate America. Retrieved May 6, 2021 from https://voxglobal.com/wp-content/uploads/VOX-Global-2012-Sustainability-Leaders-Survey-Full-Report.pdf.

Waddock, S. A. (1989). Understanding Social Partnerships: An Evolutionary Model of Partnership Organizations. *Administration & Society*, 21(1), 78–100.

Wagner, T., Lutz, R. J., & Weitz, B. A. (2009). Corporate Hypocrisy: Overcoming the Threat of Inconsistent Corporate Social Responsibility Perceptions. *Journal of Marketing*, 73(6), 77–91.

Walker, K. (2010). A Systematic Review of the Corporate Reputation Literature: Definition, Measurement, and Theory. *Corporate Reputation Review*, 12(4), 357–387.

Wang, H. C., He, J., & Mahoney, J. T. (2009). Firm-Specific Knowledge Resources and Competitive Advantage: The Roles of Economic- and Relationship-Based Employee Governance Mechanisms. *Strategic Management Journal*, 30(12), 1265–1285.

Waxman, H. (1985). Release of Poison Gases and Other Hazardous Air Pollutants from Chemical Plants. Joint Hearing before the Subcommittee on Health and the Environment and the Subcommittee on Commerce, Transportation, and Tourism of the Committee on Energy and Commerce, House of Representatives, 99th Congress, First Session, March 26.

Wenzel, E. (2020). New Leaders at Patagonia, McDonald's, Netflix. Greenbiz.com, October 7. Retrieved April 14, 2021 from www.greenbiz.com/article/new-leaders-patagonia-mcdonalds-netflix.

Werbach, A. (2009). *Strategy for Sustainability: A Business Manifesto*, Harvard Business Press.

Wernerfelt, B. (1984). A Resource-Based View of the Firm. *Strategic Management Journal*, 5(2), 171–180.

White, K., Habib, R., & Hardisty, D. J. (2019). How to SHIFT Consumer Behaviors to Be More Sustainable: A Literature Review and Guiding Framework. *Journal of Marketing*, 83(3), 22–49.

Wiedmann, K.-P., Hennigs, N., Behrens, S. H., & Klarmann, C. (2014). Tasting Green: An Experimental Design for Investigating Consumer Perception of Organic Wine. *British Food Journal*, 116(2), 197–211.

Williams, D. E., & Treadaway, G. (1992). Exxon and the Valdez Accident: A Failure in Crisis Communication. *Communication Studies*, 43(1), 56–64.

Williamson, O. E. (1985). *The Economic Institutions of Capitalism*, Free Press.

Winston, A. (2014). *The Big Pivot: Radically Practical Strategies for a Hotter, Scarcer, and More Open World*, Harvard Business Review Press.

Wright, B. G. (2000). Environmental NGOs and the Dolphin-Tuna Case. *Environmental Politics*, 9(4), 82–103.

Zaitchik, A. (2020). "This Is Not a Symbolic Action": Indigenous Protesters Occupy Oil Platforms in Radicalized Fight against Pollution in the Amazon. *The Intercept*, December 17. Retrieved April 14, 2022 from https://theintercept.com/2017/12/27/peru-amazon-oil-pollution-indigenous-protest/.

Zdravkovic, S., Magnusson, P., & Stanley, S. M. (2010). Dimensions of Fit between a Brand and a Social Cause and Their Influence on Attitudes. *International Journal of Research in Marketing*, 27(2), 151–160.

Zink, T., & Geyer, R. (2017). Circular Economy Rebound. *Journal of Industrial Ecology*, 21(3), 593–602.

Zink, T., & Geyer, R. (2019). Material Recycling and the Myth of Landfill Diversion. *Journal of Industrial Ecology*, 23(3), 541–548.

Index

activist campaigns, 1, 3, 59, 148, 152,
  155, 158, 152–163
    channels, 148, 158–161
    co-benefits, 155–157
    collective goods, 156
    company strategy, 159
    credibility, 161–163
    emotional co-benefits, 156
    functional co-benefits, 156
    Greenpeace, 146–148
    holdup problem, 161–163
    participants, 155–157
    resolution, 161
    social co-benefits, 157
    social license to operate, 158
    stakeholders, 155–157
    targets, 148, 153–155, 158
Adam, Smith, 48
Adidas, 147, 160
Amazon ecosystem, 1, 5, 47, 116, 146,
  147, 149, 155, 160–163
American Cyanamid, 68
Apple, 79
Audi, 147

Ben & Jerry's, 2, 4, 7, 46
benefit corporation, 10
Bhopal, India, 61
BirdReturns, 18
board of directors, 89
The Body Shop, 161
Bowerman, Bill, 175
boycotts, 37, 39, 44, 59, 148, 149,
  152, 156–158, 161, 175, 186
brands, 1, 4, 6, 41, 45, 78, 83, 84,
  109, 171
    competitive advantage. See Brands,
      Strategic resource
    costly signal, 45, 46, 83, 162
    green products, 119

British Petroleum, (BP), 41, 101
Burbano, Vanessa, 131, 132
Burns, Ken, 114
business strategy, 75–79
    competitive advantage, 48–50, 77
    low cost, 81
    market strategy, 38, See market
      strategy
    nonmarket strategy. See nonmarket
      strategy
    product differentiation, 49, 81,
      103–105, 109. see also green
      products
    resource-based view. See resource-
      based view

Carbon Disclosure Project (CDP), 45
CBA. See community benefit
  agreement, (CBA)
CEO. See Chief Executive Officer,
  (CEO)
certifications, 6, 43, 47–48, 82, 113,
  116–117, 167
    Dolphin-safe, 108
    ISO 14001. See ISO 14001
    LEED. See LEED certification
    Marine Stewardship Council,
      (MSC), 82
    organic, 99, 113
channels, 6, 81–82
    activist campaigns, 59, 158–161
    defined, 40
    employee engagement, 130–133
    environmental partnerships,
      166–171
    financial, 42
    government regulations, 61
    green products, 40–41
    human resources, 43
    industry self-regulation, 61

market channels, 40–43
non-market channels, 59
social license to operate, 59
strategic resources, 81–82
Chemical Manufacturers Association.
    See International Council of
    Chemical Associations
Chief Executive Officer, (CEO), 89
chief sustainability officer, (CSO),
    88–93, 96, 97
    resources, 91–92
    responsibilities, 90
China, 58
chlorofluorocarbons, 67
chocolate, 111
Chouinard, Yvon, 7
circular economy, 11
Coase, Ronald, 17, 31
    Coase theorem, 17
Coasian exchange, 17–19, 21–32, 95,
    179, 181
co-benefits, 14, 36, 106–111, 113,
    129–131, 136–139, 155–157
    credibility, 117–118
    emotional, 107–109, 118, 130,
        133, 137, 156, *See* emotional
        co-benefits
    functional, 106–107, 129, 137,
        156
    social, 109–110, 130, 138, 157
Coca-Cola, 47, 73, 74, 83, 171, 181
    brand, 74
coffee, 111, 115
Cohen, Ben, 7
cold shadow, 110
collective action, 39, 61, 156
collective goods, 39, 152, 156, 178
community benefit agreement, (CBA),
    172
company culture, 45–46, 76, 84, 131,
    134, 142
    costly signal, 45, 83
    credibility, 133–134
    employee engagement, 131
    Nike, 190
    resource-based view, 75–76
    Stonyfield, 121
    strategic resources, 93–94
Corbet, Harold, 68
costly signal, 28, 45, 83, 180, 187

credibility, 6, 26–27, 45–48,
    82–84, 187, *See* certifications;
    greenwashing; holdup problem;
    lemons problem; lemons market;
    transaction costs, monitoring and
    enforcement
    activist campaigns, 161–163
    brands, 45–47, 78, 119
    certifications, 47–48, 116–117
    co-benefits, 117–118
    company culture, 45–47, 83
    employee engagement, 133–134
    employee environmental engagement
        programs, (EEE programs),
        142–144
    environmental groups, 151
    environmental partnerships, 160,
        170–173
    green products, 117–119
    holdup problem, 28
    information, 26–27
    measurement, 45
    reporting, 45
    strategic resources, 82–84
CSO. *See* chief sustainability officer, (CSO)

Dawn dish soap, 108
Deepwater Horizon, 108
Deloitte, 47
Dow, 68, 163, 169
Ducks Unlimited, 170
DuPont, 67, 68

Earth First!, 59, 153
EarthLight, 118
Eco-Dentistry Association, 2
Emergency Planning and Community
    Right-to-Know Act (EPCRA), 68
employee engagement, 123–145, 181
    channels, 130–133
    co-benefits, 129–130
    company culture, 134
    credibility, 133–134
    emotional co-benefits, 130
    employee demand, 129–130
    environmental impacts, 129
    functional co-benefits, 129
    labor costs, 131–132
    productivity, 132
    social co-benefits, 130

employee environmental engagement
  programs, (EEE programs), 128,
  134–144
  co-benefits, 136–139
  credibility, 142–144
  emotional co-benefits, 138
  employee demand, 136–139
  environmental impacts, 128–129
  functional co-benefits, 137
  social co-benefits, 138
Environmental Defense Fund, (EDF),
  164, 167, 171
environmental ethics, 9
environmental groups, 3, 60, 146–174
  activist campaigns. *See* activist
    campaigns
  competition among, 150
  credibility, 151
  partnerships. *See* environmental
    partnerships
  strategy, 149–152
environmental impacts, 1–2, 16,
  19–20, 24, 27, 80, 184
  activist campaigns, 153–155
  assessment, 80
  definition, 20
  employee engagement, 128
  employee engagement programs,
    128–129
  environmental partnerships,
    164–165
  externalities, 19–20
  green products, 103–105
  identifying, 32–35
  observability, 27
  stakeholders, 21
  Stonyfield, 105
  TD Bank, 124
environmental insurance, 42
environmental partnerships, 163–173
  benefits, 170–171
  brands, 171
  channels, 166–171
  contributions, 169–170
  credibility, 171–173
  environmental impacts, 164–165
  forms, 166–167
  holdup problems, 171–173
  stakeholder demand, 166
  synergies, 167–168

environmental product differentiation.
  See green products
environmental strategy, 4, 5, 7, 31–51
  channels. *See* channels
  competitive advantage, 6, 50,
    77–79, 188
  credibility. *See* credibility
  definition, 4
  environmental impacts, 32–35
  framework, 5–9, 179, 184
  stakeholders. *See* stakeholders
  strategic resources. *See* strategic
    resources
externalities, 15–19
  negative, 15–21, 178
  positive, 15–20
Exxon, 37, 68
Exxon Valdez, 37

Facebook, 157
first mover advantage, 48, 50
Forest Stewardship Council, (FSC), 48
Foron, 172, 173
Friedman, Milton, 9

Gary Hirshberg, 182
General Motors, (GM), 56, 77
Glassman, Diana, 123–127, 135–136,
  138, 142–145, 181, 183
Governing the Commons, xi
government regulations, 17, 61
  command and control, 56
  Toxic Release Inventory. *See* Toxic
    Release Inventory, (TRI)
green lemons problem, 43, 116
Green marketing myopia, 118
green products, 50, 98–122
  brands, 119
  certifications, 116–117
  channels, 115
  co-benefits, 106–111, 117–118
  consumer demand, 105–106
  definition, 103
  emotional co-benefits, 107–109
  environmental impacts, 103–105
  functional co-benefits, 106–107
  Hallo effects, 111
  lemons market, 115–116
  Nike, 177
  social co-benefits, 109–110

strategy, 100–102
green teams, 92–93
Greenfield, Jerry, 7
Greenpeace, 1, 5, 47, 59, 146–149,
    155, 157, 160–163, 170,
    172–174, 181, 185, 190
greenwashing, 27, 104, 116, 144,
    180
Group Danone, 100, 183

Hangzhou, 58
Healey, Sarah, 125, 138
Hirshberg, Gary, 98–100, 102, 104,
    113–115, 119–122
holdup problem, 43
HP Inc., 90
Huawei, 69, 72
human resources, 123–145
    employee engagement, 42
    employee recruitment, 42
    employee retention, 42
    informal labor contracts, 6, 44, 130,
    131, 143

industry associations, 61
International Council of Chemical
    Associations, 61
ISO 9000, 81
ISO 14001, 20, 91, 117

Joint Auditing Cooperation (JAC), 72
JAC. *See* Joint Auditing Cooperation,
    (JAC)
Jones, Hannah, 176
Joppa, Lucas, 182

Kaymen, Samuel, 98–100, 102, 104,
    119–122
Kent, Muhtar, 74
Kerala, India, 181
Kimberly-Clark, 59
King, Andrew, 87
Knight, Phil, 175, 189
Kraft, 98, 147
Kramer, Kane, 79

LaBuddle, Sam, 108
Lactalis, 100
LCA. *See* life cycle assessment, (LCA)
LEED certification, 48, 124

lemons market, 116
Levi Strauss, 90
life cycle assessment, (LCA), 80,
    103
LimnoTech, 47
luxury goods, 110

Marine Stewardship Council, (MSC),
    82
market failure, 15
market strategy, 48–50, 78
McDonald's, 59, 161, 164
Microsoft, 182
Monsanto, 68
Moonlight Slumber, 43
MP3, 79
MSCI, 42
Mueller, Matthias, 41

National Public Radio, 109
natural-resource-based view, 78
The Nature Conservancy, (TNC), 18,
    47, 124, 150, 163, 169
Naturewatch Foundation, 161
Nestlé, 53, 59
Netflix, 90
Nike, 108, 154, 160, 179, 182,
    184–190
    brand, 175, 187, 188
    Considered Boot, 176–178,
    185–190
    Considered Design Principles, 178
    Considered Design Tool, 177
    Considered Index, 178, 184–190
    stakeholders, 185–187
nonmarket strategy, 78
The North Face, 105
NUMMI, 77, *See* New United Motor
    Manufacturing, Inc. (NUMMI)

organic, 38, 41
organic certification, 183
organizational structure, 75, 89–93,
    96, *See* chief sustainability
    officers, (CSO); Green teams;
    Human resources
    incentive problem, 88
    information problem, 88
    Nike, 190
Ostrom, Elinor, xi

Patagonia, 2, 4, 7, 33, 90, 188
Peirce, Brad, 125, 135
Pepsi, 74
Philips, 118
Poland Springs, 171
Porter hypothesis, 34
Porter's Five Forces, 49
property rights, 17
Protest Against Air Pollution, 58

recycling, 11, 92, 177
Redwood Summer, 153
Reinhardt, Forrest, 9
resource-based view, 75–79, *See*
    Strategic resources
competitive advantage, 77
Responsible Care, 61

shared value, 52
Smith, Adam, 13
social license to operate, 4, 57, 59, 61,
    149, 158, 171, 172, 186
Sony, 79
stakeholders, 2–8, 13–15, 21, 24–28,
    32, 39–40, 88, 95, 174, 179, 181,
    182, 185, 186
    activists, 59
    analysis, 35–39, 80–81, 185
    consumers, 109–110
    credibility, 82–84
    definition, 13
    employees, 43, 129–130
    environmental groups. *See*
        environmental groups
    financial, 3, 40, 42, 158
    governments, 61
    market, 39–40
    monitoring and reporting, 43–45
    Nike. *See* Nike, stakeholders
    nonmarket, 39–40, 50
Stonyfield, 50, 98–100, 102, 104,
    113–115, 119–122, 182, 183
    certifications, 120
Stop & Shop, 98
strategic resources, 75–76, 83, 97
    assessing environmental impacts,
        79–80
    brands, 78, 83, 84
    channels, 81–82
    company culture, 84, 93–94

credibility, 82–84
human resources, 94–96
stakeholder analysis, 80–81
supply chains, 24, 82, 85, 87, 88, 96,
    147, 153, 178
    Coca-Cola, 73, 181
    McDonald's, 59
    Nike, 176, 185, 186, 188
    Timberland, 47, 148, 149, 155,
        160–63
    Walmart, 82
Sustainalytics, 42
Swartz, Jeff, 1, 5, 146–148, 160–163,
    174, 181
switching costs, 75

TD Bank, 123–127, 135–136, 138,
    143–144, 181, 183
350.org, 157
Timberland, 1, 5, 47, 146–149, 155,
    157, 160–163, 174, 181, 185
    brand, 1, 155
Tom's Shoes, 119
Total Quality Management, 82
Toxic Release Inventory, (TRI), 56
Toyota, 56, 76, 109
Toyota Prius, 109, 110
Toyota Production System, (TPS), 76
transaction costs, 21–28, 178
    bargaining and transfer, 178
    monitoring and enforcement, 25–28,
        178
    search and screening, 23–24, 178
TRI. *See* Toxic Release Inventory,
    (TRI)
triple bottom line, 5, 8, 15, 178

Unilever, 163
Union Carbide, 61, 68
US Federal Trade Commission, 43

Volkswagen, 41, 47
    emissions scandal, 41

Walmart, 44, 82, 107, 147, 158
warm glow, 36, 41, 46, 107, 110, 130,
    137, 139, 157
wine, 29, 100, 110, 111
World Wildlife Fund, (WWF), 74,
    163, 171

Lightning Source UK Ltd.
Milton Keynes UK
UKHW050221010323
417839UK00009B/19